POPE FRANCIS
HYMN BOOK

More than 200 Traditional Hymns

Complete Kyriale ◆ 19 Masses, 6 Creeds

N.B. Those seeking a pew book elevating and celebrating the beauty of the Vatican II Mass should consider:

St. Isaac Jogues Illuminated Missal, Lectionary, & Gradual

- — Approved by the Committee on Divine Worship (USCCB);
- — *Imprimatur* by Bishop Edward J. Slattery (Tulsa, OK);
- — Stunning full-color images of the Priest;
- — Gorgeous illuminations & ancient liturgical manuscripts;
- — Complete Lectionary Readings (USA);
- — For the first time ever, the complete Propers in Latin/English;
- — Unbelievably large & legible font sizes;
- — Many more features, such as Funeral & Wedding Masses.

For details about this publication, visit:
CCWATERSHED.ORG/JOGUES

Whereas the *Pope Francis Hymn Book* uses a medium quality binding (allowing for extremely low pricing) the *Jogues Missal* uses the highest quality binding imaginable.

Edition: 13 June 2014
2014 © Père Isaac Jogues Art Productions

NOTES

THE PAPACY of Francis has been marked by a certain amount of simplicity, and therein lies the inspiration for this book of hymns. Its contents could not be more straightforward:

(1) More than two hundred traditional hymns
(2) The complete Kyriale and six settings of the Credo

Since these hymns were excerpted from the *Vatican II Hymnal*, that book's numbering system has been kept. However, more than forty additional hymns have been added, and many of these came from the *St. Edmund Campion Hymnal*.

No system of hymn classification could meet with everyone's approval because hymns are often appropriate for more than one season. For example, "AT THE LAMB'S HIGH FEAST" could be used outside of Eastertide. Similarly, "LO! HE COMES WITH CLOUDS DESCENDING" could be used outside of Advent. Our catalogue system provides suggestions only, designed for inexperienced choirmasters lacking extensive knowledge of hymnody.

Finally, it must be remembered that the hymn tunes chosen are mere possibilities. For example, the organist could play the more familiar version of "AT THE CROSS HER STATION KEEPING" and the congregation would have no problem following along.

Many hymnals provide an excessive amount of hymns for Advent and Christmas (which are very brief seasons), but give only a meager amount for Ordinary Time (which is a very long season).

Furthermore, they frequently ignore feasts like the Baptism of the Lord. The user can judge how successful we were in providing a remedy for this situation.

The "simplicity" of this book extends even to the organ accompaniments, which normally provide only one harmonization—whereas the *Campion Hymnal*, for example, gave numerous key transpositions and alternate versions.

Hymnal editors must often make hard choices. For example, "WE THREE KINGS" is wildly popular in the United States, but (in our judgment) has little to offer from the point of view of melody, poetry, or theological depth. Moreover, in the Ordinary Form, the Epiphany is an extremely short season, and the hymns we provide are superb: splendid melodies, strong theology, and inspired poetry. Therefore, our omission of "WE THREE KINGS" was a conscious decision, not an error, which we hope will be respected, though others might have chosen a different path.

Our publication would not have been possible without *250 Hymns in the Public Domain* (ICEL, 1981).

* * *

A different book—the *St. Isaac Jogues Hymnal*—is currently in production and will contain more than 1,000 hymns. Whereas the *Pope Francis Hymn Book* is "simple" and straightforward, this new production has a different purpose and scope. It is being created by a coalition of "regular" priests and musicians freely sharing their knowledge via the internet. To join these efforts, please visit: CCWATERSHED.ORG/JOGUES

* SEASONAL SUGGESTIONS

*Alphabetical listings of hymns & tunes
are located at the back of the book.*

HOLY EUCHARIST

MOST PRECIOUS BLOOD

TRANSFIGURATION

OUR LADY

✠ BENEDICTION OF THE BLESSED SACRAMENT

O God, Our Help In Ages Past   203

Tune: ST. ANNE (CM)   Text: Isaac Watts (†1748)

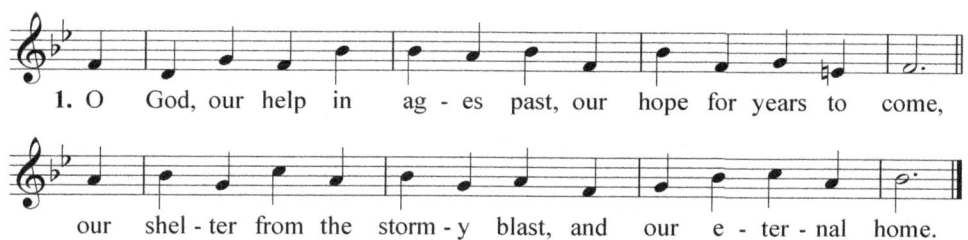

1. O God, our help in ag-es past, our hope for years to come,

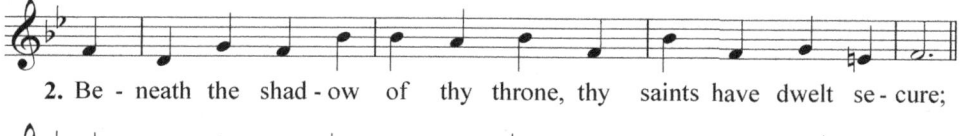

our shel-ter from the storm-y blast, and our e-ter-nal home.

2. Be-neath the shad-ow of thy throne, thy saints have dwelt se-cure;

suf-fi-cient is thine arm a-lone, and our de-fense is sure.

3. Be-fore the hills in or-der stood, or earth re-ceived her frame,
4. A thou-sand ag-es in thy sight are like an eve-ning gone;

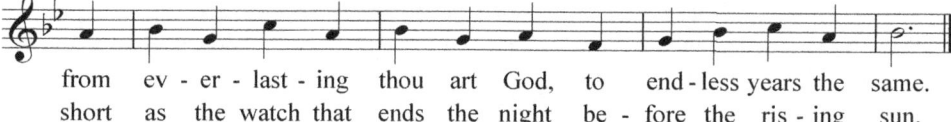

from ev-er-last-ing thou art God, to end-less years the same.
short as the watch that ends the night be-fore the ris-ing sun.

5. Time, like an ev-er-roll-ing stream, bears all its sons a-way;
6. O God, our help in ag-es past, our hope for years to come,

they fly, for-got-ten, as a dream dies at the o-p'ning day.
be thou our guide while trou-bles last, and our e-ter-nal home!

204 All People That On Earth Do Dwell

Tune: OLD HUNDREDTH (LM)   Text: att. William Kethe (†1594)

1. All peo-ple that on earth do dwell, Sing to the
Lord with cheer-ful voice. Him serve with fear, His
praise forth tell; Come ye be-fore Him and re - joice.

2. The Lord, ye know, is God in - deed;
3. O en - ter then His gates with praise;

With - out our
Ap - proach with

aid He did us make; We are His folk, He
joy His courts un - to; Praise, laud, and bless His

doth us feed, And for His sheep He doth us take.
Name al - ways, For it is seem - ly so to do.

4. For why? the Lord our God is good; His mer - cy
5. To Fa - ther, Son and Ho - ly Ghost, The God Whom

is for ev - er sure; His truth at all times
Heav'n and earth a - dore, From men and from the

firm - ly stood, And shall from age to age en - dure.
an - gel host Be praise and glo - ry ev - er - more.

Praise To The Lord, The Almighty   205

Tune: LOBE DEN HERREN (14 14 4 7 8)   Text: Joachim Neander (†1680)

1. Praise to the Lord, the Al - might - y, the King of cre -
2. Praise to the Lord, who o'er all things so won - drous - ly

a - tion! O my soul, praise him, for he is thy
reign - eth, shel - ters thee un - der his wings, yea, so

health and sal - va - tion! All ye who hear, now to his
gen - tly sus - tain - eth! Hast thou not seen how thy de -

tem - ple draw near; praise him in glad ad - o - ra - tion.
sires e'er have been grant - ed in what he or - dain - eth?

3. Praise to the Lord, who doth pros - per thy work and de -
4. Praise to the Lord, who, when dark - ness of sin is a -
5. Praise to the Lord, O let all that is in me a -

fend thee; sure - ly his good - ness and mer - cy here
bound - ing, who, when the god - less do tri - umph, all
dore him! All that hath life and breath, come now with

dai - ly at - tend thee. Pon - der a - new what the Al -
vir - tue con - found - ing, shed - deth his light, chas - eth the
prais - es be - fore him. Let the "A - men" sound from his

might - y can do, if with his love he be - friend thee.
hor - rors of night, saints with his mer - cy sur - round - ing.
peo - ple a - gain, glad - ly for all we a - dore him.

206 All Creatures Of Our God And King

Tune: LASST UNS ERFREUEN (88 44 88 w Rfn)   Text: after Francis of Assisi (†1226)

1. All crea-tures of our God and King Lift up your voice and with us
2. Thou rush-ing wind that art so strong Ye clouds that sail in Heav'n a-
3. Thou flow-ing wa-ter, pure and clear, Make mu-sic for thy Lord to

sing, Al-le-lu-ia! Al-le-lu-ia! Thou burn-ing sun with gold en
long, O__ praise Him! Al-le-lu-ia! Thou ris-ing moon, in praise re-
hear, O__ praise Him! Al-le-lu-ia! Thou fire so mas-ter-ful and

beam, Thou sil-ver moon with soft-er gleam!   **Refrain:** O__
joice, Ye lights of eve-ning, find a voice!
bright, That giv-est man both warmth and light.

praise Him! O__ praise Him! Al-le-lu-ia! Al-le-lu-ia! Al-le-lu-ia!

4. And all ye men of ten-der heart, For-giv-ing oth-ers,
5. And thou most kind and gen-tle Death, Wait-ing to hush our
6. Let all things their Cre-a-tor bless, And wor-ship Him in

take your part, O__ sing ye! Al-le-lu-ia! Ye who long
lat-est breath, O__ praise Him! Al-le-lu-ia! Thou lead-est
hum-ble-ness, O__ praise Him! Al-le-lu-ia! Praise, praise the

pain and sor-row bear, Praise God and on Him cast your care!
home the child of God, And Christ our Lord the way hath trod.
Fa-ther, praise the Son, And praise the Spir-it, Three in One!

For The Beauty Of The Earth   207

Tune: DIX (77 77 77)   Text: Folliot Sandford Pierpoint (†1864)

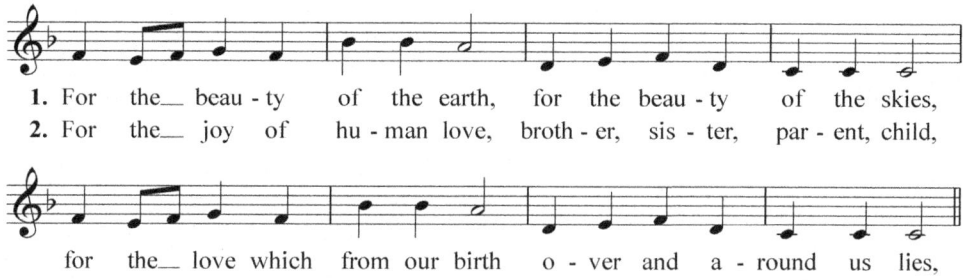

1. For the__ beau - ty of the earth, for the beau - ty of the skies,
2. For the__ joy of hu - man love, broth - er, sis - ter, par - ent, child,

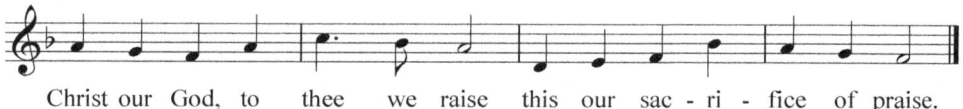

for the__ love which from our birth o - ver and a - round us lies,
friends on__ earth, and friends a - bove, for all gen - tle thoughts and mild,

Refrain:

Christ our God, to thee we raise this our sac - ri - fice of praise.

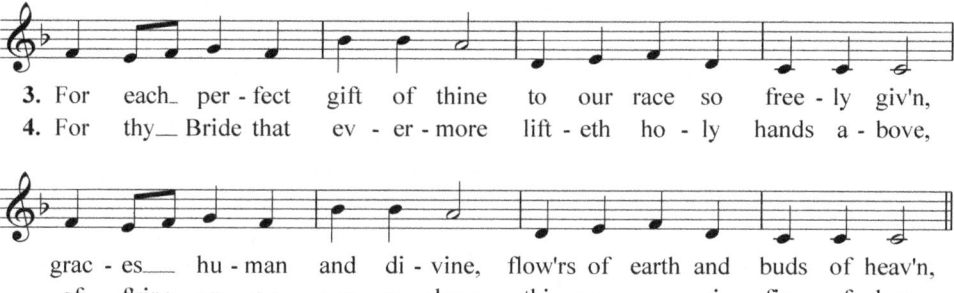

3. For each__ per - fect gift of thine to our race so free - ly giv'n,
4. For thy__ Bride that ev - er - more lift - eth ho - ly hands a - bove,

grac - es__ hu - man and di - vine, flow'rs of earth and buds of heav'n,
of - f'ring up on eve - ry shore this pure sac - ri - fice of love,

5. For the__ mar - tyrs' crown of light, for thy proph - ets' ea - gle eye,
6. For thy__ vir - gins' robes of snow, for thy maid - en Moth - er mild,

for thy__ bold con - fes - sors' might, for the lips of in - fan - cy,
for thy - self, with hearts a - glow, Je - sus, Vic - tim un - de - filed,

208 Faith Of Our Fathers

Tune: ST. CATHERINE (88 88 88)   Text: Frederick William Faber (†1863)

1. Faith of our fa - thers! liv - ing still in spite of
dun - geon, fire___ and sword: O how our hearts_ beat
high___ with joy, when - e'er we hear that glo - rious word!

Refrain:

Faith of our fa - thers, ho - ly faith! We will be true to thee till death.

2. Faith of our fa - thers! faith___ and prayer shall win all
na - tions un - to thee; and through the truth___ that
comes_ from God, man - kind shall then in - deed___ be free.

3. Faith of our fa - thers! we___ will love both friend and
foe in all___ our strife: and preach thee, too,___ as
love___ knows how, by kind - ly deeds and vir - tuous life.

Holy, Holy, Holy! Lord God Almighty 209

Tune: NICAEA (11 12 12 10)   Text: Reginald Heber (†1826)

1. Ho - ly, ho - ly, ho - ly! Lord God Al - might - y!
2. Ho - ly, ho - ly, ho - ly! All saints a - dore thee,

Ear - ly in the morn - ing our song shall rise to
cast - ing down their gold - en crowns a - round the glass - y

thee. Ho - ly, ho - ly, ho - ly! Mer - ci - ful and
sea; cher - u - bim and ser - a - phim fall - ing down be -

might - y, God in three Per - sons, bless - èd Trin - i - ty.
fore thee, which wert, and art, and ev - er - more shalt be.

3. Ho - ly, ho - ly, ho - ly! Though the dark - ness hide thee,
4. Ho - ly, ho - ly, ho - ly! Lord__ God Al - might - y!

Though the eye of sin - ful man Thy glo - ry may not
All thy works shall praise thy Name, in earth, and sky, and

see; on - ly thou art ho - ly; there is none be -
sea; Ho - ly, ho - ly, ho - ly! Mer - ci - ful and

side thee, per - fect in pow'r, in love, and pu - ri - ty.
might - y, God in three Per - sons, bless - èd Trin - i - ty.

210 Sing Praise To God In Heaven Above

Tune: GENEVA 1542/ULENBERG 1603   Text: Caspar Ulenberg (†1617)

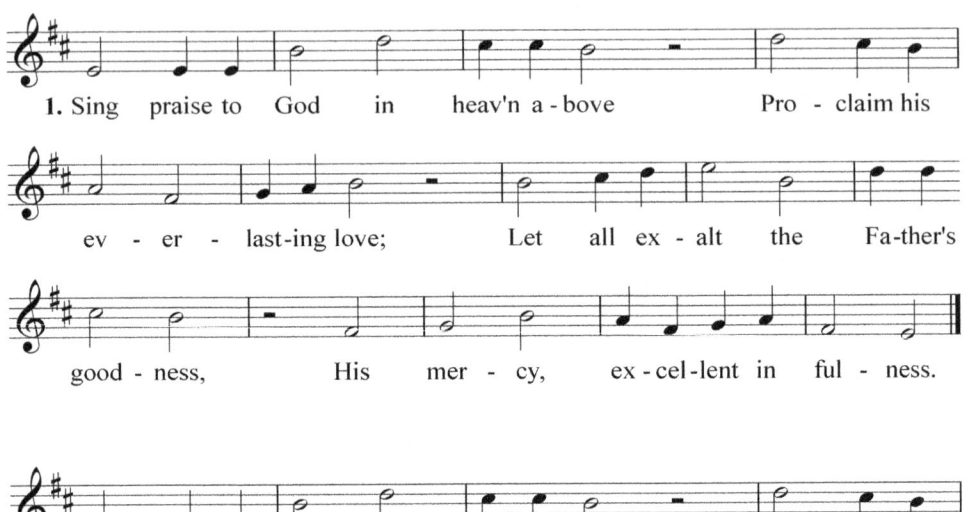

1. Sing praise to God in heav'n a-bove Pro-claim his
ev-er-last-ing love; Let all ex-alt the Fa-ther's
good-ness, His mer-cy, ex-cel-lent in ful-ness.

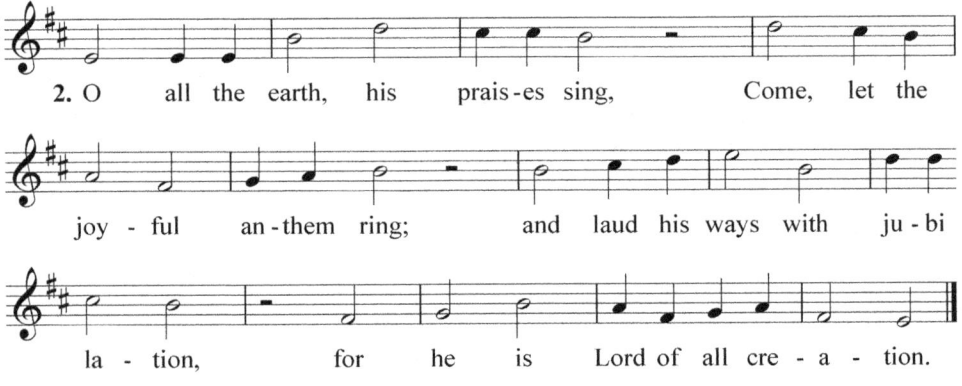

2. O all the earth, his prais-es sing, Come, let the
joy-ful an-them ring; and laud his ways with ju-bi
la-tion, for he is Lord of all cre-a-tion.

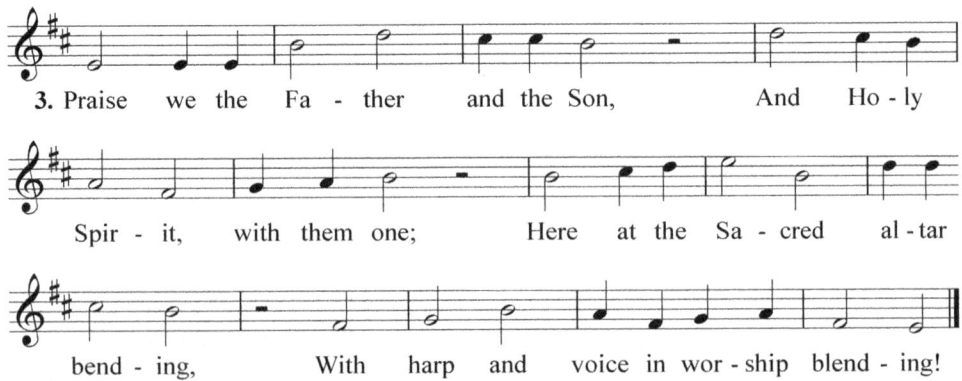

3. Praise we the Fa-ther and the Son, And Ho-ly
Spir-it, with them one; Here at the Sa-cred al-tar
bend-ing, With harp and voice in wor-ship blend-ing!

Lift Up Your Heads, Ye Mighty Gates 211

Tune: TRURO (LM) Text: Georg Weissel (†1635)

1. Lift up your heads, ye might - y gates; Be-hold, the
King of glo - ry waits; The King of kings is
draw - ing near; The Sav - ior of the world is here!

2. O blest the land, the cit - y blest, Where Christ the
Rul - er is con - fessed! O hap - py hearts and
hap - py homes To whom this King in tri - umph comes!

3. Fling wide the por - tals of your heart; Make it a
4. So come, my Sov - 'reign, en - ter in! Let new and

tem - ple, set a - part From earth - ly use for
nobl - er life be - gin; Thy Ho - ly Spir - it

heav'n's em - ploy, A-dorned with prayer and love and joy.
guide us on, Un - til the glo - rious crown is won.

212 On This Day, The First Of Days

Tune: GOTT SEI DANK (77 77)   Text: Die parente temporum

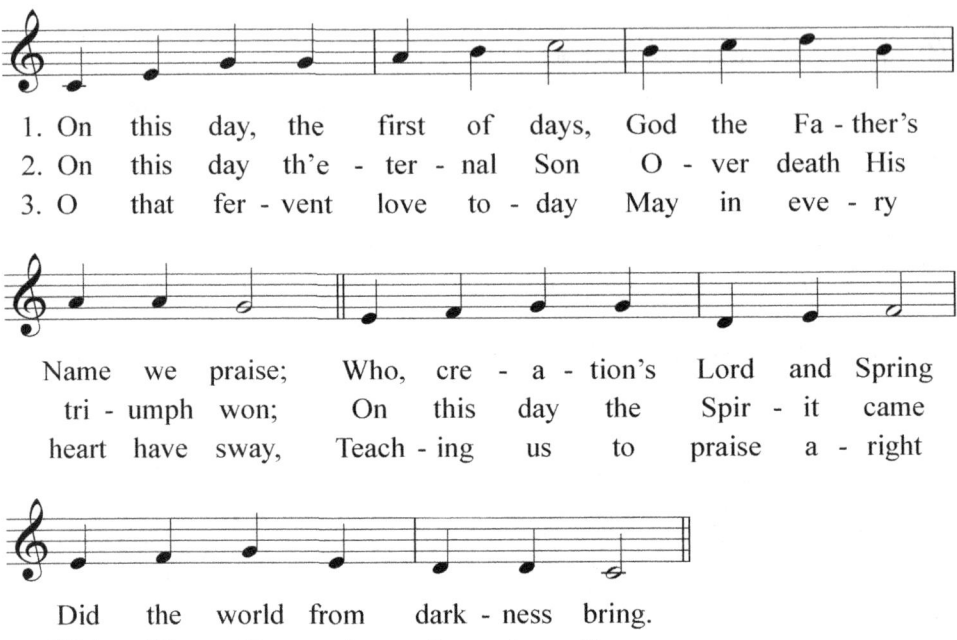

1. On this day, the first of days, God the Fa-ther's
2. On this day th'e-ter-nal Son O-ver death His
3. O that fer-vent love to-day May in eve-ry

Name we praise; Who, cre-a-tion's Lord and Spring
tri-umph won; On this day the Spir-it came
heart have sway, Teach-ing us to praise a-right

Did the world from dark-ness bring.
With His gifts of liv-ing flame.
God, the Source of life and light.

4. Father, who didst fashion me
   Image of Thyself to be,
   Fill me with Thy love divine,
   Let my every thought be Thine.

5. Thou, who dost all gifts impart,
   Shine, sweet Spirit, in my heart;
   Best of gifts Thyself bestow;
   Make me burn Thy love to know.

6. God, the blessèd Three in One,
   Dwell within my heart alone;
   Thou dost give Thyself to me;
   May I give myself to Thee.

Thy Hand, O God, Has Guided   213

Tune: KING'S LYNN (76 76D)   Text: Edward Plumptre (†1891)

1. Thy hand, O God, has guid - ed thy_ flock, from age to age;
2. Thy her - alds brought glad tid - ings to_ great - est as to least;

their_ won-drous tale is_ writ - ten, full clear, on eve - ry page;
they_ bade men rise, and_ has - ten to share the great King's feast;

thy_ peo - ple owned thy_ good - ness, and we their deeds re - cord;
and_ this was all their_ teach - ing, in eve - ry deed and word,

and both of this bear wit - ness; one_ Church, one Faith, one Lord.
to all a - like pro - claim - ing one_ Church, one Faith, one Lord.

3. And we, shall we be faith - less? shall hearts fail, hands hang down?
4. Thy mer - cy will not fail_ us, nor_ leave thy work un - done;

shall_ we e - vade the_ con - flict, and cast a - way our crown?
with_ thy right hand to_ help us, thy vic - t'ry shall be won;

Not_ so: in God's deep_ coun - sels some bet - ter thing is stored;
and_ then, by all cre - a - tion, thy name shall be a - dored,

we will main-tain, un - flinch - ing, one_ Church, one Faith, one Lord.
and this shall be their an - them: one_ Church, one Faith, one Lord.

214 Crown Him With Many Crowns

Tune: DIADEMATA (DSM)   Text: Matthew Bridges (†1894)

1. Crown Him with man-y crowns, The Lamb up-on His throne; Hark how the heav'n-ly an-them drowns All mu-sic but its own! A-wake, my soul,– and sing Of Him Who died for thee, And hail Him as thy match-less King Through all E-ter-ni-ty.

2. Crown Him the Vir-gin's Son, The God In-car-nate born,– Whose Arm those crim-son tro-phies won Which now His brow a-dorn! Fruit of the Mys-tic Rose, As of that Rose the Stem, The Root, whence Mer-cy ev-er flows, The Babe of Beth-le-hem!

3. Crown him the Lord of Love! Be-hold his hands and side,– Rich Wounds, yet vis-i-ble a-bove, In beau-ty glo-ri-fied: No an-gel in the sky, Can ful-ly bear that sight, But down-ward bends his burn-ing eye At mys-ter-ies so bright!

4. Crown Him the Lord of Peace!
Whose pow'r a scepter sways
From pole to pole, that wars may cease
Absorb'd in prayer and praise:
His reign shall know no end,
And round His piercèd Feet
Fair flow'rs of paradise extend
Their fragrance ever sweet.

5. Crown Him the Lord of Heaven!
One with the Father known,—
And the Blest Spirit through Him giv'n
From yonder Triune Throne!
All hail! Redeemer,—Hail!
For Thou hast died for me:
Thy praise shall never, never fail
Throughout eternity!

Be Thou My Vision   215

Tune: SLANE (10 11 11 11)   Text: Traditional Irish (8th cent.)

1. Be thou my vi - sion, O Lord of my heart,
2. Be thou my wis - dom, be thou my true word
3. Be thou my breast - plate, my sword for the fight,

Be all else but naught to me, save that thou art,
Be thou ev - er with me, and I with thee, Lord,
Be thou my whole ar - mor, be thou my true might,

Be thou my best thought in the day and the night,
Be thou my great Fa - ther, and I thy true son,
Be thou my soul's shel - ter, be thou my strong tower,

Both wak - ing and sleep - ing, thy pres-ence my light.
Be thou in me dwell - ing, and I with thee one.
O raise thou me heav - en - ward, great Pow'r of my pow'r.

4. Riches I heed not, nor man's empty praise,
Be thou my inheritance now and always,
Be thou and thou only the first in my heart,
O Sov'reign of heaven, my treasure thou art.

5. High King of heaven, thou heaven's bright Sun,
O grant me its joys after vict'ry is won,
Great Heart of my own heart, whatever befall,
Still be thou my vision, O Ruler of all.

216   Praise, My Soul, The King Of Heaven

Tune: LAUDA ANIMA (87 87 87)   Text: Henry Francis Lyte (†1847)

1. Praise, my soul, the King of heav-en; to his feet thy trib-ute bring;
ran-somed, healed, re-stored, for-giv-en, ev-er-more his prais-es
sing: Al-le-lu-ia, al-le-lu-ia! Praise the ev-er-last-ing King.

2. Praise him for his grace and fa-vor to our fa-thers in dis-tress;
praise him still the same for ev-er, slow to chide and swift to
bless: Al-le-lu-ia, al-le-lu-ia! Glo-rious in his faith-ful-ness.

3. Fa-ther-like, he tends and spares us; well our fee-ble frame he knows;
in his hand he gen-tly bears us, res-cues us from all our
foes. Al-le-lu-ia, al-le-lu-ia! Wide-ly yet his mer-cy flows.

4. An-gels, help us to a-dore him; ye be-hold him face to face;
sun and moon, bow down be-fore him, dwell-ers all in time and
space. Al-le-lu-ia, al-le-lu-ia! Praise with us the God of grace.

Holy God, We Praise Thy Name   217

Tune: GROSSER GOTT (78 78 77)   Text: Fr. Ignaz Franz (†1790)

1. Ho - ly God, we praise thy Name; Lord of all,_ we bow_ be-
2. Hark! the loud_ ce - les - tial hymn an - gel choirs a - bove_ are
3. Lo! the ap - os - tol - ic train join the sa - cred Name to

fore thee! All on earth_ thy scep - ter claim, all in heav'n a-
rais-ing, cher - u - bim_ and ser - a - phim, in un - ceas - ing
hal - low; proph - ets swell the loud_ re - frain, and the white robed

bove a - dore thee; in - fi - nite_ thy vast do - main, ev - er-
cho - rus prais-ing; fill the heav'ns with sweet ac - cord: Ho - ly,
mar - tyrs fol - low; and from morn_ to set of sun, through the

last - ing is_ thy reign.   4. Ho - ly Fa - ther, Ho - ly Son,
ho - ly, ho - ly, Lord.   5. Thou art King of glo - ry, Christ:
Church the song goes on.   6. Spare Thy peo - ple, Lord, we pray,

Ho - ly Spir - it, Three we name thee; while in es - sence
Son of God,_ yet born_ of Mar - y; For us sin - ners
By a thou - sand snares sur - round-ed: Keep us with - out

on - ly One, un - di - vid - ed God_ we claim thee; and a-
sac - ri - ficed, And to death a trib - u - tar - y: First to
sin_ to - day, Nev - er let_ us be_ con-found-ed. Lo, I

dor - ing bend the knee, while we own_ the mys - ter - y.
break the bars of death, Thou has o - pened Heav'n_ to faith.
put_ my trust in Thee; Nev - er, Lord, a - ban - don me.

218   I Sing The Mighty Power Of God

Tune: ELLACOMBE (76 76D)   Text: Isaac Watts (†1748)

1. I sing the_might-y pow'r of God, that made the moun-tains rise,
that spread the_ flow-ing seas a-broad, and built the loft-y skies.
I_ sing the wis-dom that or-dained the_ sun to rule the day;
the moon shines full at His com-mand, and all_ the stars o-bey.

2. I sing the_ good-ness of the Lord, That fill'd_ the earth with food: He form'd the_ crea-tures with his word, And then_ pro-nounced them good. Lord,_ how thy won-ders are dis-play'd Where 'er I turn mine eye, If I sur-vey the ground I tread, Or gaze_ up-on the sky!

3. There's not a_ plant or flow'r be-low, But makes thy glo-ries known; And clouds a-rise and tem-pests blow, By or-der from thy throne. While_ all that bor-rows life from Thee Is_ ev-er in Thy care, And eve-ry-where that man can be, Thou, God, art pre-sent there.

Sing Praise To God, Who Reigns Above 219

Tune: MIT FREUDEN ZART (87 87 88 7)   Text: Johann Jakob Schütz (†1690)

1. Sing praise to God who reigns a - bove, the__ God of all cre -
2. The an - gel host, O King of kings, thy__ praise for ev - er__

-a - tion, the God of pow'r, the God of love, the__
tell - ing, in earth and sky all liv - ing things be -

God of our sal - va - tion; with heal - ing balm my
neath thy shad - ow__ dwell - ing, a - dore the wis - dom

soul he fills, and eve - ry faith - less mur - mur stills: to
which could span and pow'r which formed cre - a - tion's plan: to

God all praise and__ glo - ry.
God all praise and__ glo - ry.

3. What God's al - might - y
4. O ye who name Christ's

pow'r hath made, his__ gra - cious mer - cy__ keep - eth; by
ho - ly name give__ God all praise and__ glo - ry; let

morn - ing glow or eve - ning shade his__ watch - ful eye ne'er
all who know his pow'r pro - claim a - loud the won - drous

sleep - eth. With - in the king - dom of his might, lo!
sto - ry! Cast each false i - dol from its throne, the

all is just and all is right: to God all praise and__ glo - ry.
Lord is God, and he a - lone: to God all praise and__ glo - ry.

220 To Jesus Christ, Our Sovereign King

Tune: ICH GLAUB AN GOTT (87 87 with Refrain)   Text: Martin B. Hellriegel (†1981)

1. To Je - sus Christ, our Sov-'reign King, Who is the world's sal - va - tion,

All praise and hom - age do we bring, And thanks and ad - o - ra - tion.

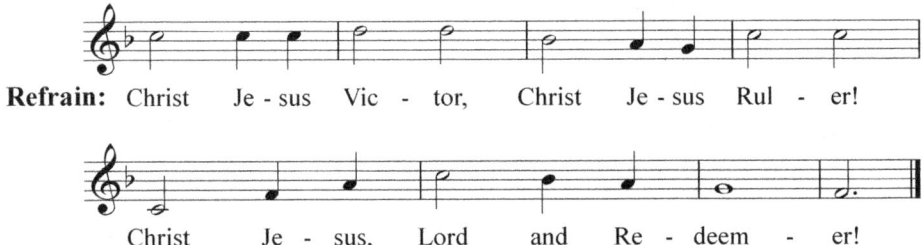

Refrain: Christ Je - sus Vic - tor, Christ Je - sus Rul - er!

Christ Je - sus, Lord and Re - deem - er!

2. Thy reign ex - tend, O King be - nign, To eve - ry land and na - tion,

For in thy king - dom, Lord di - vine, A - lone we find sal - va - tion.

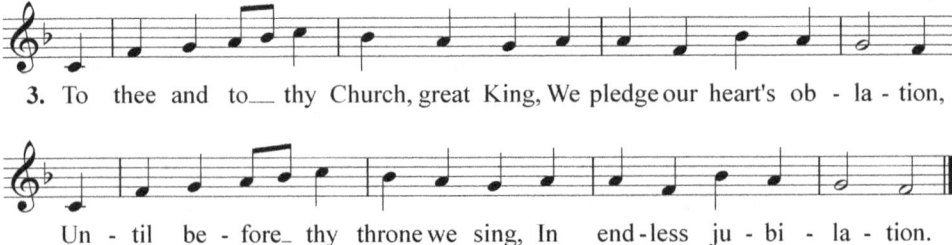

3. To thee and to__ thy Church, great King, We pledge our heart's ob - la - tion,

Un - til be - fore_ thy throne we sing, In end - less ju - bi - la - tion.

Now Thank We All Our God   221

Tune: NUN DANKET ALLE GOTT (67 67 66 66)   Text: Martin Rinkart (†1649)

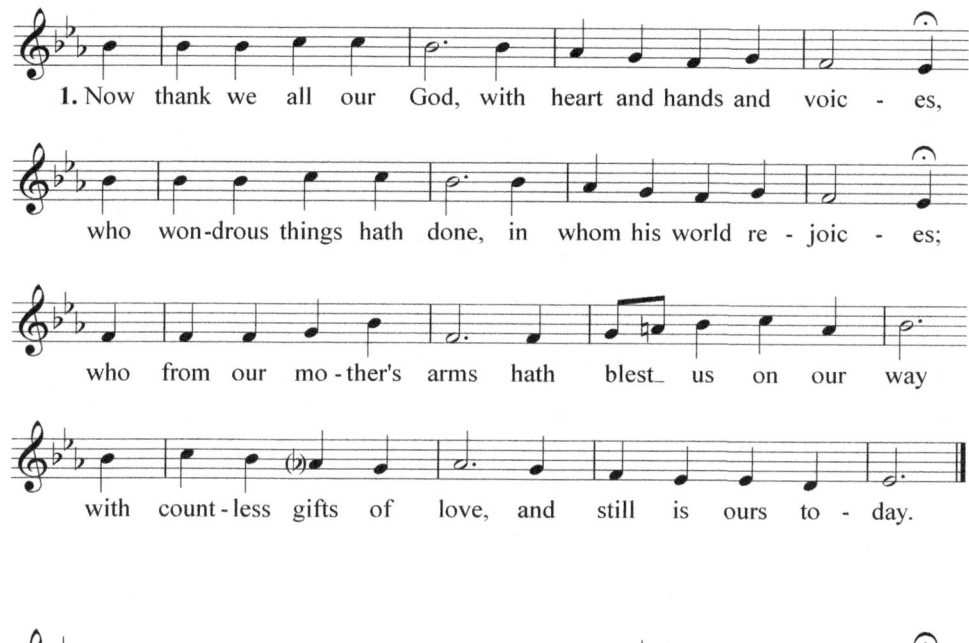

1. Now thank we all our God, with heart and hands and voic - es,
who won-drous things hath done, in whom his world re - joic - es;
who from our mo -ther's arms hath blest_ us on our way
with count - less gifts of love, and still is ours to - day.

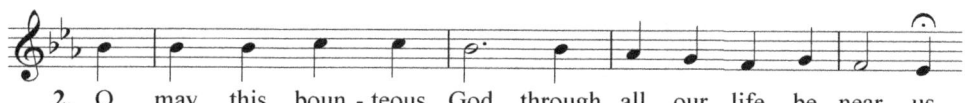

2. O   may   this   boun - teous   God   through   all   our   life   be   near   us,
3. All   praise   and   thanks   to   God   the   Fa - ther   now   be   giv - en,

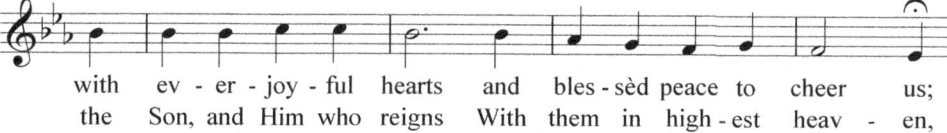

with   ev - er - joy - ful   hearts   and   bles - sèd   peace   to   cheer   us;
the   Son, and   Him who reigns   With   them   in   high - est   heav - en,

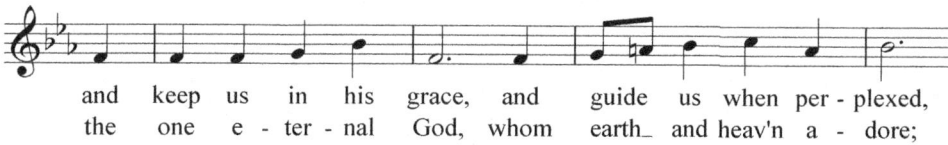

and   keep   us   in   his   grace,   and   guide   us   when   per - plexed,
the   one   e - ter - nal   God,   whom   earth_   and heav'n   a - dore;

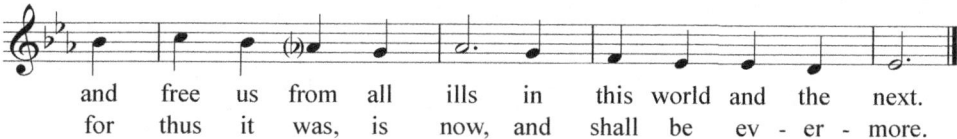

and   free   us   from   all   ills   in   this   world   and   the   next.
for   thus   it   was,   is   now,   and   shall   be   ev - er - more.

222   Triumphantly Doth Christ Unfurl

Tune: ST. HUGH (CM)   Text: Vexilla Christus Inclyta

1. Tri - um -phant - ly doth Christ un - furl His   ban - ners far and   wide!

Ye   na - tions, come, give praise, ap -plaud The   King Who for   us   died!

2. He   con - quers king - doms not   by wars, Nor   bru - tal force, nor   fear;

But raised on high up - on   the Cross, He   draws His sub - jects near.

3. O   lov - ing King, Thy light we seek, To   shine by night and   day!

And   may the world, blest with Thy peace, A - dore Thee and o - bey!

4. To   Thee be glo - ry, Christ our King, Who   rul - est all with might,

For - ev - er with the   Fa - ther, God, and   Spir - it, Lord of Light!

O Lord Of Heaven, Whose Love Profound 223

Tune: DEO GRACIAS (LM)   Text: Edward Cooper (†1833)

1. O Lord of heav'n whose love pro - found a ran - som for__ our__ souls hath found, be - fore thy throne we sin -ners bend; to us thy par - d'ning love ex - tend.

2. Al - might - y Son, In - car - nate Word, our Proph - et, Priest, Re - deem - er, Lord, be - fore thy throne we sin - ners bend; to us thy sav - ing grace ex - tend.

3. E - ter - nal Spir - it, by whose breath the soul__ is raised__ from sin and death, Be - fore thy throne we sin - ners bend; to us thy quick - 'ning pow'r ex - tend.

4. Thrice Ho - ly! Fa - ther, Spir - it, Son, mys - te - rious God - head, Three in One, be - fore thy throne we sin - ners bend; grace, par - don, life to us ex - tend.

224 Joyful, Joyful, We Adore Thee

Tune: HYMN TO JOY (87 87D)   Text: Henry Van Dyke (†1933)

1. Joy-ful, joy-ful, we a-dore thee, God of glo-ry, Lord of love;
2. All thy works with joy sur-round thee, earth and heav'n re-flect thy rays,

hearts un-fold like flow'rs be-fore thee, open-ing to the sun a-bove.
stars and an-gels sing a-round thee, cen-ter of un-bro-ken praise.

Melt the clouds of sin and sad-ness; drive the dark of doubt a-way;
Field and for-est, vale and moun-tain, flow-'ry mead-ow, flash-ing sea,

Giv-er of im-mor-tal glad-ness, fill us with the light of day!
sing-ing bird and flow-ing foun-tain call us to re-joice in thee.

3. Thou art giv-ing and for-giv-ing, ev-er bless-ing, ev-er blest,
4. Mor-tals, join the might-y cho-rus, which the morn-ing stars be-gan;

well-spring of the joy of liv-ing, o-cean depth of hap-py rest!
Fa-ther-love is reign-ing o'er us, broth-er love binds man to man.

Thou our Fa-ther, Christ our Broth-er, all who live in love are thine;
ev-er sing-ing, march we on-ward, vic-tors in the midst of strife,

teach us how to love each oth-er, lift us to the joy di-vine.
joy-ful mu-sic leads us sun-ward in the tri-umph song of life.

All Hail The Power Of Jesus' Name   225

Tune: Based on CORONATION (86 86 86)   Text: Edward Perronet (†1792)

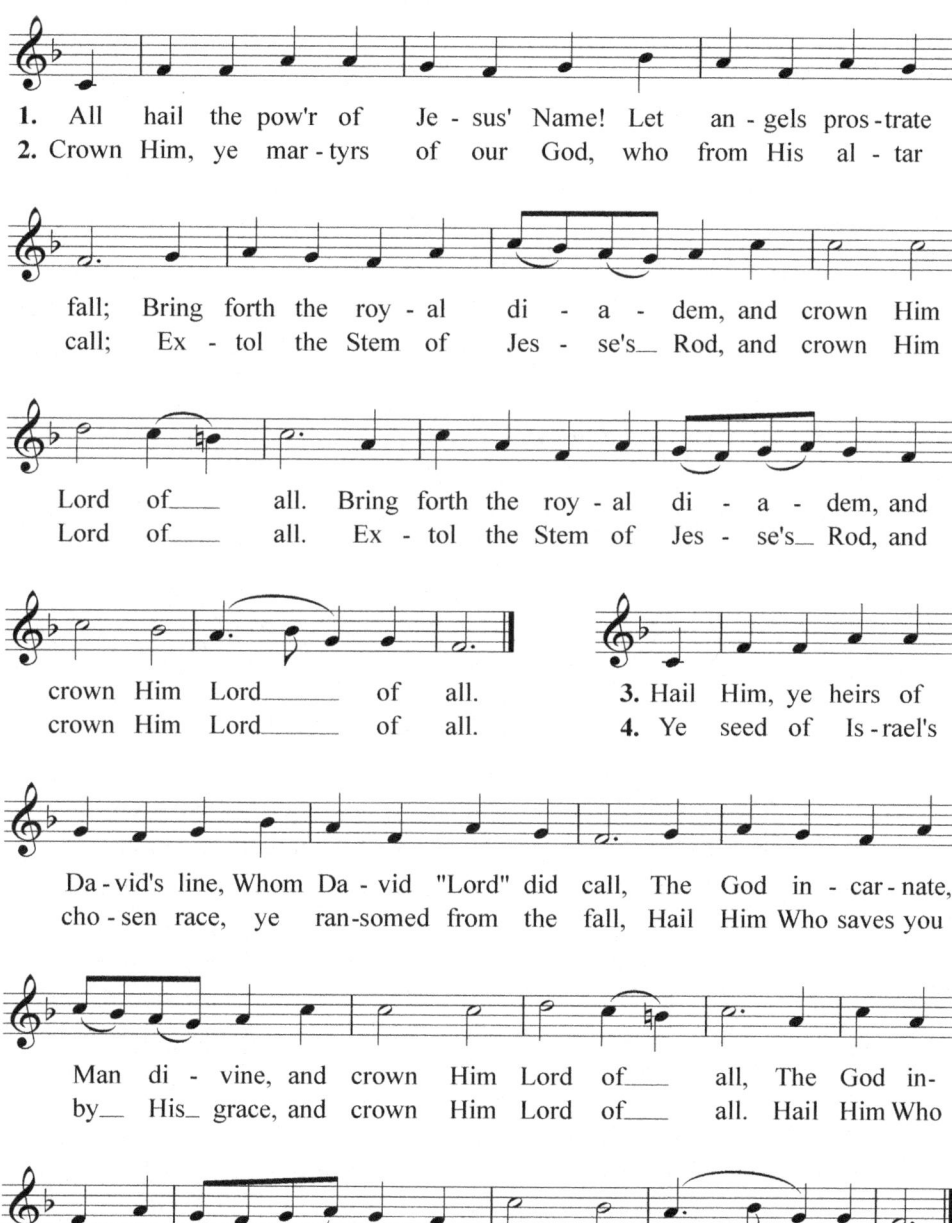

1. All hail the pow'r of Je-sus' Name! Let an-gels pros-trate
2. Crown Him, ye mar-tyrs of our God, who from His al-tar

fall; Bring forth the roy-al di-a-dem, and crown Him
call; Ex-tol the Stem of Jes-se's_ Rod, and crown Him

Lord of___ all. Bring forth the roy-al di-a-dem, and
Lord of___ all. Ex-tol the Stem of Jes-se's_ Rod, and

crown Him Lord___ of all.   3. Hail Him, ye heirs of
crown Him Lord___ of all.   4. Ye seed of Is-rael's

Da-vid's line, Whom Da-vid "Lord" did call, The God in-car-nate,
cho-sen race, ye ran-somed from the fall, Hail Him Who saves you

Man di-vine, and crown Him Lord of___ all, The God in-
by_ His_ grace, and crown Him Lord of___ all. Hail Him Who

car-nate, Man_ di-vine, and crown Him Lord___ of all.
saves you by_ His_ grace, and crown Him Lord___ of all.

226 Veni, Veni Emmanuel

Tune: VENI EMMANUEL   Text: Veni, Veni Emmanuel

1. Ve - ni, ve - ni Em - má - nu - el, Cap - tí - vum sol - ve
1. O come, O come, Em - ma - nu - el, and ran-som cap-tive

Is - ra - ël, Qui ge - mit in e - xí - li - o Pri -
Is - ra - el, that mourns in lone-ly ex - ile here un -

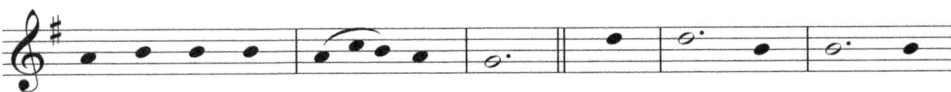

vá - tus De - i Fí - li - o. ℟. Gau - de, gau - de! Em -
til the Son of God_ ap - pear. ℟. Re - joice! Re - joice! Em -

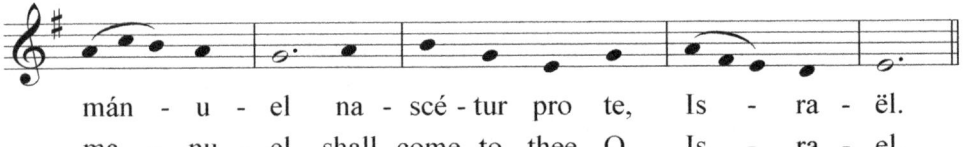

mán - u - el na - scé - tur pro te, Is - ra - ël.
ma - nu - el shall come to thee, O Is - ra - el.

2. Veni, O Jesse vírgula,
   Ex hostis tuos úngula,
   De specu tuos tártari
   Educ et antro bárathri.
   ℟. Gaude!

3. Veni, veni O Oriens!
   Soláre nos advéniens,
   Noctis depélle nébulas,
   Dirásque noctis ténebras.
   ℟. Gaude!

4. Veni, Clavis Davídica,
   Regna reclúde cælica,
   Fac iter tutum súperum,
   Et claude vias ínferum.
   ℟. Gaude!

5. Veni, veni Adonái!
   Qui pópulo in Sínai
   Legem dedísti vértice,
   In Majéstate glóriæ.
   ℟. Gaude!

Text: Psalteriolum Cantionum Catholicarum, Cologne, 1722.
Melody: 15th Century Franciscan Processionale.

O Come, O Come, Emmanuel   227

Tune: VENI EMMANUEL   Text: Veni, Veni Emmanuel

1. *See facing page.*

2. O come, Thou Rod of Jesse, free
   Thine own from Satan's tyranny;
   From depths of hell Thy people save,
   And give them victory over the grave.
                          ℟. Rejoice!

3. O come, Thou Day-spring, come and cheer
   Our spirits by Thine advent here;
   Disperse the gloomy clouds of night,
   And death's dark shadows put to flight.
                          ℟. Rejoice!

4. O come, Thou Key of David, come,
   And open wide our heavenly home;
   Make safe the way that leads on high,
   And close the path to misery.
                          ℟. Rejoice!

5. O come, O come, great Lord of Might,
   Who to Thy tribes on Sinai's height
   In ancient times once gave the law
   In cloud and majesty and awe.
                          ℟. Rejoice!

English Translation by Dr. John Neale (†1866).
Melody: 15th Century Franciscan Processionale.

228   Savior Of The Nations Come

Tune: NUN KOMM DER HEIDEN HEILAND (77 77)   Text: St. Ambrose (†397)

1. Sav-ior of the na - tions, come; Vir-gin's Son, here make thy home!
Mar - vel now, O heav'n and earth, that the Lord chose such a birth.

2. Not by hu - man flesh and blood; by the Spir - it of our God
3. Won-drous birth! O won - drous child of the Vir - gin un - de - filed!
4. From the Fa - ther forth he came and re - turn - eth to the same,

was the Word of God made flesh, wo - man's off - spring,
Though by all the world dis - owned, still to be in
cap - tive lead - ing death and hell high the song of

pure and fresh.   5. Thou, the Fa - ther's on - ly Son,
heav'n en - throned.   6. Bright - ly doth thy man - ger shine,
tri - umph swell!   7. Praise to God the Fa - ther sing,

hast o'er sin the vic - t'ry won. bound - less shall thy
glo - rious is its light di - vine. Let not sin o'er -
praise to God the Son, our King, praise to God the

king - dom be; when shall we its glo - ries see?
cloud this light; ev - er be our faith thus bright.
Spir - it be ev - er and e - ter - nal - ly.

On Jordan's Bank The Baptist's Cry 229

Tune: WINCHESTER NEW (LM)   Text: Charles Coffin (†1749)

1. On Jor - dan's bank the Bap - tist's cry an -
nounc - es that the Lord is nigh; a - wake and heark - en,
for he brings glad tid - ings of the King of kings.

2. Then cleansed be eve - ry soul from sin; make
3. For thou art our sal - va - tion, Lord, our

straight the way for God with - in, pre - pare we in our
ref - uge and our great re - ward; with - out thy grace we

hearts a home where such a might - y Guest may come.
waste a - way like flow'rs that with - er and de - cay.

4. To heal the sick stretch out thine hand, and
5. All praise, e - ter - nal Son, to thee, whose

bid the fall - en sin - ner stand; shine forth and let thy
ad - vent doth thy peo - ple free; whom with the Fa - ther

light re - store earth's own true love - li - ness once more.
we a - dore and Ho - ly Spir - it ev - er - more.

230 Hark! The Herald Angels Sing

Tune: Felix Mendelssohn (†1847)   Text: Charles Wesley (†1788)

1. Hark! The her - ald an - gels sing,__ "Glo - ry to the new-born King;
2. Christ, by high - est Heav'n a - dored; Christ the ev - er - last - ing Lord;

Peace on earth, and mer - cy mild,__ God and sin - ners rec - on - ciled!"
Late in time, be - hold Him come,__ Off-spring of the vir - gin's womb.

Joy - ful, all ye na - tions rise,__ Join the tri - umph of the skies;__
Veiled in flesh the God-head see;__ Hail th'in - car - nate De - i - ty,__

With th'an-gel - ic host pro-claim, "Christ is__ born in Beth - le - hem!"
Pleased as man with man to dwell, Je - sus__ our Em - ma - nu - el.

Refrain: Hark! the her - ald an - gels sing, "Glo - ry__ to the new-born King!"

3. Hail the heav'n - ly Prince of Peace! Hail the Sun of Right-eous-ness!
4. Come, De - sire of na - tions, come,__ Fix in us Thy hum - ble home;

Light and life to all He brings, Ris'n with heal - ing in His wings.
Rise, the wom - an's con-qu'ring Seed,__ Bruise in us the ser-pent's head.

Mild He lays His glo - ry by,__ Born that man no more may die.__
Now dis - play Thy sav - ing pow'r, Ru - ined na - ture now re - store;__

Born to raise the sons of earth, Born to__ give them sec - ond birth.
Now in mys - tic un - ion join Thine to__ ours, and ours to Thine.

O Come, All Ye Faithful   231

Tune: ADESTE FIDELES   Text: John Francis Wade (†1786)

1. O come, all ye faith ful, joy - ful and tri - um - phant,
2. True God of true God, Light from Light E - ter - nal,
3. Sing, choirs of an - gels, sing in ex - ul - ta - tion;

O come ye, O come ye, to Beth - le - hem.
Lo, He ab - hors not the Vir - gin's womb;
O sing, all ye cit - i - zens of heav - en a - bove!

Come and be - hold Him, born the King of an - gels;
Son of the Fa - ther, be - got - ten, not cre - at - ed;
Glo - ry to God, all glo - ry in the high - est;

Refrain: O come, let us a - dore Him, O come, let us a -
Ve - ní - te, a - do - ré - mus, ve - ní - te, a - do -

dore Him, O come, let us a - dore Him, Christ the Lord.
ré - mus, ve - ní - te, a - do - ré - mus Dó - mi - num.

4. Yea, Lord, we greet Thee, born this hap - py morn - ing,
5. *Ad - é - ste fi - dé - les, lae - ti tri - um - phán - tes,*
6. *De - um de De - o, lu - men de lú - mi - ne*

Je - sus, to Thee be glo - ry giv'n;
Ve - ní - te, ve - ní - te in Béth - le - hem.
Ge - stant pu - él - lae ví - sce - ra.

Word of the Fa - ther, now in flesh ap - pear - ing.
Na - tum vi - dé - te Re - gem an - ge - ló - rum.
De - um ve - rum, gé - ni - tum non fa - ctum.

232   Joy To The World

Tune: ANTIOCH   Text: Isaac Watts (†1748)

1. Joy to the world, the Lord is come! Let earth re-
2. Joy to the earth, the Sav - ior reigns! Let men their

ceive her King; Let ev - er - ry heart pre - pare Him
songs em - ploy; While fields and floods, rocks, hills and

room, And Heav'n and na - ture sing, And Heav'n and na - ture
plains Re - peat the sound-ing joy, Re - peat the sound-ing

sing, And Heav'n, and Heav'n and na - ture sing.
joy, Re - peat, re - peat the sound - ing joy.

3. No more let sins and sor - rows grow, Nor thorns in -
4. He rules the world with truth and grace, And makes the

fest the ground; He comes to make His bless - ings
na - tions prove The glo - ries of His right - eous -

flow Far as the curse is found, Far as the curse is
-ness, And won-ders of His love, And won-ders of His

found, Far as, far as the curse is found.
love, And won - ders, won - ders of His love.

God Rest You Merry, Gentlemen   233

Tune: GOD REST YOU MERRY   Text: Traditional

1. God rest you mer - ry, gen - tle - men, Let noth - ing you dis - may,
2. From God our heav'n - ly Fa - ther A bless - èd an - gel came,

For Je - sus Christ, our Sav - ior, Was born up - on this day
And un - to cer - tain shep - herds Brought tid - ings of the same,

To save us all from Sa - tan's pow'r When we were gone a - stray.
How that in Beth - le - hem was born The Son of God by name.

Refrain: O___ tid - ings of com - fort and joy, com-fort and

joy; O___ tid - ings of com - fort and joy!

3. The shep-herds at these tid - ings Re - joic - èd much in mind,
4. Now to the Lord sing prais - es, All you with - in this place,

And left their flocks a - feed - ing In tem-pest, storm and wind,
And with true love and broth - er - hood Each oth - er now em - brace.

And went to Beth - le - hem straight-way This bless - èd Babe to find.
The ho - ly tide of Christ - mas All oth - ers doth ef - face.

234   Angels We Have Heard On High

Tune: GLORIA (77 77 R)   Text: French Carol

1. An - gels we have heard   on high   Sweet - ly   sing - ing
2. Shep-herds, why this   ju - bi-lee?   Why your joy - ous
3. Come to Beth - le - hem   and see   Him Whose birth the

o'er   the plains,   And   the moun-tains   in   re - ply
strains pro- long?   What the glad-some   tid - ings be
an - gels sing;   Come, a - dore on   bend - ed knee

Ech - o   back   their   joy - ous strains.
Which   in - spire   your   heav'n - ly song?
Christ   the   Lord,   the   new - born King.

℟. Gló - - - - ri - a   in ex-cél-sis De - o,

Gló - - - - ri - a, in ex-cél-sis De - o.

4. See Him in a manger laid,
   Whom the choirs of angels praise;
   Mary, Joseph, lend your aid,
   While our hearts in love we raise.
            ℟. Glória.

*Traditional French Melody.   English Translation of "Les Anges
dans nos campagnes" by Bishop James Chadwick (†1882).*

The First Nowell 235

Tune: THE FIRST NOWELL (Irregular) Text: Traditional

1. The first No - ël the an - gel did say was to
2. They look - èd up and saw a star shin - ing
3. And by the light of that same star three
cer - tain poor shep-herds in fields as they lay; in
in the east be - yond them far, and
wise men came from coun - try far; to
fields as they lay, keep - ing their sheep, on a
to the earth it gave great light, and
seek for a king was their in - tent, and to
cold win - ter's night that was so deep. ℟. No -
so it con - tin - ued both day and night.
fol - low the star wher - ev - er it went.
- ël, No - ël, No - ël, No - ël, born is the King of Is - ra - el.

4. This star drew nigh to the northwest / O'er Bethlehem it took its rest
And there it did both pause and stay / Right o'er the place where Jesus lay. ℟.

5. Then entered in those Wise men three / Full reverently upon their knee
And offered there in His presence / Their gold and myrrh and frankincense. ℟.

6. Then let us all with one accord / Sing praises to our heavenly Lord | That hath made Heav'n and earth of nought / And with his blood mankind has bought. ℟.

236   As With Gladness Men Of Old

Tune: DIX (77 77 77)   Text: William Dix (†1898)

1. As with gladness, men of old Did the guiding star behold
As with joy they hailed its light Leading onward, beaming bright
So, most glorious Lord, may we Evermore be led to Thee.

2. As with joyful steps they sped To that lowly manger bed
There to bend the knee before Him Whom Heav'n and earth adore;
So may we with willing feet Ever seek Thy mercy seat.

3. As they offered gifts most rare At that manger rude and bare;
So may we with holy joy, Pure and free from sin's alloy,
All our costliest treasures bring, Christ, to Thee, our heav'nly King.

4. Holy Jesus, every day Keep us in the narrow way;
And, when earthly things are past, Bring our ransomed souls at last
Where they need no star to guide, Where no clouds Thy glory hide.

5. In the heav'nly country bright, Need they no created light;
Thou its Light, its Joy, its Crown, Thou its Sun which goes not down;
There forever may we sing Alleluias to our King!

Songs Of Thankfulness And Praise   237

Tune: ST. GEORGE'S WINDSOR (77 77D)   Text: Christopher Wordsworth (†1885)

1. Songs of thank-ful-ness and praise, Je-sus, Lord, to thee we raise,
2. Man-i-fest at Jor-dan's stream, Proph-et, Priest and King su-preme;

man-i-fest-ed by the star to the sag-es from a-far;
and at Ca-na, wed-ding guest, in thy God-head man-i-fest;

branch of roy-al Da-vid's stem in thy birth at Beth-le-hem;
man-i-fest in pow'r di-vine, chang-ing wa-ter in-to wine;

an-thems be to thee ad-dressed, God in man made man-i-fest.
an-thems be to thee ad-dressed, God in man made man-i-fest.

3. Man-i-fest in mak-ing whole pal-sied limbs and faint-ing soul;
4. Sun and moon shall dark-ened be, stars shall fall, the heav'ns shall flee;
5. Grant us grace to see thee, Lord, mir-rored in thy ho-ly Word;

man-i-fest in val-iant fight, quell-ing all the dev-il's might;
Christ will then like light-ning shine, all will see his glo-rious sign;
may we im-i-tate thee now, and be pure, as pure art thou;

man-i-fest in gra-cious will, ev-er bring-ing good from ill;
all will then the trum-pet hear, all will see the Judge ap-pear;
that we like to thee may be at thy great E-piph-a-ny;

an-thems be to thee ad-dressed, God in man made man-i-fest.
thou by all wilt be con-fessed, God in man made man-i-fest.
and may praise thee, ev-er blest, God in man made man-i-fest.

238 "I Come," The Great Redeemer Cries

Tune: FOREST GREEN (DCM)   Text: Christian Hymnbook, 1865, alt.

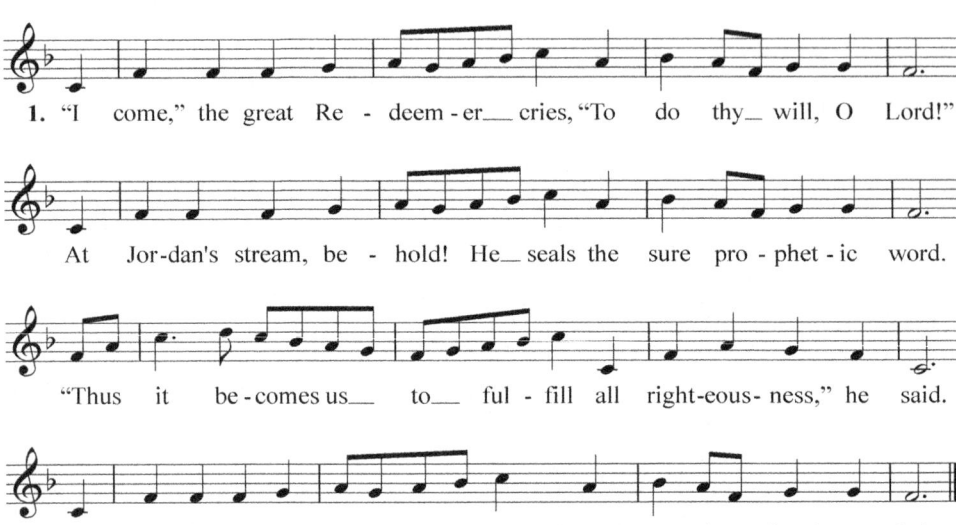

1. "I come," the great Re - deem - er cries, "To do thy will, O Lord!"

At Jor-dan's stream, be - hold! He seals the sure pro - phet - ic word.

"Thus it be - comes us to ful - fill all right-eous- ness," he said.

Then, faith-ful to the Lord's com-mands, through Jor - dan's flood was led.

2. O glo - rious voice! The Fa - ther speaks from heav'n's ex - alt - ed height:
3. True Lamb of God made man - i - fest, the Fa - ther's bless-èd Son.

"This is my Son, my well - be - loved, in whom I take de - light."
And he who sin had nev - er known hath all our sins un - done.

The Sav - ior Je - sus, Ho - ly Lord! His Name we will pro - fess,
No more we'll count our - selves our own but his in bonds of love.

like him de - sir - ous to ful - fill God's will in right-eous - ness.
Oh, may such bonds for ev - er draw our souls to things a - bove!

Blest Author Of This Earthly Frame   239

Tune: TALLIS CANON (LM)   Text: Sedulius (5th century), alt.

1. Blest Au-thor of this earth-ly frame, To take a ser-vant's form He came,
That, lib-er-at-ing flesh by flesh, Whom He had made might live a-fresh.

2. In that chaste pa-rent's ho-ly womb Ce-les-tial grace hath found its home;
And she, as earth-ly bride un-known, Yet calls that Off-spring blest her own.

3. That Son, that Roy-al Son she bore, Whom Ga-briel's voice had told a-fore;
Whom, in his moth-er yet con-cealed, The in-fant Bap-tist had re-vealed.

4. Lo, dipped in Jor-dan's cleans-ing stream, The Lamb of God would whit-er seem;
Yet 'twas our sins, in foul ar-ray, He bore, and bear-ing washed a-way.

5. All hon-or, laud, and glo-ry be, O Je-sus, Vir-gin-born to Thee:
All glo-ry, as is ev-er meet, To Fa-ther and to Par-a-clete.

240 Lord, Who Throughout These Forty Days

Tune: ST. FLAVIAN (CM)   Text: Claudia Hernaman (†1898)

1. Lord, who through-out these for-ty days for us didst fast and pray, teach us with thee to mourn our sins, and close by thee to stay.

2. As thou with Sa-tan didst con-tend and didst the vic-t'ry win, O give us strength in thee to fight, in thee to con-quer sin.

3. As thou didst hun-ger bear and thirst, so teach us, gra-cious Lord, to die to self, and chief-ly live by thy most ho-ly word.

4. And through these days of pen-i-tence, and through thy Pas-sion-tide, yea, ev-er-more, in life and death, Je-sus! with us a-bide.

5. A-bide with us, that so, this life of suf-fer-ing o'er-past, an East-er of un-end-ing joy we may at-tain at last!

Forty Days And Forty Nights   241

Tune: AUS DER TIEFE (77 77)   Text: George Smyttan (†1870)

1. For-ty days and for-ty nights thou wast fast-ing in the wild; for-ty days and for-ty nights tempt-ed, and yet un-de-filed.

2. Should not we thy sor-row share and from world-ly joys ab-stain, fast-ing with un-ceas-ing prayer, strong with thee to suf-fer pain?

3. Then if Sa-tan on us press, Je-sus, Sav-ior, hear our call! Vic-tor in the wil-der-ness, grant we may not faint or fall!

4. So shall we have peace di-vine: ho-lier glad-ness ours shall be; round us, too, shall an-gels shine, such as min-is-tered to thee.

5. Keep, O keep us, Sav-ior dear, ev-er con-stant by thy side; that with thee we may ap-pear at th'e-ter-nal East-er-tide.

242　All Glory, Laud, And Honor

Tune: ST. THEODULPH (76 76D)　　Text: Theodulph of Orleans (†821)

Refrain: All glo-ry, laud and hon-or, To Thee, Re-deem-er, King, To Whom the lips of chil-dren Made sweet ho-san-nas ring.

1. Thou art the King of Is-ra-el, Thou Da-vid's roy-al Son, Who in the Lord's Name com-est, The King and Bless-èd One.

2. The com-pa-ny of an-gels Are prais-ing Thee on High, And mor-tal men and all things Cre-at-ed make re-ply.

3. The peo-ple of the He-brews With palms be-fore Thee went; Our prayer and praise and an-thems Be-fore Thee we pre-sent.

4. To Thee, be-fore Thy pas-sion, They sang their hymns of praise;
5. Thou didst ac-cept their prais-es; Ac-cept the prayers we bring,

To Thee, now high ex-alt-ed, Our mel-o-dy we raise.
Who in all good de-light-est, Thou good and gra-cious King.

The Glory Of These Forty Days 243

Tune: ERHALT UNS, HERR (LM)   Text: Pope St. Gregory (†604)

1. The glo-ry of these for-ty days we cel-e-brate with songs of praise; for
Christ, through whom all things were made, him-self has fast-ed and has prayed.

2. A-lone and fast-ing Mo-ses saw the lov-ing God who gave the law;
and to E-li-jah, fast-ing, came the steeds and char-i-ots of flame.

3. So Dan-iel trained his mys-tic sight, de-liv-ered from the li-ons' might;
and John, the Bride-groom's friend, be-came the her-ald of Mes-si-ah's name.

4. Then grant us, Lord, like them to be full oft in fast and prayer with thee;
our spir-its strength-en with thy grace, and give us joy to see thy face.

5. O Fa-ther, Son, and Spir-it blest, to thee be eve-ry prayer ad-dressed,
who art in three-fold Name a-dored, from age to age, the on-ly Lord.

244   Lift High The Cross

Tune: CRUCIFER (10 10 with Refrain)   Text: Kitchen (†1912) & Newbolt (†1956)

Refrain: Lift high the cross, the love of Christ pro - claim till all the world___ a - dore___ his sa - cred Name.

1. Come, breth - ren, fol - low where our Cap - tain trod, our King vic - to - rious, Christ the Son of God.
2. Led on their way by this tri - um - phant sign, the hosts of___ God in con - qu'ring ranks com - bine.

3. Each new - born sol - dier of the Cru - ci - fied bears on the___ brow the seal of him who died.
4. From far - thest re - gions let their hom - age bring, and on his___ Cross a - dore their Sav - ior King.

5. Set up thy throne, that earth's de - spair may cease be - neath the___ shad - ow of its heal - ing peace.
6. For thy blest Cross which doth for all a - tone cre - a - tion's__ prais - es rise be - fore thy throne.

O Sacred Head, Surrounded   245

Tune: PASSION CHORALE (76 76D)   Text: Bernard of Clairvaux (†1153)

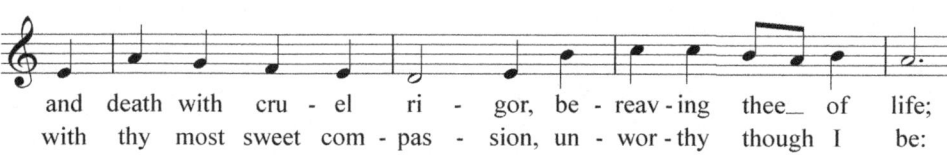

1. O sa-cred head, sur-round-ed by crown of pierc-ing thorn!

O bleed-ing head, so wound-ed, re-viled and put to scorn!

Our sins have marred the glo-ry of thy most ho-ly face,

yet an-gel hosts a-dore thee and trem-ble as they gaze.

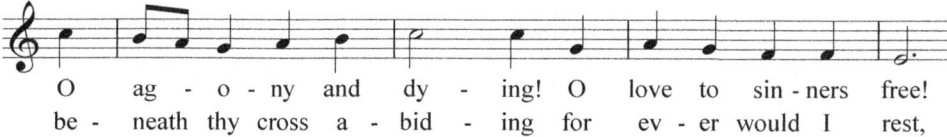

2. I see thy strength and vig-or all fad-ing in the strife,
3. In this thy bit-ter pas-sion, Good Shep-herd, think of me

and death with cru-el ri-gor, be-reav-ing thee of life;
with thy most sweet com-pas-sion, un-wor-thy though I be:

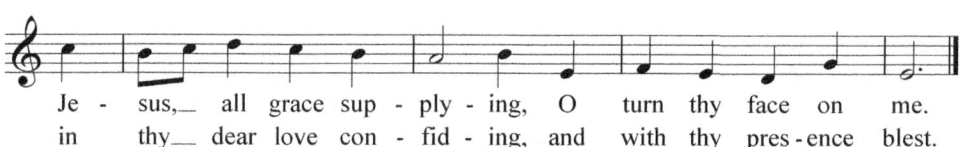

O ag-o-ny and dy-ing! O love to sin-ners free!
be-neath thy cross a-bid-ing for ev-er would I rest,

Je-sus, all grace sup-ply-ing, O turn thy face on me.
in thy dear love con-fid-ing, and with thy pres-ence blest.

246   Christ, The Lord, Is Risen Today

Tune: VICTIMAE PASCHALI (77 77D)   Text: Wipo of Burgundy (†1048)

1. Christ, the Lord is ris'n to-day; Chris-tians, haste your vows to pay;
2. Christ, the Vic-tim un-de-filed, God and man has rec-on-ciled,

Make your joy and prais-es known At the Pas-chal Vic-tim's throne.
When in fierce and blood-y strife Met to-geth-er Death and Life.

For the sheep the Lamb has bled, Sin-less in the sin-ner's stead;
Chris-tians, on this hap-py day, Raise your hearts with joy and say:

Christ, the Lord, is ris'n on high; Now He lives, no more to die!
Christ, the Lord, is ris'n on high; Now He lives, no more to die!

3. Say, O wond'ring Mar-y, say What you saw a-long the way.
4. Christ, Who once for sin-ners bled, Now the first-born from the dead,

"I be-held two an-gels bright, emp-ty tomb and wrap-pings white;
Throned in glo-rious maj-es-ty, Reigns through all e-ter-ni-ty.

I be-held the glo-ry bright Of the ris-en Lord of light.
Hail, e-ter-nal Hope on high! Hail, Thou King of vic-to-ry!

Christ, my hope, is ris'n a-gain; Now he lives, and lives to reign!"
Hail, Thou Prince of life a-dored! Help us, save us, gra-cious Lord!

Come, Ye Faithful, Raise The Strain   247

Tune: AVE VIRGO VIRGINUM (76 76D)   Text: St. John Damascene († c. 750)

1. Come, ye faith-ful, raise the strain of tri-um-phant glad-ness!
2. 'Tis the spring of souls to-day: Christ hath burst his pris-on,

God hath brought his Is-ra-el in-to joy from sad-ness:
and from three days' sleep in death as a sun hath ris-en;

loosed from Pha-roah's bit-ter yoke Ja-cob's sons and daugh-ters,
all the win-ter of our sins, long and dark, is fly-ing

led them with un-mois-tened foot through the Red Sea wa-ters.
from his light, to whom we give laud and praise un-dy-ing.

3. Now the queen of sea-sons, bright with the day of splen-dor,
4. Nei-ther might the gates of death, nor the tomb's dark por-tal,
5. "Al-le-lu-ia" now we cry to our King Im-mor-tal,

with the roy-al feast of feasts, comes its joy to ren-der;
nor the watch-ers, nor the seal hold thee as a mor-tal:
who tri-um-phant burst the bars of the tomb's dark por-tal;

comes to glad Je-ru-sa-lem, who with true af-fec-tion
but to-day a-midst the twelve thou didst stand, be-stow-ing
"al-le-lu-ia," with the Son God the Fa-ther prais-ing;

wel-comes in un-wea-ried strains Je-sus' res-ur-rec-tion.
that thy peace which ev-er-more pas-seth hu-man know-ing.
"al-le-lu-ia" yet a-gain to the Spir-it rais-ing.

248   Be Joyful, Mary, Heavenly Queen

Tune: REGINA CAELI JUBILA   Text: Cath. Hymn. Germanicum, 1584

1. Be joy - ful, Mar - y, heav'n - ly queen, Gau - de, Ma - rí -
2. The Son you bore by hea - ven's grace, *Be joy - ful, Ma -*

a: Your grief is changed to joy se - rene,
ry: Did all our guilt and sin ef - face,

Al - le - lú - ia, Lae - tá - re, O Ma - rí - a!
Al - le - lu - ia! Re - joice, re - joice, O Ma - ry!

3. The Lord is ris - en from the dead, Gau - de, Ma - rí -
4. Then pray to God, O Vir - gin fair, *Be joy - ful, Ma -*

a: He rose in glo - ry as He said.
ry: That He our souls to heav - en bear.

Al - le - lú - ia, Lae - tá - re, O Ma - rí - a!
Al - le - lu - ia! Re - joice, re - joice, O Ma - ry!

Jesus Christ Is Risen Today 249

Tune: EASTER HYMN (77 77 with Alleluias)   Text: Traditional

1. Je - sus Christ is ris'n to - day,__ Al - le - lu - ia!
2. Hymns of praise then let us sing,__ Al - le - lu - ia!

our tri - um - phant ho - ly day,__ Al - le - lu - ia!
un - to Christ, our heav'n - ly King, Al - le - lu - ia!

who did once up - on the cross, Al - le - lu - ia!
who en - dured the cross and grave, Al - le - lu - ia!

suf - fer_ to re - deem our loss._ Al - le - lu - ia!
sin - ners to re - deem and save. Al - le - lu - ia!

3. But the pains which he en - dured, Al - le - lu - ia!
4. Lives a - gain our glo - rious King, Al - le - lu - ia!

our sal - va - tion have pro - cured, Al - le - lu - ia!
Where, O death, is now thy sting? Al - le - lu - ia!

now a - bove the sky he's King, Al - le - lu - ia!
Once He died our souls to save, Al - le - lu - ia!

where the_ an - gels ev - er sing._ Al - le - lu - ia!
Where thy_ vic - to - ry, O grave? Al - le - lu - ia!

250   Ye Choirs of New Jerusalem

Tune: ST. MAGNUS (CM)   Text: St. Fulbert of Chartres (†1028)

1. Ye choirs of new Je - ru - sa - lem, your sweet-est notes em - ploy,
the pas-chal vic-to - ry to hymn in strains of___ ho - ly joy.

2. How Ju-dah's Li - on burst his chains, and crushed the ser-pent's head;
and brought with him, from death's do-mains the long - im - pris- oned dead.

3. From hell's de - vour-ing jaws the prey a - lone our lead - er bore;
4. Tri - um-phant in his glo - ry now his scep - tre rul - eth all;
his ran - somed hosts pur - sue their way where he has__ gone be - fore.
earth, heav'n and hell be - fore him bow and at his__ foot-stool fall.

5. While joy - ful thus his praise we sing, his mer - cy we im - plore,
6. All glo - ry to the Fa - ther be, all glo - ry to the Son,
in - to his pal - ace bright to bring and keep us__ ev - er - more.
all glo - ry, Ho - ly Ghost to thee, while end - less__ ag - es run.

He, Who Gave For Us His Life   251

Tune: WÜRTTEMBURG (77 77 with Alleluia)   Text: Michael Weisse (†1534)

1. He, who gave for us His life, Who for us en-dured the strife, Is our
Pas-chal Lamb to-day; We, too, sing for joy, and say: Al - le - lu - ia!

2. He, who bore all pain and loss Com - fort - less up -
3. He Who slum - bered in the grave, Is ex - alt - ed
4. He Whose path no re - cords tell, Who de - scend - ed

on the cross, Lives in glo - ry now on high,
now to save; Now through Chris - ten - dom it rings
in - to hell; Who the strong man armed hath bound,

Pleads for us,___ and hears our cry; Al - le - lu - ia!
That the Lamb is King of kings. Al - le - lu - ia!
Now in high - est Heav'n is crowned. Al - le - lu - ia!

5. Now He bids us tell a - broad How the lost may
6. Thou, our Pas - chal Lamb in - deed, Christ, Thy ran - somed
7. Christ the Lord is ris'n a - gain; Christ hath bro - ken

be re - stored, How the pen - i - tent for - giv'n,
peo - ple feed: Take our sins and guilt a - way,
eve - ry chain; Hark! An - gel - ic voic - es cry,

How we, too,___ may en - ter Heav'n. Al - le - lu - ia!
Let us sing___ by night and day: Al - le - lu - ia!
Sing - ing ev - er - more on high, Al - le - lu - ia!

252   Hail The Day That Sees Him Rise

Tune: LLANFAIR (77 77 with Alleluias)   Text: Charles Wesley (†1788)

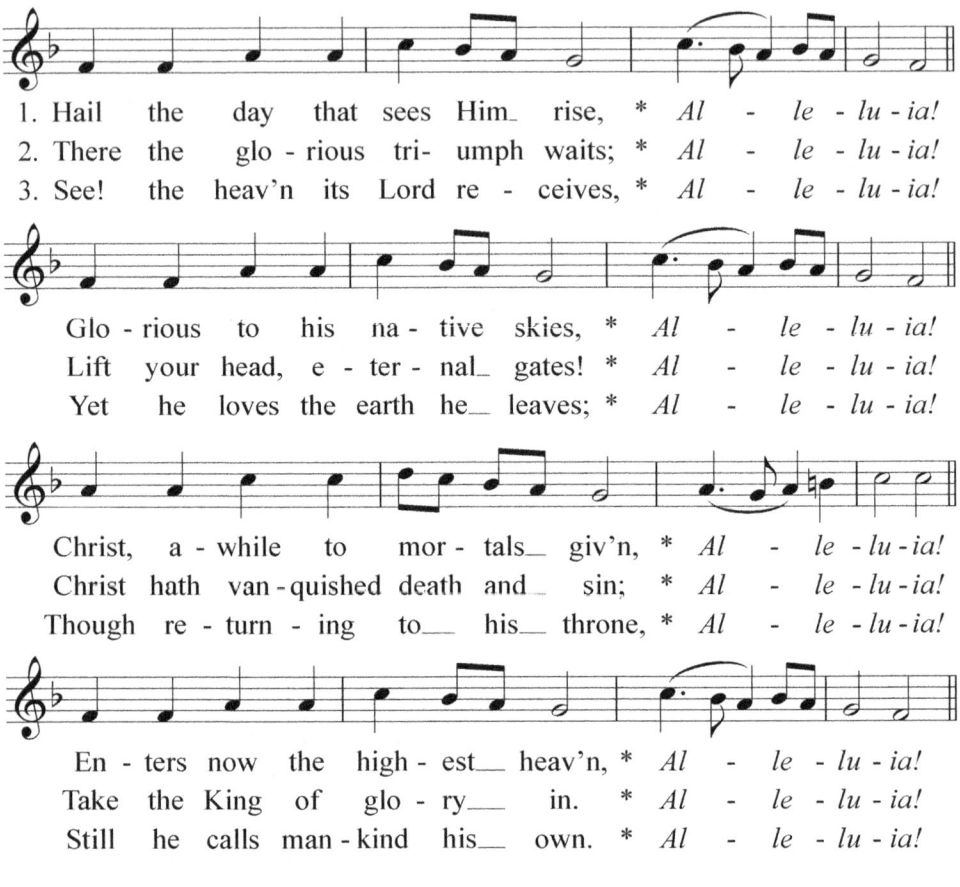

1. Hail the day that sees Him rise, * Al - le - lu - ia!
   Glo - rious to his na - tive skies, * Al - le - lu - ia!
   Christ, a - while to mor - tals giv'n, * Al - le - lu - ia!
   En - ters now the high - est heav'n, * Al - le - lu - ia!

2. There the glo - rious tri - umph waits; * Al - le - lu - ia!
   Lift your head, e - ter - nal gates! * Al - le - lu - ia!
   Christ hath van - quished death and sin; * Al - le - lu - ia!
   Take the King of glo - ry in. * Al - le - lu - ia!

3. See! the heav'n its Lord re - ceives, * Al - le - lu - ia!
   Yet he loves the earth he leaves; * Al - le - lu - ia!
   Though re - turn - ing to his throne, * Al - le - lu - ia!
   Still he calls man - kind his own. * Al - le - lu - ia!

4. Still for us he intercedes, * / His prevailing death he pleads, *
   Near himself prepares our place, * / Harbinger of human race. *

5. Lord, though parted from our sight, * / Far above yon azure height, *
   Grant our hearts may thither rise, * / Seeking thee beyond the skies. *

6. There we shall with thee remain, * / Partners of thine endless reign; *
   There thy face unclouded see, * / Find our heaven of heavens in thee. *

The Head Once Crowned With Thorns 253

Tune: ST. MAGNUS (CM)   Text: Thomas Kelly (†1855)

1. The head that once was crowned with thorns is crowned with glo - ry now;

a roy - al di - a - dem a - dorns the might - y___ Vic - tor's brow.

2. The high - est place that heav'n af - fords is his, is his by right,

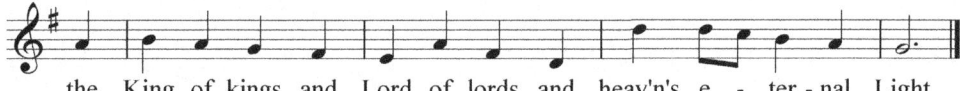

the King of kings, and Lord of lords, and heav'n's e - ter - nal Light.

3. The joy of all who dwell a - bove, the joy of all be - low,
4. To them the cross with all its shame, with all its grace is giv'n;

to whom he man - i - fests his love and grants his___ Name to know.
their name, an ev - er - last - ing name; their joy, the___ joy of heav'n.

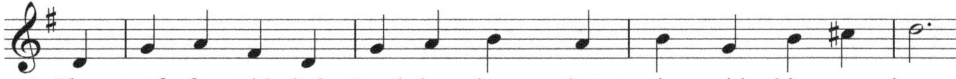

5. They suf - fer with their Lord be - low, they reign with him a - bove,
6. The cross he bore is life and health, though shame and death to him:

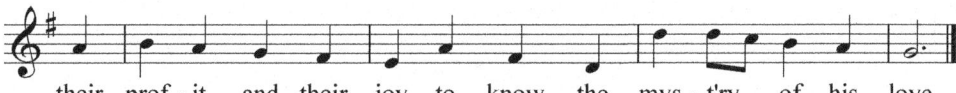

their prof - it and their joy to know the mys - t'ry___ of his love.
his peo-ple's hope, his peo-ple's wealth, their ev - er - last - ing theme.

254 Come, Holy Ghost

Tune: LOUIS LAMBILLOTTE (LM with Repeat)   Text: Rabanus Maurus (†856)

1. Come, Ho - ly Ghost, Cre - a - tor blest, And in our
2. O Com - fort - er, to Thee we cry, Thou heav'n - ly

hearts__ take up__ Thy rest; Come with Thy grace
Gift__ of God__ most high; Thou fount of life

and heav'n - ly aid, To fill the hearts which Thou hast
and fire of love, And sweet a - noint - ing__ from a -

made, To fill the hearts which_ Thou hast made.
bove, And sweet a - noint - ing__ from a - bove.

3. O Ho - ly Ghost, through Thee a - lone, Know we the
4. Praise we the Lord, Fa - ther and Son, And the blest

Fa - ther and__ the Son; Be this our firm,
Spir - it with__ Them one; And may the Son

un - chang - ing creed: That Thou dost from Them both pro -
on us be - stow The gifts that from the__ Spir - it

ceed, That Thou dost from Them_ both pro - ceed.
flow, The gifts that from the__ Spir - it flow.

The Holy Spirit Was Outpoured 255

Tune: TALLIS CANON (LM)   Text: Beata Nobis Gaudia

1. Re - joice! the year up - on its way has
2. On each the fire, de - scend - ing, stood, in

brought a - gain that bless - èd day, when on the cho - sen
quiv -'ring tongues' si - mil - i - tude, tongues, that their words might

of the Lord the Ho - ly Spir - it was out - poured.
read - y prove, and fire, to make them flame with love.

3. To all in eve - ry tongue they spoke; a -
4. These things were done in type that day, when

maze - ment in the crowd a - woke, who mocked, as o - ver -
East - er - tide had passed a - way, the num - ber told which

come with wine, those who were filled with pow'r di - vine.
once set free the cap - tive at the ju - bi - lee.

5. And now, O ho - ly God, this day re -
6. To God the Fa - ther, God the Son, and

gard us as we hum - bly pray, and send us, from thy
God the Spir - it, praise be done; may Christ the Lord up -

heav'n - ly seat, the bless - ings of the Par - a - clete.
on us pour the Spir - it's gift for ev - er - more.

256 Most Ancient Of All Mysteries

Tune: ST. FLAVIAN (CM)   Text: Frederick Faber (†1863)

1. Most an-cient of all mys-ter-ies, be-fore thy throne we lie;
have mer-cy now, most mer-ci-ful, most ho-ly Trin-i-ty.

2. When heav'n and earth were yet un-made, when time was yet un-known,
thou in thy bliss and maj-es-ty didst live and love a-lone.

3. Thou wast not born; there was no fount from which thy be-ing flowed;
there is no end which thou canst reach: but thou art sim-ply God.

4. How won-der-ful cre-a-tion is, the work which thou didst bless!
And O what then must thou be-like, e-ter-nal Love-li-ness!

5. Most an-cient of all mys-ter-ies, low at thy throne we lie;
have mer-cy now, most mer-ci-ful, most ho-ly Trin-i-ty.

O Trinity Of Blessed Light   257

Tune: TALLIS CANON (LM)   Text: Aeterna Lux Divinitas

1. O Trin - i - ty of bless - èd light, O
U - ni - ty of prince - ly might, Thy ho - ly name Thy
ser - vants bless, to Thee we pray, and Thee con - fess.

2. We praise the Fa - ther, might - y One; We
3. Thou First and Last, from whom there springs the
praise the sole - be - got - ten Son; We praise the Ho - ly
Fount of all cre - at - ed things, Thou art the Life which
Ghost a - bove, Who joins Them in one bond of love.
moves the whole, sure hope of each be - liev - ing soul.

4. As from the Fa - ther in - fi - nite His
5. O Fa - ther, Son and Ho - ly Ghost, Al -
Son and Word e - ter - nal came, So too from both the
might - y God of heav'n and earth, All mor - tals and the
Par - a - clete Pro - creeds, in De - i - ty the same.
heav'n - ly host Pro - claim Thy ev - er - last - ing worth.

258   O Glorious Maid, Exalted Far

Tune: WINCHESTER NEW (LM)   Text: O Gloriosa Femina

1. O glo - rious Maid, ex - alt - ed far be -
yond the light of burn - ing star, from him who made thee
thou hast won grace to be Moth - er of his Son.

2. That which was lost in hap - less Eve thy
ho - ly Sci - on did re - trieve; the tear - worn sons of
Ad - am's race through thee have seen the heav'n - ly place.

3. Thou wast the gate of heavn's high Lord, the
4. All hon - or, laud and glo - ry be, O

door through which the light hath poured. Chris - tians re - joice, for
Je - sus, Vir - gin - born to thee! All glo - ry, as is

through a Maid to all man - kind is life con - veyed!
ev - er meet, to Fa - ther and to Par - a - clete.

Immaculate Mary   259

Tune: FRENCH MELODY (11 11 with Refrain)   Text: Traditional

1. Im - mac - u - late Mar - y, thy prais - es we___ sing,

Who reign - est in splen - dor with Je - sus our___ King.

Refrain: A - ve, A - ve, A - ve Ma - rí - a!

A - ve, A - ve Ma - rí - a!

2. In heav - en the bless - èd thy glo - ry pro - claim,

On earth we thy chil - dren in - voke thy fair___ name.

3. Thy name is our pow - er, thy vir - tues our___ light,
4. We pray for our Moth - er, the Church up - on___ earth,

Thy love is our com - fort, thy plead - ing our___ might.
And bless, dear - est La - dy, the land of our___ birth.

260   Daily, Daily Sing To Mary

Tune: ALLE TAGE SING UND SAGE (87 87D)   Text: Omni Die Dic Mariae (12th cent.)

1. Dai - ly, dai - ly sing to Mar - y, Sing, my soul, her prais - es due.
2. She is might - y to de - liv - er. Call her, trust her lov - ing - ly.

All her feasts, her ac - tions hon - or With the heart's de - vo - tion true.
When the tem - pest rag - es round thee, She will calm the trou - bled sea.

Lost in won - d'ring con - tem - pla - tion, Be her Maj - es - ty con - fess'd.
Gifts of heav - en she has giv - en, No - ble La - dy, to our race.

Call her Moth - er, call her Vir - gin, Hap - py Moth - er, Vir - gin blest.
She, the Queen, who decks her sub - jects With the light of God's own grace.

3. Sing, my tongue, the Vir - gin's tro - phies Who for us her Mak - er bore.
4. All my sens - es, heart, af - fec - tions, Strive to sound her glo - ry forth:

For the curse of old in - flict - ed, Peace and bless - ing to re - store.
Spread a - broad the sweet me - mo - rials Of the Vir - gin's price - less worth:

Sing in songs of peace un - end - ing, Sing the world's ma - jes - tic Queen.
Where the voice of mu - sic thrill - ing, Where the tongue of el - o - quence,

Wea - ry not nor faint in tell - ing. All the gifts she gives to men.
That can ut - ter hymns be - seem - ing All her match - less ex - cel - lence?

Hail, Holy Queen Enthroned Above   261

Tune: SALVE REGINA CAELITUM (84 84 77 79)   Text: att. Hrm. Contractus (11th cen.)

1. Hail, ho - ly Queen en - thron'd a - bove, O Ma - rí - a!

Hail Moth-er of mer - cy and of love, O Ma - rí - a! **R.**

Refrain:

Tri - umph all ye Cher - u - bim, Sing with us ye

Ser - a - phim, Heav'n and earth re - sound the hymn;

Sal - ve, Sal - ve, Sal - ve Re - gí - na!

2. Our life, our sweet-ness, here be - low, O Ma - rí - a!

Our hope in sor - row and in woe, O Ma - rí - a! **R.**

3. To thee we cry, poor sons of Eve, O Ma - rí - a!
4. Turn then most gra - cious Ad - vo - cate, O Ma - rí - a!

To thee we sigh, we mourn, we grieve, O Ma - rí - a! **R.**

T'ward us thine eyes com - pas - sion - ate, O Ma - rí - a! **R.**

262 From All Thy Saints In Warfare

Tune: KING'S LYNN (76 76D)   Text: Horatio Nelson (†1913)

1. From all thy saints in war - fare, for_ all thy saints at rest,
2. Praise, Lord, for thy dis - ci - ples, who see thee face to Face.

to_ thee, O bless - èd_ Je - sus, all prais - es be ad - dressed;
One love, one zeal im - pelled them, re - spon - sive to thy Grace.

thou, Lord, didst win the_ bat - tle, that they might con - quer'rs be;
May_ we with zeal as_ ear - nest the faith of Christ main - tain,

their crowns of liv - ing glo - ry are_ lit with rays from thee.
and, bound in love as breth - ren, at_ length thy rest at - tain.

3. A - pos - tles, proph - ets, mar - tyrs, and_ all the sa - cred throng,
4. Then praise we God the Fa - ther, and_ praise we God the Son,

who_ wear the spot - less_ rai - ment, who raise the cease - less song,
and_ God the Ho - ly_ Spir - it, e - ter - nal Three in One;

for_ these, passed on be - fore us, Sav - ior, we thee a - dore,
till_ all the ran - somed num - ber fall down be - fore the throne,

and, walk - ing in their foot - steps, would serve thee more and more.
and hon - or, pow'r, and glo - ry, as - cribe to God a - lone.

For All The Saints   263

Tune: SINE NOMINE (10 10 10 4)   Text: William How (†1897)

1. For all the saints, who from their la - bors rest, who thee by
faith be - fore the world con - fessed, thy Name, O Je - sus,
be for - ev - er__ blest.

Refrain: Al - le - lu - ia, Al - le - lu - ia!

2. Thou wast their Rock, their For - tress and their Might; thou, Lord, their
Cap - tain in the well fought fight; thou, in the dark - ness
drear, their one__ true__ Light. **R.**

3. But lo! there breaks a yet more glo - rious day; the
4. From earth's wide bounds, from o - cean's far - thest coast, through

saints tri - um - phant rise in bright ar - ray; the
gates of pearl streams in the count - less host, and

King of__ glo - ry pass - es on__ his__ way. **R.**
sing - ing to Fa - ther, Son and Ho - ly__ Ghost: **R.**

264   Hearken, Shepherd Of The Sheep

Tune: ST. THOMAS (87 87 87)   Text: De Profundis Exclamantes (1502)

1. Christ, en-throned in high-est heav-en, Hear us, cry-ing from the deep
2. King of glo-ry, hear our voic-es, Grant the faith-ful rest, we pray;

For the faith-ful ones de-part-ed, For the souls of all that sleep;
We have sinned and may not 'bide it, If Thou mark our steps a-stray,

As Thy kneel-ing Church en-treat-eth, Heark-en, Shep-herd of the sheep.
Yet we plead that sav-ing vic-tim, Which for them we bring to-day.

3. That which Thou, Thy-self, hast of-fered To Thy Fa-ther, of-fer we:
4. They are Thine, O take them to Thee; Thou their hope, O raise them high;

By Thy sac-ri-fice, O Je-sus, From sin's bur-den set them free;
In Thy mer-cy ev-er trust-ing, Con-fi-dent we make our cry

Hear us, lov-ing friend of sin-ners, Mer-ci-ful and gra-cious be.
That the souls whom Thou hast pur-chased May un-to Thy heart be nigh.

5. Let Thy plen-teous lov-ing-kind-ness On them ev-er-more be poured;
6. Where the saints, Thy throne sur-round-ing, Join in the an-gel-ic song,

Let them through Thy bound-less mer-cy Be to bound-less life re-stored,
Where Thy Moth-er, raised in glo-ry, Leads the great re-deem-èd throng,

And with-in Thy Fa-ther's man-sions Give to each a place, O Lord.
Grant that we, with souls de-part-ed, May through grace at length be-long.

In Paradisum – *Two Options*   265

Tune: Adaptation from the Graduale Romanum   Text: ICEL Adaptation

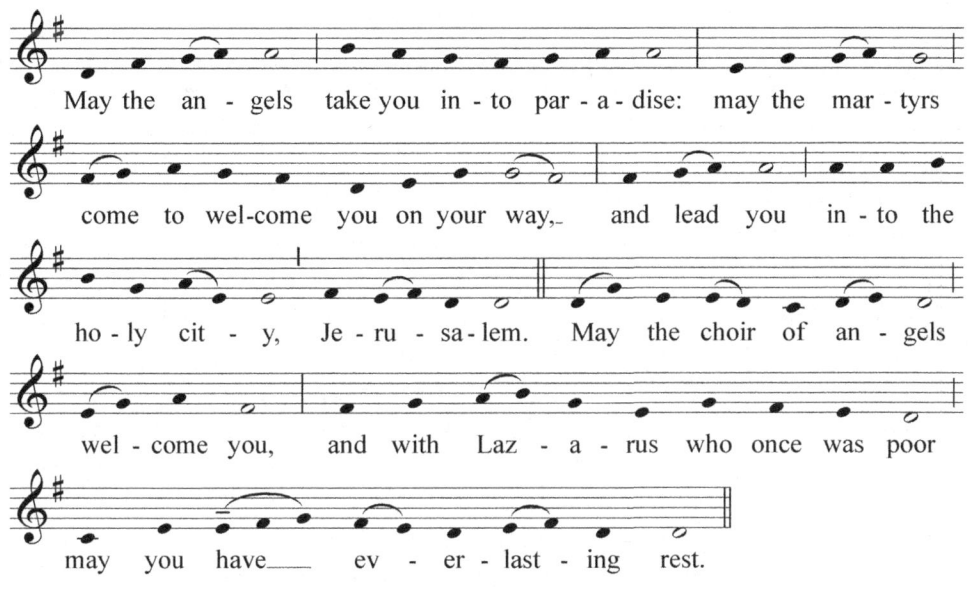

May the an - gels take you in - to par - a - dise: may the mar - tyrs
come to wel-come you on your way,_ and lead you in - to the
ho - ly cit - y, Je - ru - sa - lem. May the choir of an - gels
wel - come you, and with Laz - a - rus who once was poor
may you have__ ev - er - last - ing rest.

Editio Vaticana

In pa - ra - dí - sum: de - dú - cant te An - ge - li:
in tu - o ad - vén - tu sus - cí - pi - ant te Már - ty - res,__
et per - dú - cant te in ci - vi - tá - tem san - ctam Je - rú - sa - lem.
Cho - rus An - ge - ló - rum te__ su - scí - pi - at,
et cum Lá - za - ro quon - dam páu - pe - re ae - tér-
-nam__ há - be - as__ ré - qui - em.

266   For The Dead

Tune: ST FLAVIAN (CM)

1. Help, Lord, the souls which Thou hast made, The
2. Those ho - ly souls, they suf - fer on, Re -
3. For dai - ly falls, for par - don'd crime, They

souls to Thee so dear, In pris - on for the
sign'd in heart and will, Un - til Thy high be -
joy to un - der - go The shad - ow of Thy

debt un - paid Of sins com - mit - ted here.
hest is done, And jus - tice has its fill.
cross sub - lime, The rem - nant of Thy woe.

4. Oh, by their patience of delay, / Their hope amid their pain,
   Their sacred zeal to burn away / Disfigurement and stain;

5. Oh, by their fire of love, not less / In keenness than the flame,
   Oh, by their very helplessness, / Oh, by Thy own great Name,

6. Good Jesu, help! sweet Jesu, aid / The souls to Thee most dear,
   In prison for the debt unpaid / Of sins committed here.

*Text by Blessed Cardinal Newman (†1890), Priest of the
Oratory of St. Philip Neri. Melody by John Day (†1584).*

When The Patriarch Was Returning 267

Tune: ALL SAINTS (87 87 77)   Text: Hoste dum victo triumphans

1. When the Pa - tr'arch was re - turn - ing Crown'd with
2. On the truth, thus dim - ly shad - ow'd, Lat - er
3. Won - d'rous gift!– The Word who fash - ion'd All things

tri - umph from the fray, Him the peace - ful king of Sa - lem
days a lus - tre shed; When the great High-Priest e - ter - nal,
by his might di - vine, Bread in - to His Bod - y chang - es,

Came to meet up - on his way; Meek - ly bear - ing
Un - der form of Wine and Bread, For the world's im -
In - to His own Blood the wine;– What though sense no

Bread and Wine, Ho - ly Priest - hood's aw - ful sign.
mor - tal food Gave His Flesh and gave his Blood.
change per - ceives, Faith ad - mires, a - dores, be - lieves.

4. He who once to die a Victim / On the Cross, did not refuse,
Day by day, upon our altars, / That same Sacrifice renews;
Through His holy Priesthood's hands, / Faithful to His last commands.

5. While the people all uniting / In the Sacrifice sublime
Offer Christ to His high Father, / Offer up themselves with Him;
Then together with the Priest / On the living Victim feast.

6. Praise the Universal Maker, / Father of the world of men;
Praise the Son, whose life-blood flowing / Bought our captive souls again;
Gracious Breath of Life Divine— / Praise, O Triune God, be Thine!

English Translation by Fr. Edward Caswall (†1878), Priest of the
Oratory of St. Philip Neri.   German Melody (†1698).

268 What Wondrous Love Is This

Tune: WONDROUS LOVE (12 9 12 12 9)

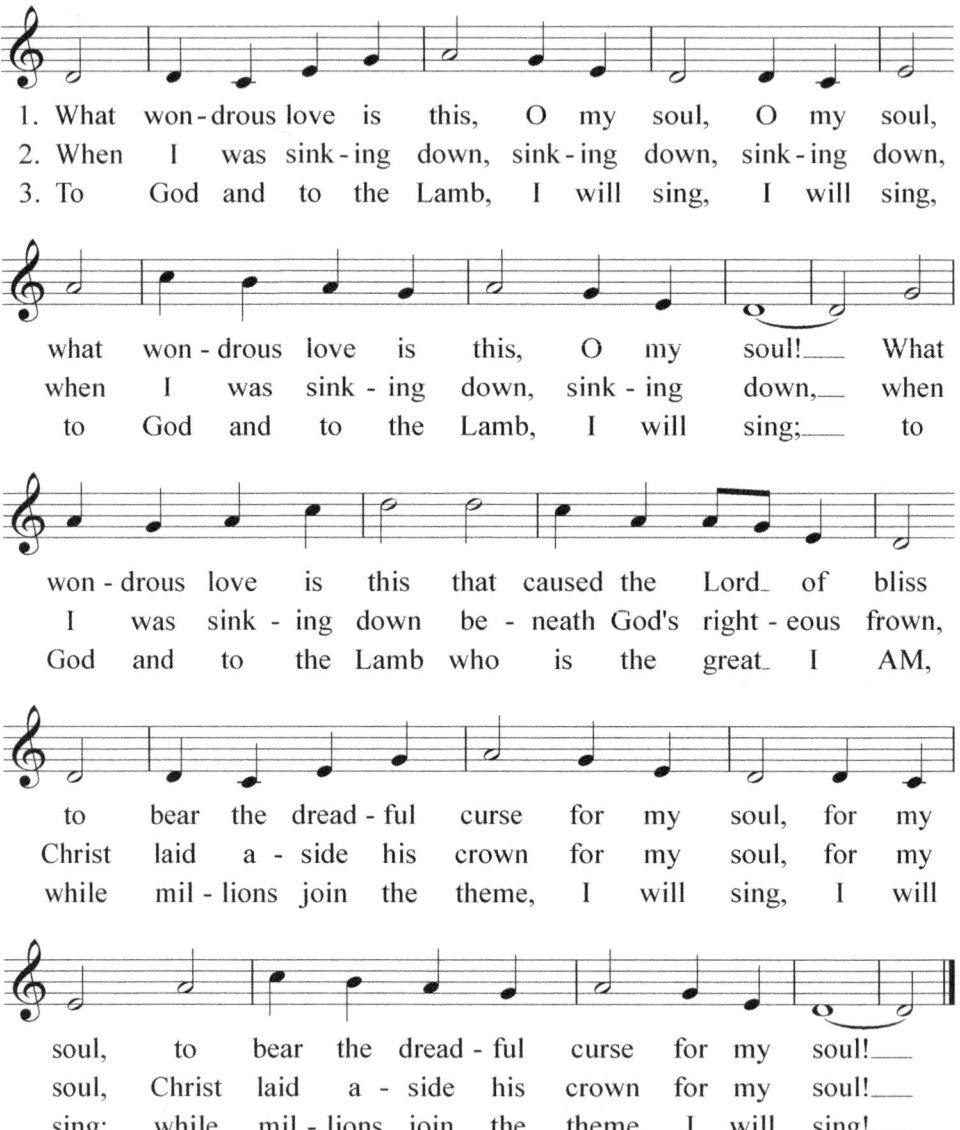

1. What won-drous love is this, O my soul, O my soul,
2. When I was sink-ing down, sink-ing down, sink-ing down,
3. To God and to the Lamb, I will sing, I will sing,

what won-drous love is this, O my soul!___ What
when I was sink-ing down, sink-ing down,___ when
to God and to the Lamb, I will sing;___ to

won-drous love is this that caused the Lord_ of bliss
I was sink-ing down be-neath God's right-eous frown,
God and to the Lamb who is the great_ I AM,

to bear the dread-ful curse for my soul, for my
Christ laid a-side his crown for my soul, for my
while mil-lions join the theme, I will sing, I will

soul, to bear the dread-ful curse for my soul!___
soul, Christ laid a-side his crown for my soul!___
sing; while mil-lions join the theme, I will sing!___

4. And when from death I'm free, I'll sing on, I'll sing on;
and when from death I'm free, I'll sing on;
and when from death I'm free, I'll sing and joyful be,
and through eternity, I'll sing on, I'll sing on;
and through eternity I'll sing on.

The King Of Love My Shepherd Is   269

Tune: ST. COLUMBA (87 87)   Text: Henry Baker (†1877)

1. The___ King of love my___ shep - herd is, whose good - ness
2. Where streams of liv - ing___ wa - ter flow, my___ ran - somed

fail - eth___ nev - er; I noth - ing lack if I am his, and
soul he___ lea - deth, and where the ver - dant pas - tures grow, with

he is mine for ev - er.   3. Per - verse and fool - ish___
food ce - les - tial fee - deth.   4. In___ death's dark vale I___

oft I strayed, but___ yet in love He___ sought me, and on his
fear no ill with thee, dear Lord, be - side me; thy rod and

shoul - der gen - tly laid, and home, re - joic - ing, brought me.
staff my com - fort still, thy cross be - fore to guide me.

5. Thou spread'st a ta - ble___ in my sight; thy___
6. And___ so through all the___ length of days thy___

unc - tion grace be - stow - eth; and O what trans - port
good - ness fail - eth___ nev - er: Good Shep - herd, may I

of de - light from thy pure chal - ice flow - eth!
sing thy praise with - in thy house for ev - er.

270 O Thou, Who At Thy Eucharist (I)

Tune: UNDE ET MEMORES (10 10 10 10 10 10)   Text: Based on John 17: 22

1. O Thou, Who at Thy Eu-cha-rist didst pray
2. For all thy Church, O Lord, we in-ter-cede;
3. We pray thee too for wan-d'rers from Thy fold;

That all Thy Church might be for ev-er one,
Make Thou our sad di-vi-sions soon to cease;
O bring them back, good Shep-herd of the sheep,

Grant us at eve-ry Eu-cha-rist to say
Draw us the near-er each to each, we plead,
Back to the faith which saints be-lieved of old,

With long-ing heart and soul, "Thy will be done." O
By draw-ing all to thee, O Prince of Peace; Thus
Back to the Church which still that faith doth keep; Soon

may we all one Bread, one Bod-y be,

Through this blest Sac-ra-ment of u-ni-ty.

4. So, Lord, at length when Sacraments shall cease, / May we be one with
   all thy Church above, | One with thy saints in one unbroken peace, /
   One with thy saints in one unbounded love; | More blessèd still, in
   peace and love to be / One with the Trinity in Unity.

O Esca Viatorum   271

Tune: HAYDN (776 D)   Text: O esca viatórum

1. O___ es - ca vi - a - tó - rum   O pa - nis an - ge -
2. O___ lym - pha fons a - mó - ris   Qui pu - ro Sal - va -
3. O___ Je - su tu - um vul - tum   Quem có - li - mus oc -

ló - rum   O man - na cæ - li - tum.   E - su - ri - én - tes___
tó - ris   E cor - de pró - flu - is   Te si - ti - én - tes___
cúl - tum   Sub pa - nis spé - ci - e.   Fac ut, re - mó - to___

ci - ba   Dul - cé - di - ne non___ pri - va   Cor -
po - ta   Haec so - la nos - tra___ vo - ta.   His
ve - lo,   Post lí - be - ra in___ cæ - lo   Cer -

da quæ - rén - ti - um,   Cor - da quæ - rén - ti - um.
u - na súf - fi - cis,   His u - na súf - fi - cis.
ná - mus fá - ci - e,   Cer - ná - mus fá - ci - e.

1. O Food of wayworn exiles, / O Bread of all the Angels, | O Manna of the Blest! / Come down to us that hunger, | And do not hide Thy sweetness / From hearts that truly seek, / From hearts that truly seek.

2. O Love's unfailing well-spring / That from the Heart of Jesus | Dost pour thy shining flood, / Refresh our thirsty spirit | And drown all baser longing, / Thyself be all in all, / Thyself be all in all.

3. Thy blessed Face, O Savior, / That even now we worship | Beneath the Bread's disguise; / May we at last in Heaven | Behold unveiled for ever / With free, enraptured eyes, / With free, enraptured eyes.

272   The Blessed Sacrament Of The Altar

Tune: SONG I (10 10 10 10 10 10)   Text: Saint Robert Southwell (†1595)

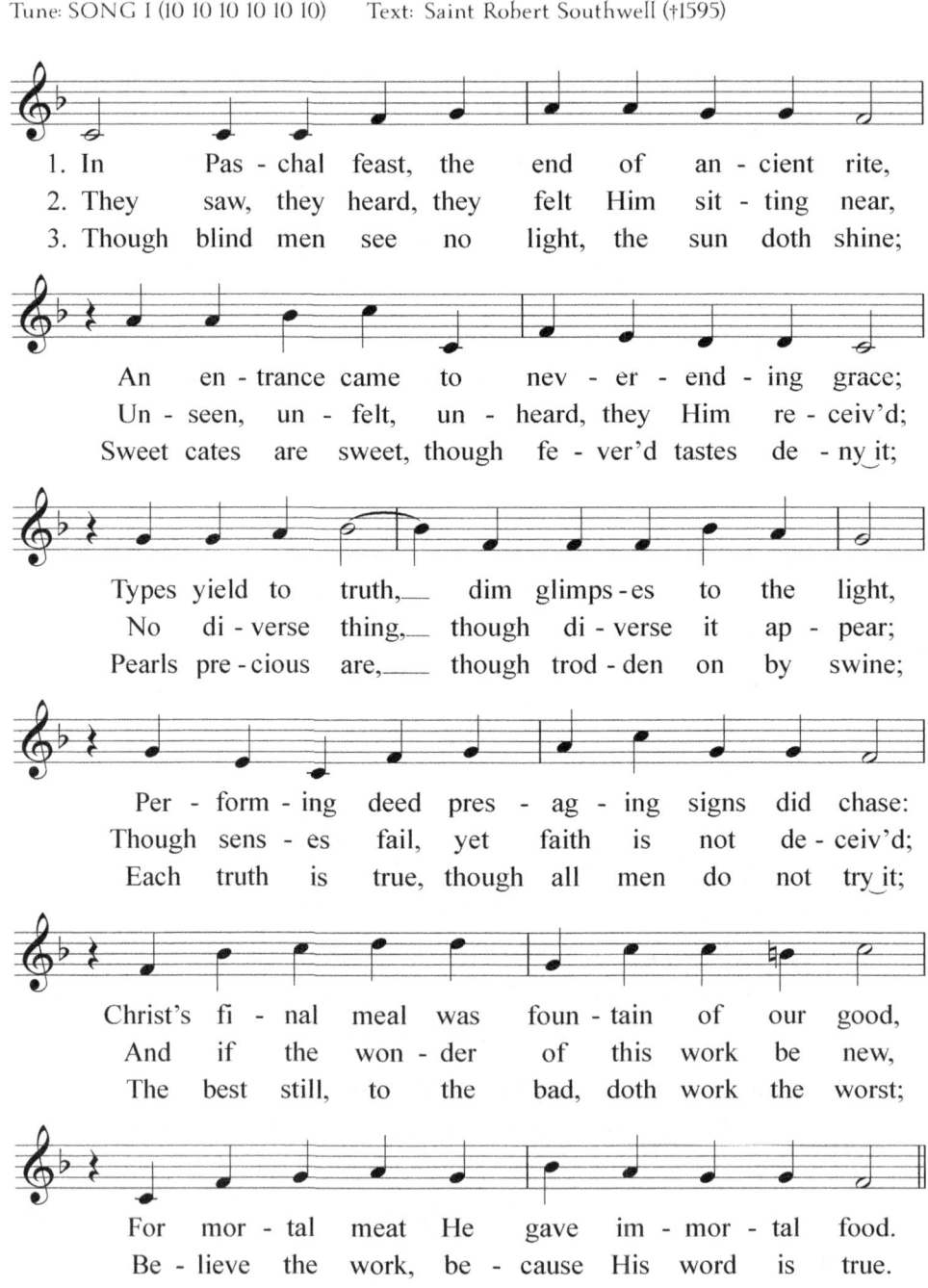

1. In Pas - chal feast, the end of an - cient rite,
2. They saw, they heard, they felt Him sit - ting near,
3. Though blind men see no light, the sun doth shine;

An en - trance came to nev - er - end - ing grace;
Un - seen, un - felt, un - heard, they Him re - ceiv'd;
Sweet cates are sweet, though fe - ver'd tastes de - ny it;

Types yield to truth,— dim glimps - es to the light,
No di - verse thing,— though di - verse it ap - pear;
Pearls pre - cious are,— though trod - den on by swine;

Per - form - ing deed pres - ag - ing signs did chase:
Though sens - es fail, yet faith is not de - ceiv'd;
Each truth is true, though all men do not try it;

Christ's fi - nal meal was foun - tain of our good,
And if the won - der of this work be new,
The best still, to the bad, doth work the worst;

For mor - tal meat He gave im - mor - tal food.
Be - lieve the work, be - cause His word is true.
Things bred to bliss do make them more ac - curs'd.

4. The God of hosts in slendor Host doth dwell;
    Yea, God and Man, with all to other due,
    That God, who rules the Heav'ns and rifled hell,
    That Man, Whose Death did us to life renew:
    That God and Man, who is the Angels' bliss,
    In form of bread and wine our nurture is.

5. Whole may His body be in smallest bread,
    Whole in the whole, yea whole in every crumb;
    With which be one or e'en ten thousand fed,
    All to each one, to all but one doth come;
    And tho' each one as much as all receive,
    Not one too much, nor all too little have.

6. One soul in man is all in every part;
    One face at once in many mirrors shines;
    One fearful noise doth make a thousand start;
    One eye at once a thousand things defines;
    If proofs of one in many Nature frame,
    God may in stronger sort perform the same.

7. God present is at once in every place,
    Yet God in every place is ever one;
    So various may be the gifts of grace,
    Suited to many minds, alike in none.
    Since angels may effects of bodies show,
    God angels' gifts on bodies may bestow.

8. What God, as author, made, He alter may;
    No change so hard as making all of nought;
    If Adam fashion'd were of slime and clay,
    Bread may to Christ's most sacred flesh be wrought:
    He may do this, that made, with mighty hand,
    Of water wine, a snake of Moses' wand.

*Text by St. Robert Southwell (†1595), Priest of the Society of Jesus
and one of the Forty Martyrs of England and Wales.
Melody by Orlando Gibbons (†1625).*

274 Sing, My Tongue, The Mystery Holy

Tune: A MONK OF GETHSEMANI (87 87 87)   Text: Pange Lingua Gloriosi

1. Sing, my tongue, the mys-t'ry ho-ly   Of the Bod-y of my Lord,
2. Of a pure and spot-less vir-gin, Born for us, His love to show,
3. On the night be-fore His pas-sion, His A-pos-tles by His side,

And His Pre-cious Blood, the ran-som Which up-on the earth was poured.
He, as man, with man con-vers-ing, Stayed, the seeds of truth to sow;
He ful-filled the law com-plete-ly With the food He pu-ri-fied;

Fruit of Mar-y's womb all ho-ly, May He ev-er be a-dored.
Then He closed in won-drous fash-ion, This His life on earth be-low.
Then He gave Him-self un-to them, Bread His hands had sanc-ti-fied.

4. The In-car-nate Word now chang-es Bread to flesh at His com-mand,
5. Down in ad-o-ra-tion fall-ing, This great sac-ra-ment we hail;
6. Praise to the Al-might-y Fa-ther; Hon-or, glo-ry to the Son;

And the wine be-comes His life-blood. Sens-es fail to un-der-stand;
O-ver an-cient forms of wor-ship New-er rites of grace pre-vail;
Ad-o-ra-tion to the Spir-it, Who with Them is ev-er one,

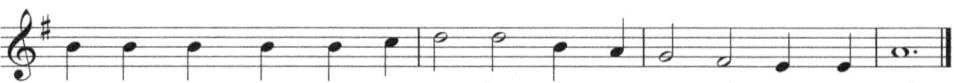

But the heart that is in ear-nest Can by faith its doubt with stand.
Faith re-minds us Christ is pre-sent When our hu-man sens-es fail.
And pro-cedes from both for-ev-er, As e-ter-nal ag-es run.

Sing, My Tongue, The Savior's Glory 275

Tune: C. EARLS (87 87 87)   Text: Pange Lingua Gloriosi

1. Sing, my tongue, the Sav-ior's glo-ry, Of His flesh the mys-t'ry sing;
2. Of a pure and spot-less vir-gin Born for us on earth be-low,

Of the blood, all price ex-ceed-ing, Shed by our im-mor-tal king,
He, as man, with man con-vers-ing, Stayed, the seeds of truth to sow;

Des-tined, for the world's re-demp-tion, From a no-ble womb to spring.
Then He closed in sol-emn or-der Won-drous-ly His life of woe.

3. On the night of that Last Sup-per Seat-ed with His cho-sen band,
4. Word made flesh, the bread of na-ture By His word to flesh He turns;

He, the pas-chal vic-tim eat-ing, First ful-fills the Law's com-mand:
Wine in-to His blood He chang-es: What though sense no change dis-cerns?

Then as food to all His Breth-ren Gives Him-self with His own hand.
On-ly be the heart in ear-nest, Faith her les-son quick-ly learns.

5. Down in ad-o-ra-tion fall-ing, Lo! the sa-cred host we hail;
6. To the ev-er-last-ing Fa-ther, And the Son who reigns on high,

Lo! o'er an-cient forms de-part-ing, New-er rites of grace pre-vail;
With the Ho-ly Ghost pro-ceed-ing Forth from Each e-ter-nal-ly,

Faith for all de-fects sup-ply-ing, Where the fee-ble sens-es fail.
Be sal-va-tion, hon-or, bless-ing. Might, and end-less maj-es-ty.

276 Love Divine, All Loves Excelling

Tune: HYFRYDOL (87 87D)   Text: Charles Wesley (†1788)

1. Love di - vine,___ all loves ex - cel - ling, Joy of
2. Come, Al - might - y to de - liv - er, Let us
3. Fin - ish, then,___ Thy new cre - a - tion; Pure and

heav'n to earth_ come down; Fix in us___ thy hum - ble
all Thy life_ re - ceive; Sud - den - ly___ re - turn and
spot - less let_ us be. Let us see___ Thy great sal -

dwell - ing; All thy faith - ful mer - cies crown!
nev - er, Nev - er more Thy tem - ples leave.
va - tion Per - fect - ly re - stored_ in Thee;

Je - sus, Thou_ art all com - pas - sion, Pure un -
Thee we would_ be al - ways bless - ing, Serve Thee
Changed from glo - ry in - to glo - ry, Till in

bound - ed love_ Thou art; Vis - it us___ with Thy_ sal -
as___ Thy hosts_ a - bove, Pray_ and praise Thee with - out
heav'n we take_ our place, Till_ we cast_ our crowns be -

va - tion; En - ter eve - ry trem - bling heart.
ceas - ing, Glo - ry in___ Thy per - fect love.
fore___ Thee, Lost in won - der, love, and praise.

Alleluia, Sing To Jesus   277

Tune: HYFRYDOL (87 87D)   Text: William Dix (†1898)

1. Al - le - lu - ia! sing to Je - sus! His the scep - ter, his_ the throne.
2. Al - le - lu - ia! not as or - phans are we left in sor - row now;

Al - le - lu - ia! His the tri - umph, his the vic - to - ry_ a -
Al - le - lu - ia! He is near_ us, faith be - lieves, nor ques - tions

lone. Hark! the songs of peace - ful Zi - on thun - der like_ a
how; Though the cloud from sight re - ceived him when the for - ty

might - y flood. Je - sus out_ of eve - ry na - tion hath re -
days_ were o'er shall_ our hearts for - get_ his prom - ise, "I am

deemed us by his blood.
with_ you ev - er - more"?

3. Al - le - lu - ia! bread of heav - en,
4. Al - le - lu - ia! King e - ter - nal,

here on earth our food_ and stay! Al - le - lu - ia! here the sin - ful
thee the Lord of lords we own; Al - le - lu - ia! born of Mar - y,

flee to thee from day_ to day. In - ter - ces - sor, Friend of
earth thy foot - stool, heav'n thy throne. Thou with - in_ the veil hast

sin - ners, earth's Re - deem - er, plead_ for me. Where the
en - tered, robed in flesh,_ our great_ High Priest. Thou_ on

songs of all_ the sin - less sweep a - cross the crys - tal sea.
earth both Priest and Vic - tim in the Eu - cha - ris - tic Feast.

278 Draw Nigh, And Take – *Version I*

Tune: SONG 46 (10 10 10 10)   Text: Sancti Venite Christi Corpus Sumite

1. Draw nigh and take the Bod-y of the Lord,
2. Saved by that Bod-y and that pre-cious Blood,

and drink the ho-ly Blood for you out-poured.
with souls re-freshed, we ren-der thanks to God.

3. Sal-va-tion's Giv-er, Christ, the on-ly Son,
4. Of-fered was he for great-est and for least,

by his dear Cross and Blood the vic-t'ry won.
him-self the Vic-tim, and him-self the Priest.

5. Ap-proach ye then with faith-ful hearts sin-cere,
6. He that in this world rules his saints and shields,

and take the safe-guard of sal-va-tion here.
to all be-liev-ers life e-ter-nal yields.

7. With heav'n-ly bread makes them that hun-ger whole,
8. Al-pha O-me-ga un-to whom shall bow

gives liv-ing wa-ters to the thirst-ing soul.
all na-tions at the Doom, is with us now.

Draw Nigh, And Take – *Version II*   279

Tune: ALL SOULS (10 10 10 10)   Text: Sancti Venite Christi Corpus Sumite

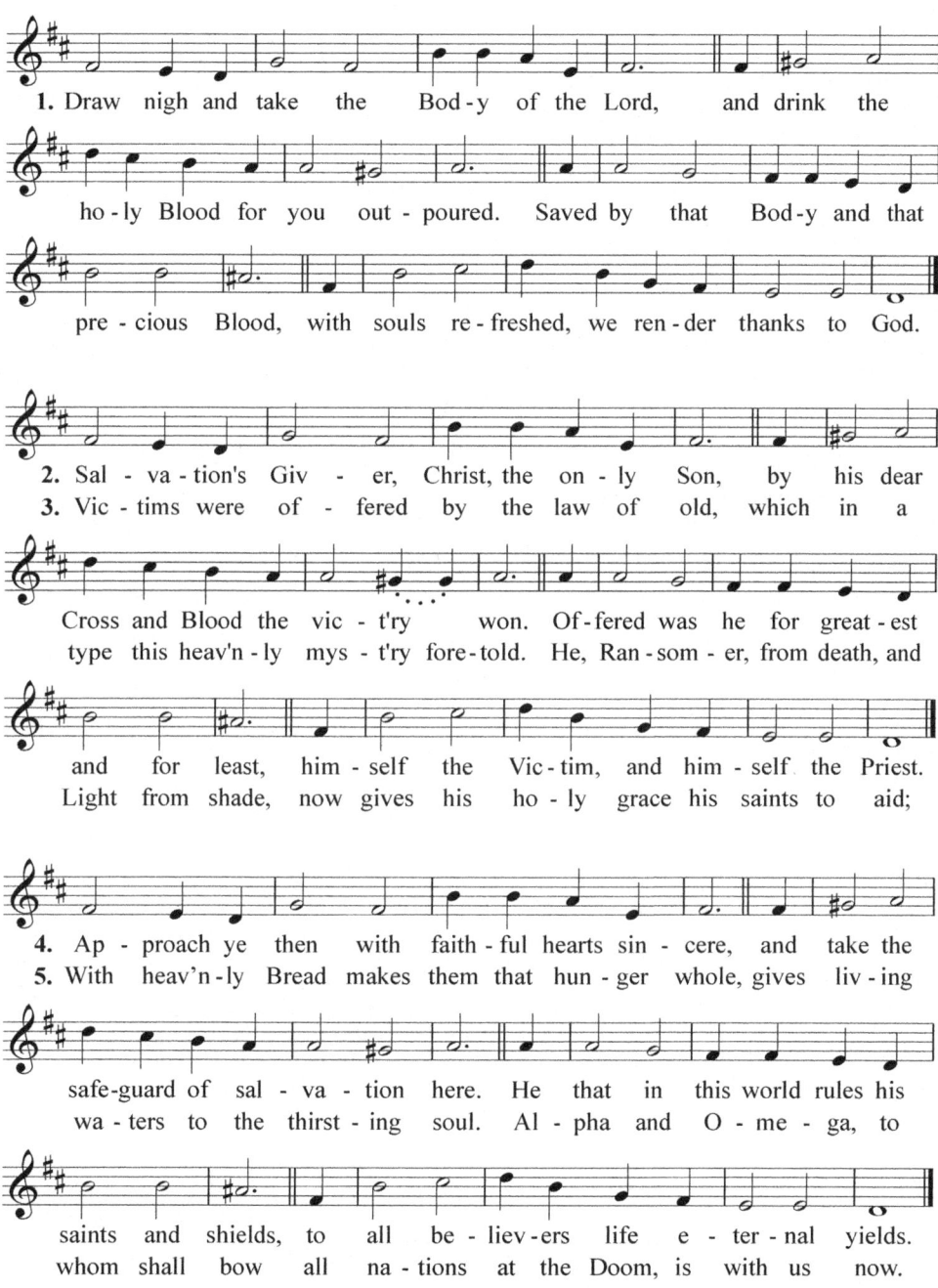

1. Draw nigh and take the Bod-y of the Lord, and drink the
ho-ly Blood for you out-poured. Saved by that Bod-y and that
pre-cious Blood, with souls re-freshed, we ren-der thanks to God.

2. Sal-va-tion's Giv-er, Christ, the on-ly Son, by his dear
Cross and Blood the vic-t'ry won. Of-fered was he for great-est
and for least, him-self the Vic-tim, and him-self the Priest.

3. Vic-tims were of-fered by the law of old, which in a
type this heav'n-ly mys-t'ry fore-told. He, Ran-som-er, from death, and
Light from shade, now gives his ho-ly grace his saints to aid;

4. Ap-proach ye then with faith-ful hearts sin-cere, and take the
safe-guard of sal-va-tion here. He that in this world rules his
saints and shields, to all be-liev-ers life e-ter-nal yields.

5. With heav'n-ly Bread makes them that hun-ger whole, gives liv-ing
wa-ters to the thirst-ing soul. Al-pha and O-me-ga, to
whom shall bow all na-tions at the Doom, is with us now.

280 O Thou, Who At Thy Eucharist (II)

Tune: SONG 1 (10 10 10 10 10 10)   Text: William Turton (†1938)

1. O thou, who at thy Eu - cha-rist didst pray that all thy Church might
2. For all thy Church, O Lord, we in - ter - cede; make thou our sad di -

be for ev - er one, grant us at eve - ry Eu - cha-rist to say
vi - sions soon to cease; draw us the near - er each to each, we plead,

with long-ing heart and soul, "Thy will be done." O may we all one
by draw-ing all to thee, O Prince of Peace; thus may we all one

Bread, one Bod - y be, through this blest Sac - ra - ment of u - ni - ty.
Bread, one Bod - y be, through this blest Sac - ra - ment of u - ni - ty.

3. We pray thee too for wan-d'rers from thy fold; O bring them back, good
4. So, Lord, at length when sac - ra - ments shall cease, may we be one with

Shep-herd of the sheep, back to the faith__ which saints be - lieved of
all thy Church a - bove, one with thy saints__ in one un - bro - ken

old, back to the Church which still that faith doth keep; soon may we
peace, one with thy saints in one un - bound-ed love; more bless - èd

all one Bread, one Bod - y be, through this blest Sac - ra - ment of u - ni - ty.
still, in peace and love to be one with the Trin - i - ty in U - ni - ty.

And Now, O Father, Mindful Of The Love 281

Tune: UNDE ET MEMORES (10 10 10 10 10 10)   Text: William Bright (†1901)

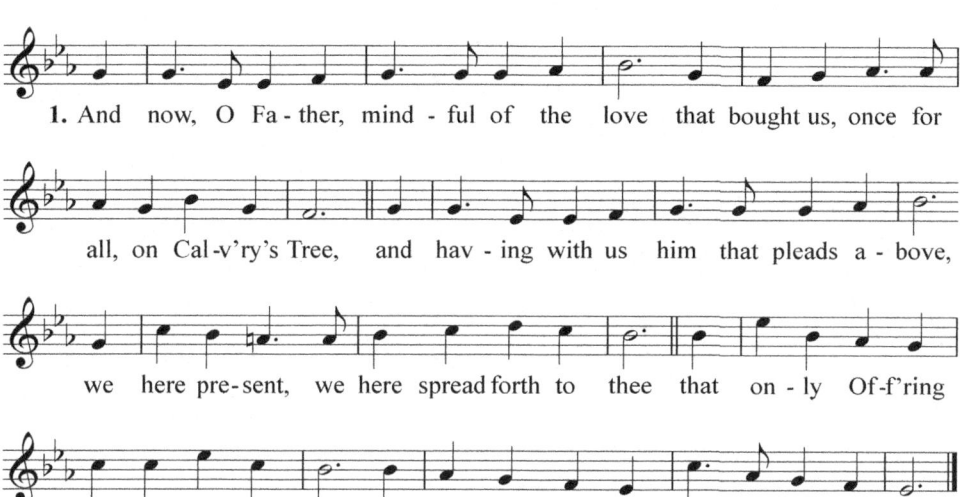

1. And now, O Fa-ther, mind-ful of the love that bought us, once for
all, on Cal-v'ry's Tree, and hav-ing with us him that pleads a-bove,
we here pre-sent, we here spread forth to thee that on-ly Of-f'ring
per-fect in thine eyes, the one, true, pure, im-mor-tal Sac-ri-fice.

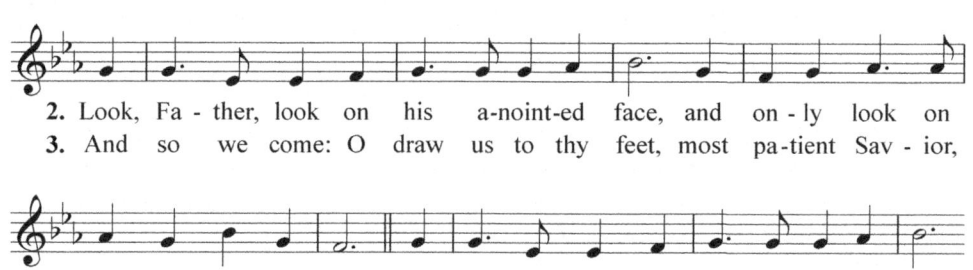

2. Look, Fa-ther, look on his a-noint-ed face, and on-ly look on
3. And so we come: O draw us to thy feet, most pa-tient Sav-ior,

us as found in him; look not on our mis-us-ings of thy grace,
who canst love us still; and by this Food, so awe-ful and so sweet,

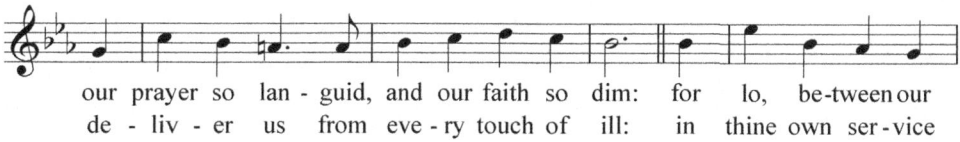

our prayer so lan-guid, and our faith so dim: for lo, be-tween our
de-liv-er us from eve-ry touch of ill: in thine own ser-vice

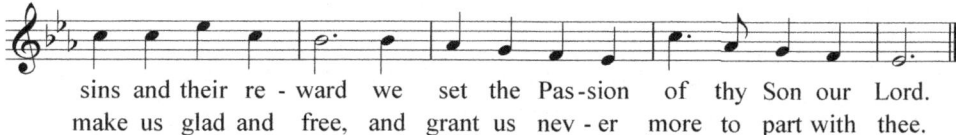

sins and their re-ward we set the Pas-sion of thy Son our Lord.
make us glad and free, and grant us nev-er more to part with thee.

282   O Food Of Men Wayfaring – *Version I*

Tune: O ESCA VIATORUM (776D)   Text: Athelstan Riley (†1945)

1. O Food of men way - far - ing, The bread of an - gels shar - ing, O Man-na from on high! We hun - ger; Lord, sup - ply us, Nor Thy de - lights de - ny us, Whose hearts to Thee draw nigh.

2. O stream of love past tell - ing, O pur - est foun - tain, well - ing From out the Sav - ior's side! We faint with thirst; re - vive us, Of Thine a - bun-dance give us, And all we need pro - vide.

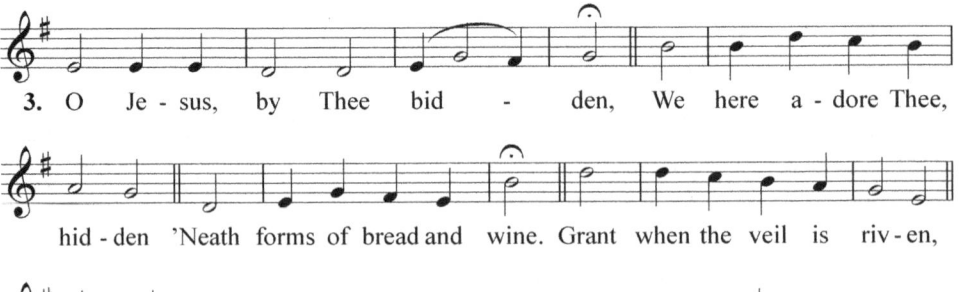

3. O Je - sus, by Thee bid - den, We here a - dore Thee, hid - den 'Neath forms of bread and wine. Grant when the veil is riv - en, We may be - hold, in heav - en, Thy coun - te - nance di - vine.

O Food Of Men Wayfaring – *Version II* 283

Tune: IN ALLEN MEINEN THATEN (776D)   Text: Athelstan Riley (†1945)

1. O Food of men way - far - ing, the bread of an - gels shar - ing,
O Man - na from on high! We hun - ger; Lord, sup - ply us,
nor thy de - lights de - ny us, whose hearts to__ thee draw nigh.

2. O stream of love past tell - ing, O pur - est foun - tain, well - ing
from out the Sav - ior's side! We faint with thirst; re - vive us,
of thine a - bun-dance give us, and all we__ need pro - vide.

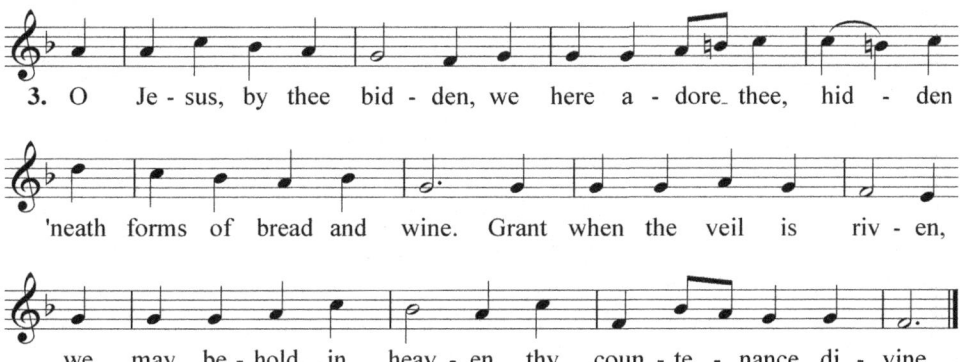

3. O Je - sus, by thee bid - den, we here a - dore_ thee, hid - den
'neath forms of bread and wine. Grant when the veil is riv - en,
we may be - hold, in heav - en, thy coun - te - nance di - vine.

284   O Food Of Exiles Lowly

Tune: HEINRICH ISAAC (776D)   Text: O Esca Viatorum

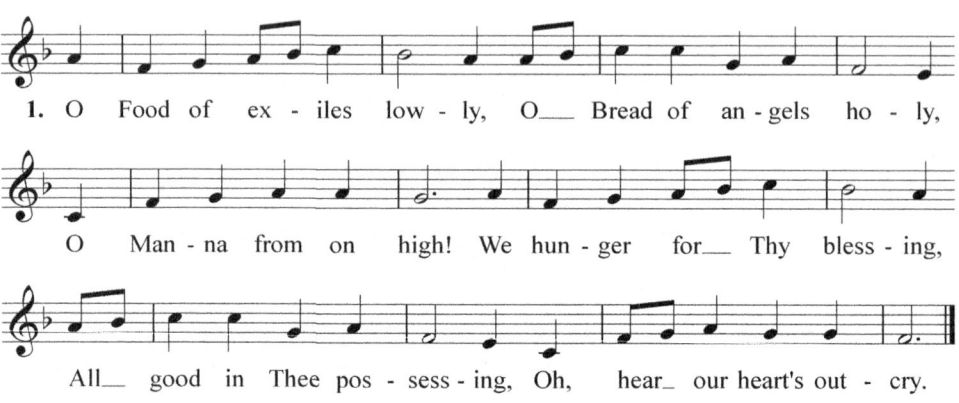

1. O Food of ex - iles low - ly, O__ Bread of an - gels ho - ly,
O Man - na from on high! We hun - ger for__ Thy bless - ing,
All__ good in Thee pos - sess - ing, Oh, hear__ our heart's out - cry.

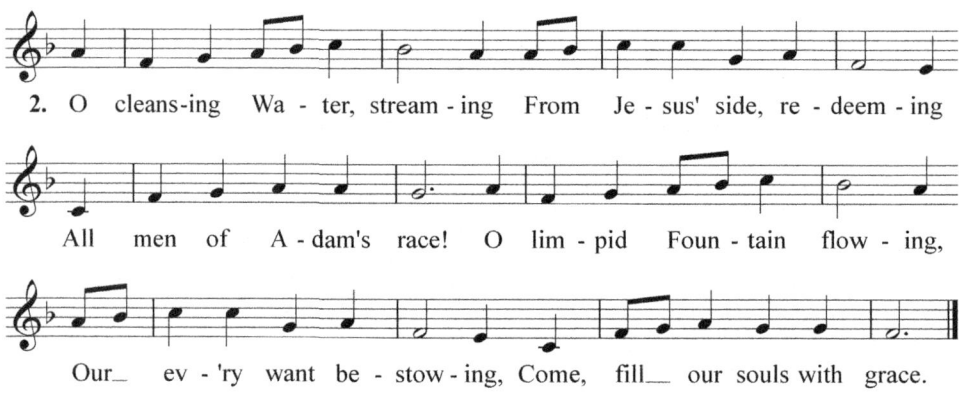

2. O cleans-ing Wa - ter, stream - ing From Je - sus' side, re - deem - ing
All men of A - dam's race! O lim - pid Foun - tain flow - ing,
Our__ ev - 'ry want be - stow - ing, Come, fill__ our souls with grace.

3. O Lord! We kneel be - fore Thee, And__ fer - vent - ly a - dore Thee,
From hu - man sight con - cealed. In heav'n, Thy mer - cies prais - ing,
May__ we, with glad -ness gaz - ing, Be - hold__ Thy face re - vealed.

My Faith Looks Up To Thee   285

Tune: OLIVET (664 6664)   Text: Ray Palmer (†1887)

1. My faith looks up to Thee, Thou Lamb of
2. May Thy rich grace im-part Strength to my

Cal - va - ry, Sav - ior di - vine! Now hear me
faint - ing heart, my zeal in - spire! As Thou hast

while I pray, take all my guilt a - way,
died for me, O may my love to Thee,

O let me from this day be whol - ly Thine!
Pure warm, and change - less be, a liv - ing fire!

3. While life's dark maze I tread, And griefs a -
4. When ends life's tran - sient dream, When death's cold

round me spread, be Thou my Guide; Bid dark-ness
sul - len stream o - ver me roll; Blest Sav - ior,

turn to day, wipe sor - row's tears a - way,
then in love, fear and dis - trust re - move;

Nor let me ev - er stray from Thee a - side.
O bear me safe a - bove, a ran - somed soul!

286 Let All Mortal Flesh Keep Silence

Tune: PICARDY (87 87 87)   Text: Gerald Moultrie (†1885)

1. Let all mor-tal flesh keep si-lence, and with fear and
2. King of kings, yet born of Mar-y, as of old on

trem-bling stand; pon-der noth-ing earth-ly mind-ed,
earth he stood, Lord of lords in hu-man ves-ture,

for with bless-ing in his hand Christ our God to earth des-
in the Bod-y and the Blood he will give to all the

cend-eth, our full hom-age to de-mand.
faith-ful his own self for heav'n-ly food.

3. Rank on rank the host of heav-en spreads its van-guard
4. At his feet the six-winged ser-aph; cher-u-bim with

on the way, as the Light of Light des-cend-eth
sleep-less eye, veil their fac-es to the Pres-ence,

from the realms of end-less day, that the pow'rs of hell may
as with cease-less voice they cry, "Al-le-lu-ia, al-le-

van-ish as the dark-ness clears a-way.
lu-ia! Al-le-lu-ia, Lord Most High!"

Praise To The Holiest In The Height   287

Tune: NEWMAN (CM)   Text: Blessed Cardinal Newman (†1890)

1. Praise to the Ho-liest in the height, and in___ the depth be
2. O lov-ing wis-dom of our God! When all___ was sin and

praise; in all his words most won-der-ful, most sure_ in
shame, a sec-ond Ad-am to___ the fight and to___ the

all his ways!   3. O wis-est love! that flesh and
res-cue came.   4. And that the high-est gift of

blood, which did___ in Ad-am fail, should strive a-
grace should flesh___ and blood re-fine: God's pres-ence

fresh a-gainst_ the foe, should strive,_ and should pre-vail.
and his ver-y self, and es-sence all-di-vine.

5. O gener-ous love! that he who smote in man_ for man the foe, the
6. And in the gar-den se-cret-ly, and on_ the cross on high, should

dou-ble ag-o-ny_ in Man for man_ should un-der-go.
teach his breth-ren, and_ in-spire to suf-fer and to die.

288 O With Thy Benediction

Tune: THAXTED (13 13 13 13 13 13)   Text: Vincent Coles (†1929)

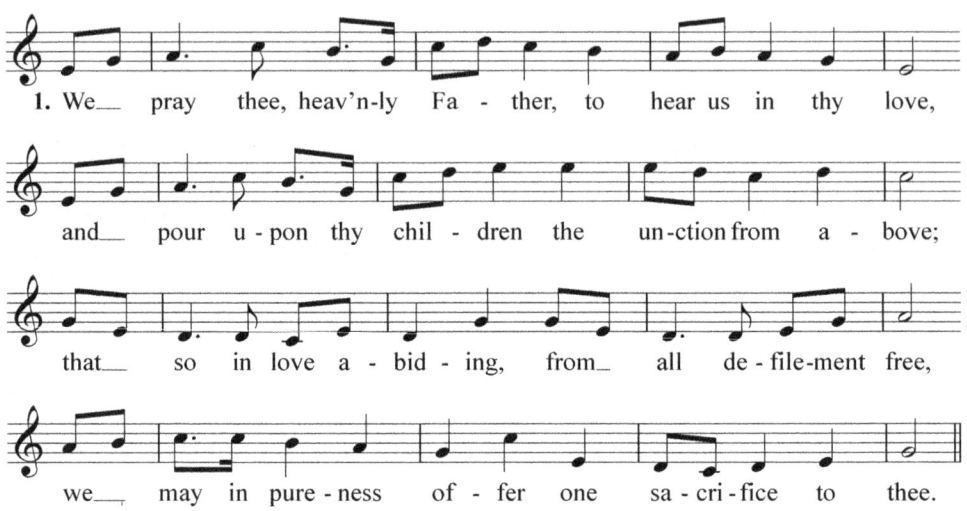

1. We__ pray thee, heav'n-ly Fa - ther, to hear us in thy love,

and__ pour u - pon thy chil - dren the un-ction from a - bove;

that__ so in love a - bid - ing, from__ all de - file-ment free,

we__ may in pure - ness of - fer one sa - cri -fice to thee.

Refrain:

O__ with Thy be - ne - dic - tion, u - pon our souls out - poured,

may we now pro-ceed in glad - ness to glo - ri - fy the Lord.

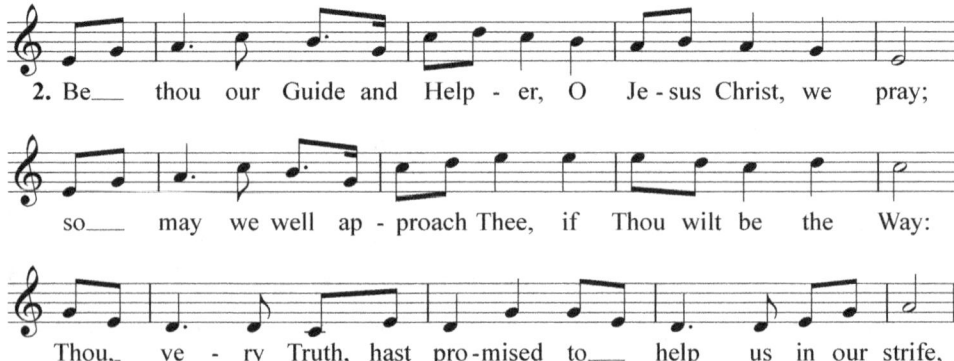

2. Be__ thou our Guide and Help - er, O Je - sus Christ, we pray;

so__ may we well ap - proach Thee, if Thou wilt be the Way:

Thou,_ ve - ry Truth, hast pro-mised to__ help us in our strife,

food_ of the wea - ry pil - grim, e - ter - nal Source of life. **R.**

3. And_ thou, Cre - a - tor Spi - rit, look on us, we are Thine;

re - new us in Thy grac - es, up - on our dark - ness shine;

One_ thing a - lone we bring not, The_ will - ful-ness of sin,

And_ all we bring is noth - ing Save that which is with - in. **R.**

4. Where - fore, though all un - wor - thy To of - fer sa - cri - fice,
5. O_ Tri - ni - ty of Per - sons! O U - ni - ty most high!

We_ pray that this our du - ty be pleas - ing in Thine eyes;
On_ Thee a - lone re - ly - ing Thy ser - vants would draw nigh;

For_ praise, and thanks and wor - ship, For_ mer - cy and for aid,
un - wor - thy in our weak - ness, on_ Thee our hope is stayed,

The_ Ca - tho - lic ob - la - tion Of Je - sus Christ is made. **R.**
and_ blest by Thy for - give - ness we will not be a - fraid. **R.**

290 O Jesus, King Most Wonderful

Tune: ST. MATTHEW (DCM)   Text: Jesu Rex Admirabilis

1. O Je - sus, King most won - der - ful Thou con - quer - or___ re - nowned,
2. O Je - sus, light of all___ be - low, Thou font of life___ and fire,

Thou sweet - ness most in - ef - fa - ble,___ In whom all joys_ are found!
Sur - pas - sing all the joys_ we know, And all we can_ de - sire.

When once Thou vis - it - est___ the heart, Then truth be - gins to shine;
May eve - ry heart con - fess_ Thy Name, And ev - er___ Thee a - dore;

Then earth - ly van - i - ties de - part;_ Then kin - dles love_ di - vine.
And, seek - ing Thee, it - self in - flame_ To seek Thee more and more.

3. Thee may our tongues for - ev - er bless; Thee may we love_ a - lone;
4. Thou, Sav - ior, cause that eve - ry soul Which Thou hast loved so well,

And ev - er in our lives_ ex - press The im - age of___ Thine own.
May will, with - in Thine o - pen Heart, In life and death to dwell.

Stay with us, Lord, and with_ Thy light Il - lume the_ soul's a - byss;
O Je - sus, spot - less Vir - gin-flow'r, Our life and_ joy; to Thee

Scat - ter the dark - ness of our night,_ And fill the world_ with bliss.
Be praise, be - at - i - tude, and pow'r, Through all e - ter - ni - ty.

To Christ, The Prince Of Peace 291

Tune: TRADITIONAL (66 86)   Text: Summi Parentis Filio

1. To Christ the Prince of Peace, And Son of God most high, The Father of the world to come, Sing we with ho - ly joy.

2. Deep in His heart, for us, The wound of love He bore; That love where-with He still in-flames The hearts that Him a - dore.

3. O Je - sus, vic - tim blest, What else but love di - vine Could Thee con-strain to o - pen thus That Sa - cred Heart of thine?

4. O fount of end - less life, O spring of wa - ter clear, O flame ce - les - tial, cleans-ing all Who un - to Thee draw near!

5. Praise to the Fa - ther be, And sole - be - got - ten Son; Praise, Ho - ly Par - a - clete, to thee While end - less ag - es run.

292 Word Of God To Earth Descending

Tune: DRAKES BROUGHTON (87 87)   Text: Verbum Supernum Prodiens

1. Word of God to earth descending With the Father present still,
Near his earthly journey's ending Hastes his mission to fulfill.

2. Well the traitor's kiss foreknowing Miracle of love divine;
See his hands himself bestowing In the hallowed bread and wine.

3. Holy body, blood all precious, Giv'n by him to be our food,
With them both he doth refresh us, Formed like him of flesh and blood.

4. Mighty Victim, earth's salvation, Heav'n's own gate unfolding wide,
Help thy people in temptation, Feed them from thy bleeding side.

5. Unto thee, the hidden manna, Father, Spirit, unto thee,
Let us raise the loud hosanna, And adoring bend the knee.

The Word, Descending From Above   293

Tune: W. RATCLIFFE (LM)   Text: Verbum Supernum Prodiens

1. The Word, de - scend - ing from a - bove, Though with the Fa - ther still on high, Went forth up - on His work of love, And soon to life's last eve drew nigh.

2. He short - ly to a death ac - cursed By a dis - ci - ple shall be giv'n; But, to His twelve dis - ci - ples, first He gives Him - self the Bread from heav'n.

3. Him - self in ei - ther kind He gave; He gave His Flesh, He gave His Blood; Of flesh and blood all men are made; And He of man would be the Food.

4. At birth our Broth - er He be - came; And now Him - self as food He gives; To ran - som us He died in shame; As our re - ward, in bliss He lives.

294 The Heavenly Word, Proceeding Forth

Tune: WAREHAM (LM)   Text: Verbum Supernum Prodiens

1. The Heav'n-ly Word pro - ceed - ing forth, Yet leav - ing
2. By false dis - ci - ple to be giv'n To foe - men

not the Fa - ther's side, And go - ing to His
for His Blood a - thirst, Him - self, the liv - ing

work on earth Had reached at length life's e - ven - tide.
Bread from Heav'n, He gave to His dis - ci - ples first.

3. To them He gave, in two - fold kind, His ver - y
4. By birth, our fel - low - man was He; Our meat, while

Flesh, His ver - y Blood: In love's own ful - ness
sit - ting at the board; He died, our ran - som -

thus de - signed Of the whole man to be the food.
er to be; He ev - er reigns, our great re - ward.

5. O sav - ing Vic - tim, o - p'ning wide The gate of
6. To Thy great Name be end - less praise, Im - mor - tal

Heav'n to man be - low: Our foes press on from
God - head, One in Three! O grant us end - less

eve - ry side; Thine aid sup - ply, Thy strength be - stow.
length of days In our true na - tive land, with Thee.

Christ The Word To Earth Descended   295

Tune: Based on BATTY (87 87)   Text: Verbum Supernum Prodiens

1. Christ the Word to earth de-scend-ed, Yet re-mained in heav-en still;

When His earth-ly jour-ney end-ed He ful-filled the Fa-ther's will.

2. While the false dis - ci - ple wait-ed To be-tray his Mas-ter's life,

Christ for men, though by men hat-ed, Gave in love the bread of life.

3. Un - der two-fold spe-cies giv-en, Flesh as bread and blood as wine,

He be-came a pledge of heav-en: Man par-took of Life Di-vine.

4. Might-y Vic-tim, earth's sal - va-tion, Heav-en's gates un - fold-ing wide,

See, we cry in des - o - la-tion: Be our strength, be at our side.

5. To Thee, God-head, three-fold es-sence, Be un - end-ing praise and love;

Make us wor-thy of Thy pres-ence In our heav'n-ly home a - bove.

296 Sanctify Me Wholly

Tune: ANIMA CHRISTI (10 10 10 10)   Text: Thomas Ball (†1916)

1. Sanc-ti-fy me whol-ly, Soul of Christ a-dored; Be my sure sal-va-tion, Bod-y of the Lord; Fill my yearn-ing spir-it, O Thou Blood un-priced: Wash me, Sa-cred Wa-ter from the side of Christ.

2. Pas-sion of my Sav-ior, be my strength in need; Good and gra-cious Je-sus, to my prayer give heed. In Thy wounds most pre-cious, let me ref-uge find: All the en-vious pow-er of the foe-man bind.

3. At death's fi-nal hour_ call me to Thy face; Bid me stand be-side Thee in the heav'n ly place: There with saints and an-gels I shall sing to Thee Through the count-less ag-es of e-ter-ni-ty.

Soul Of My Savior   297

Tune: ANIMA CHRISTI (10 10 10 10)   Text: Anima Christi (14th century)

1. Soul of my Sav - ior sanc - ti - fy my breast, Bod - y of
Christ, be thou my sav - ing guest, Blood of my Sav - ior, bathe me
in thy tide, wash__ me with wa - ters flow - ing from thy side.

2. Strength and pro - tec - tion may thy pas - sion be, O bless - èd
Je - sus, hear and an - swer me; deep in thy wounds, Lord,
hide and shel - ter me, so__ shall I nev - er, nev - er part from thee.

3. Save me from e - vil, make me Thine a - lone; In my last
mo - ments take me for Thine own; Call me and bid me has - ten
to Thy side, That__ I may see Thee praised and glo - ri - fied.

298   Lead, Kindly Light

Tune: SANDON (10 4 10 4 10 10)   Text: Blessed Cardinal Newman (†1890)

1. Lead, Kind-ly Light, a-mid th'en-cir-cling gloom,
2. I was not ev-er thus, nor prayed that Thou

Lead Thou me on! The night is dark, and I am far from
shouldst lead me on; I loved to choose and see my path; but

home, Lead Thou me on! Keep Thou my feet; I do not
now lead Thou me on! I loved the gar-ish day, and,

ask to see The dis-tant scene; one step e-nough for me.
spite of fears, Pride ruled my will. Re-mem-ber not past years!

3. So long Thy pow'r hath blest me, sure it still
4. Mean-time, a-long the nar-row rug-ged path,

will lead me on. O'er moor and fen, o'er crag and tor-rent,
Thy-self hast trod, Lead, Sav-iour, lead me home in child-like

till the night is gone, And with the morn those an-gel
faith, home to my God. To rest for-ev-er af-ter

fac-es smile, which I Have loved long since, and lost a-while!
earth-ly strife In the calm light of ev-er-last-ing life.

Let Thy People Praise Thee, Lord   299

Tune: HEATHLANDS (77 77 77)   Text: Henry Lyte (†1847)

1. Let thy peo-ple praise thee, Lord; be by all that live a-dored.
Let the na-tions shout and sing glo-ry to their Sav-ior King;
at thy feet their trib-ute pay, and thy ho-ly will o-bey.

2. Let thy peo-ple praise thee, Lord; earth shall then her fruits af-ford;
God to man his bless-ing give, man to God de-vot-ed live;
all be-low, and all a-bove, one in joy, and light, and love.

3. God of mer-cy, God of grace, show the bright-ness of thy face.
Shine up-on us, Sav-ior, shine, fill thy Church with light di-vine,
and thy sav-ing health ex-tend un-to earth's re-mot-est end.

300   May The Grace Of Christ Our Savior

Tune: WALTHAM (87 87) alt.   Text: John Newton (†1807)

1. May the grace of Christ our Sav-ior And the Fa-ther's bound-less love
With the Ho-ly Spir-it's fa-vor, Rest up-on us from a-bove.

2. Thus may we a-bide in un-ion With each oth-er and the Lord,
And pos-sess, in sweet com-mun-ion, Joys which earth can-not af-ford.

3. To this tem-ple, where we call Thee, Come, O Lord of Hosts, to-day;
With Thy wont-ed lov-ing-kind-ness Hear Thy peo-ple as they pray.

4. Vouch-safe to un-wor-thy ser-vants What they sup-pli-cate to gain;
And here-af-ter in Thy glo-ry With Thy bles-sèd ones to reign.

5. Laud to Fa-ther, Son, and Spir-it; Ev-er Three, and ev-er One:
Con-sub-stan-tial, co-e-ter-nal, While un-end-ing ag-es run.

Lord, Enthroned In Heavenly Splendor   301

Tune: STUTTGART (87 87)   Text: O Sola Magnarum Urbium

1. Lord, en-throned in heav'n-ly splen-dor, first - be - got - ten from the dead.

Thou a - lone, our strong de - fend - er, lift - est up thy peo-ple's head.

2. Here our humbl-est hom-age pay we, here in lov - ing rev-'rence bow;

here for faith's dis - cern-ment pray we, lest we fail to know thee now.

3. Though the low -liest form doth veil thee as of old in Beth - le - hem,

here, as there, thine an - gels hail thee, branch and flow'r of Jes - se's stem.

4. Pas -chal Lamb, thine of - f'ring, fin -ished once for all when thou was slain,

here re-newed, yet un - di - min-ished, cleans-ing souls from eve - ry stain.

5. Life - im - part - ing heav'n -ly Man - na, strick -en Rock with stream-ing side,

heav'n and earth with loud ho - san - na wor -ship thee, the Lamb who died.

302 O Thou, The Son Of God Most High

Tune: SOLEMNIS HAEC FESTIVITAS (LM)   Text: Summi Parentis Filio

1. O Thou, the Son of God most High, Thou
Fa - ther of the life to be, O Prince of Peace, to
Thee we cry, We bring our song of praise to Thee.

2. Thy Heart was wound - ed by the blow Or -
dained of ev - er - last - ing love; Such love a - mong Thy
flocks be - low Thou kindl - est at the fires a - bove.

3. Dear Christ in pit - y for our woe Thou
didst Thy - self as vic - tim give, The cru - el pangs to
un - der - go, To op'n Thy side that man might live.

4. O sa - cred fount of love sub - lime, O
liv - ing spring of wa - ters free, O fire to cleanse a -
way all crime, O Heart a - flame with char - i - ty.

5. Lord, keep us ev - er in Thy Heart, Thy
ten - der love to feel and know, The joys of heav'n to
us im - part, When we shall leave these walks be - low.

6. Glo - ry to Fa - ther and to Son, And
to the Ho - ly Ghost the same, To whom all pow'r when
time is done, And end - less rule, in end - less fame.

O Jesus Christ, Remember 303

Tune: AURELIA (76 76D)   Text: Edward Caswell (†1878)

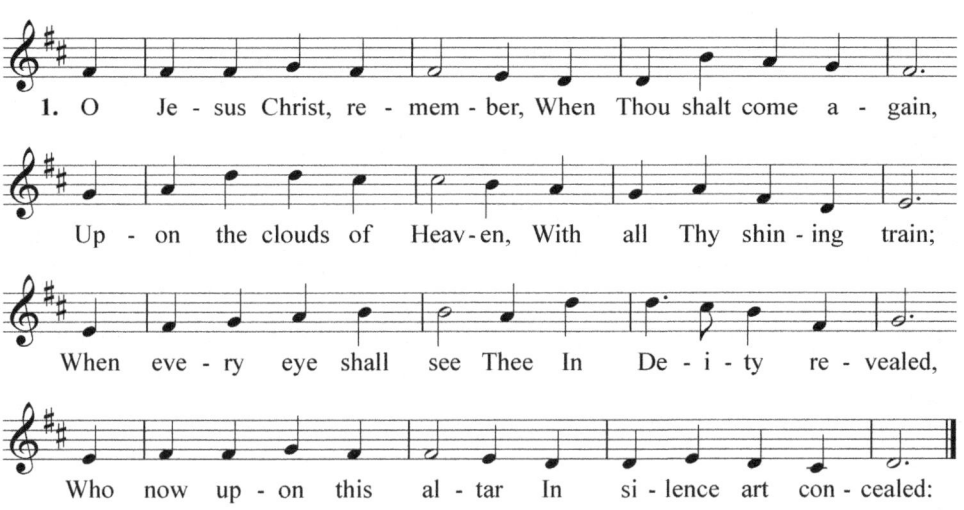

1. O Je - sus Christ, re - mem - ber, When Thou shalt come a - gain,
Up - on the clouds of Heav - en, With all Thy shin - ing train;
When eve - ry eye shall see Thee In De - i - ty re - vealed,
Who now up - on this al - tar In si - lence art con - cealed:

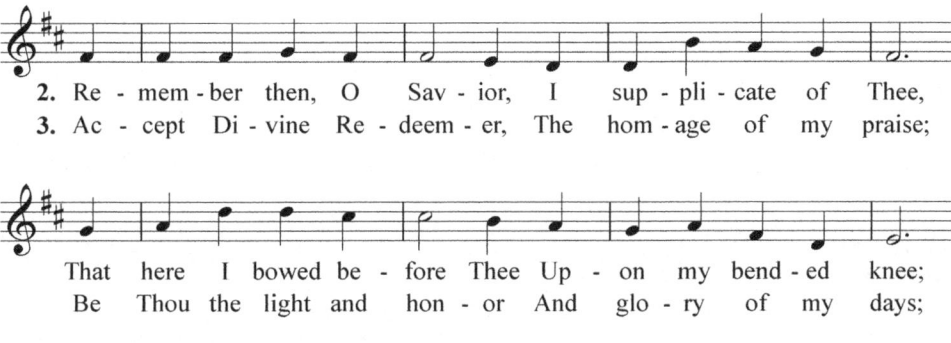

2. Re - mem - ber then, O Sav - ior, I sup - pli - cate of Thee,
3. Ac - cept Di - vine Re - deem - er, The hom - age of my praise;

That here I bowed be - fore Thee Up - on my bend - ed knee;
Be Thou the light and hon - or And glo - ry of my days;

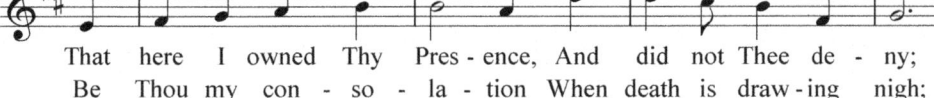

That here I owned Thy Pres - ence, And did not Thee de - ny;
Be Thou my con - so - la - tion When death is draw - ing nigh;

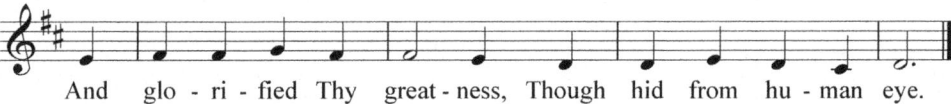

And glo - ri - fied Thy great - ness, Though hid from hu - man eye.
Be Thou my on - ly treas - ure Through all e - ter - ni - ty.

304 O Lord, I Am Not Worthy

Tune: NON DIGNUS (76 76)   Text: Landshuter Gesangbuch (1777)

1. O__ Lord, I am not wor-thy That. Thou should'st come to   me,

But__ speak the words of   mer - cy, My   spir - it healed shall   be.

2. Oh,__ come, all you who   la - bor In__ sor - row and   in   pain,

Come, eat This Bread from heav-en; Thy peace and strength re - gain.

3. O__   Je - sus, we   a - dore Thee, Our__ Vic - tim and our Priest,

Whose__ pre-cious Blood and   Bod - y Be - come our   sa - cred Feast.

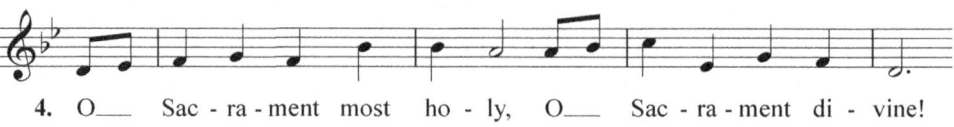

4. O__   Sac - ra - ment most ho - ly, O__   Sac - ra - ment di - vine!

All__ praise and all thanks-giv - ing Be   ev - 'ry mo-ment Thine.

O Sacrament Most Holy   305

Tune: FULDA (76 76 with Refrain)   Text: I. Udulutsch

1. O Je - sus, we a - dore thee, Who, in thy love di - vine,
2. O Je - sus, we a - dore thee, our vic - tim and our Priest,

Con - ceal thy might - y God - head In forms of bread and wine. R.
Whose pre - cious blood and bod - y Be - come our Sa - cred feast. R.

Refrain:

O sac - ra-ment most ho - ly, O sac - ra-ment di - vine,

All praise and all thanks - giv - ing Be ev - 'ry mo - ment thine!

3. O Je - sus, we a - dore thee, Our Sav - ior and our
4. O Je - sus, we a - dore thee; Come, live in us we
5. O come, all thee who la - bor In sor - row and in

King, And with the saints and an - gels Our
pray, That all our thoughts and ac - tions Be
pain; Come, eat this bread from heav - en; Thy

hum - ble hom - age bring. R.
thine a - lone to - day. R.
peace and strength re - gain. R.

306 Christ Is Made The Sure Foundation

Tune: REGENT SQUARE (87 87 87)   Text: Angularis Fundamentum

1. Christ is made the sure Foun-da-tion, Christ the Head and
2. All that ded-i-cat-ed cit-y, Dear-ly loved of
3. To this tem-ple, where we call Thee, Come, O Lord of

Cor-ner-stone; Cho-sen of the Lord, and pre-cious,
God on high, In ex-ult-ant ju-bi-la-tion,
Hosts, to-day; With Thy wont-ed lov-ing-kind-ness

Bind-ing all the__ Church in one, Ho-ly Zi-on's
Pours per-pet-ual__ mel-o-dy, God the One in
Hear Thy ser-vants as they pray. And Thy full-est

Help for-ev-er, And her Con-fi-dence a-lone.
Three a-dor-ing In glad hymns e-ter-nal-ly.
ben-e-dic-tion Shed with-in its walls for aye.

4. Here vouchsafe to all Thy servants / What they ask of Thee to gain;
   What they gain from Thee forever / With the blessèd to retain,
   And hereafter in Thy glory / Evermore with Thee to reign.

5. Laud and honor to the Father, / Laud and honor to the Son,
   Laud and honor to the Spirit, / Ever Three and ever One;
   Consubstantial, co-eternal, / While unending ages run.

English Translation by Dr. John Neale (†1866).
Melody by Henry Smart (†1879).

O God Of Earth And Altar 307

Tune: LLANGLOFFAN (76 76D)   Text: G. K. Chesterton (†1936)

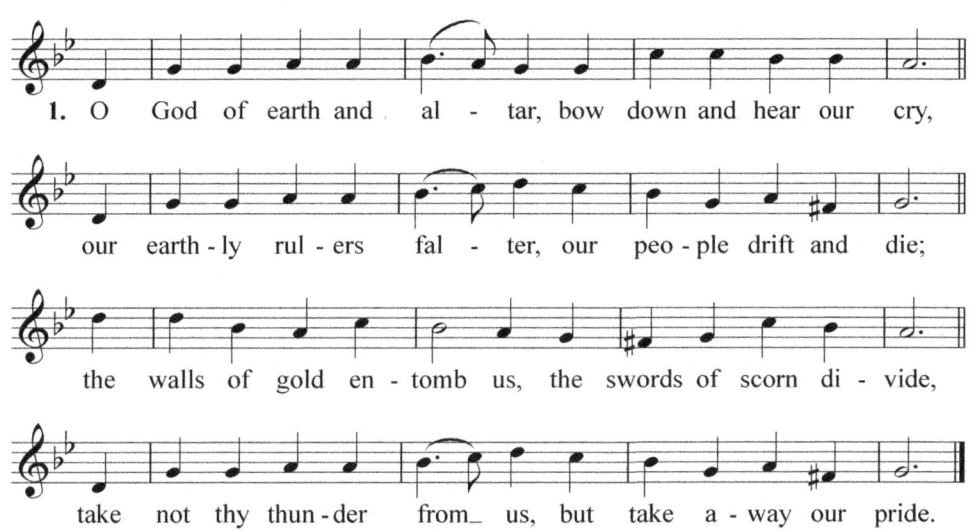

1. O God of earth and al - tar, bow down and hear our cry,
our earth - ly rul - ers fal - ter, our peo - ple drift and die;
the walls of gold en - tomb us, the swords of scorn di - vide,
take not thy thun - der from us, but take a - way our pride.

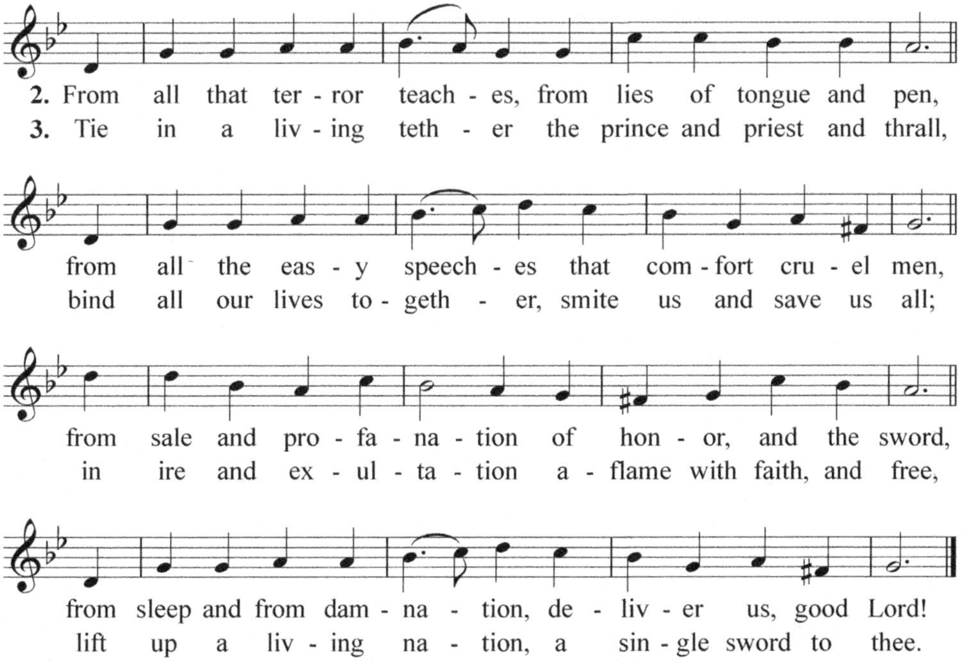

2. From all that ter - ror teach - es, from lies of tongue and pen,
from all the eas - y speech - es that com - fort cru - el men,
from sale and pro - fa - na - tion of hon - or, and the sword,
from sleep and from dam - na - tion, de - liv - er us, good Lord!

3. Tie in a liv - ing teth - er the prince and priest and thrall,
bind all our lives to - geth - er, smite us and save us all;
in ire and ex - ul - ta - tion a - flame with faith, and free,
lift up a liv - ing na - tion, a sin - gle sword to thee.

308   Blessed Jesus, At Thy Word

Tune: LIEBSTER JESU (78 78 88)   Text: Tobias Clausnitzer (†1684)

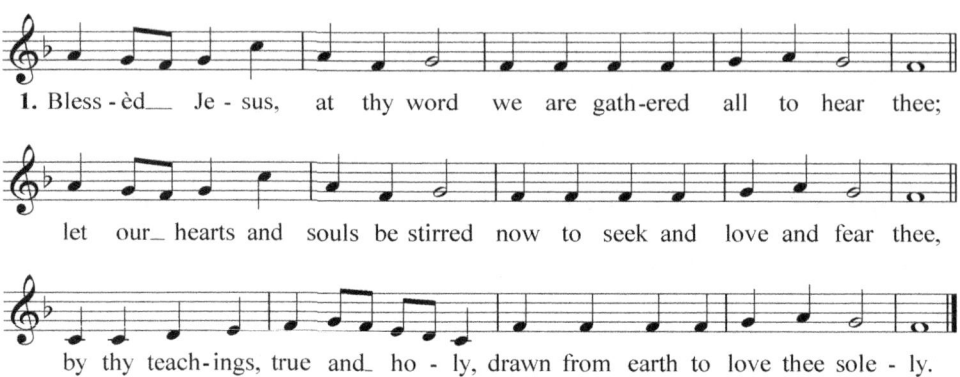

1. Bless-èd__ Je - sus, at thy word we are gath-ered all to hear thee;

let our__ hearts and souls be stirred now to seek and love and fear thee,

by thy teach-ings, true and__ ho - ly, drawn from earth to love thee sole - ly.

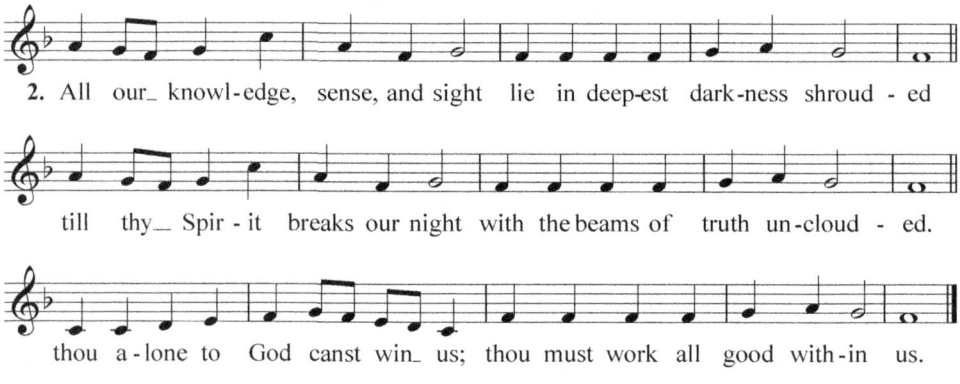

2. All our__ knowl-edge, sense, and sight lie in deep-est dark-ness shroud - ed

till thy__ Spir - it breaks our night with the beams of truth un-cloud - ed.

thou a - lone to God canst win__ us; thou must work all good with-in us.

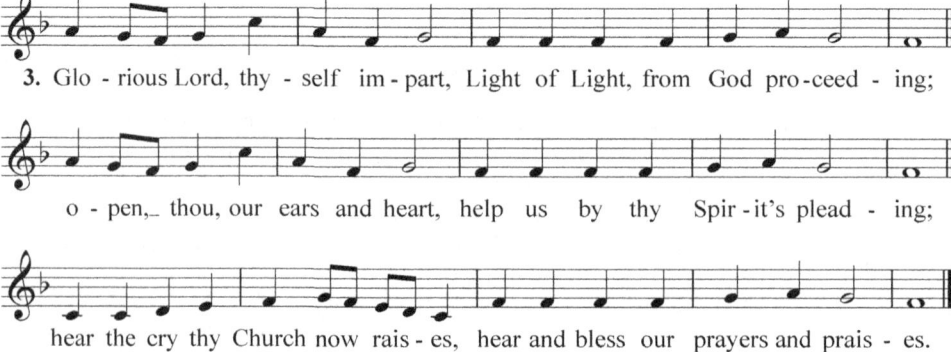

3. Glo - rious Lord, thy - self im - part, Light of Light, from God pro-ceed - ing;

o - pen,__ thou, our ears and heart, help us by thy Spir -it's plead - ing;

hear the cry thy Church now rais - es, hear and bless our prayers and prais - es.

Panis Angelicus 309

Tune: LAMBILLOTTE PANIS (12 12 12 8)   Text: St. Thomas Aquinas (†1274)

1. Pa - nis An - gé - li -cus fit___ pa - nis hó - mi-num;
Dat pa - nis caé - li -cus fi - gu - ris tér - mi - num:
O res mi - rá - bi - lis! Man - dú - cat Dó - mi-num.
Pau - per, ser - vus et hú - mi - lis.

2. Te tri - na De - i - tas, u - na-que po - sci-mus,
Sic nos tu vi - si - ta, si - cut te co - li - mus;
Per tu - as se - mi-tas duc nos quo ten - di-mus,
Ad lu - cem quam in - há - bi - tas. A - men.

"The Bread of Angels becomes the Bread of men; the Bread of Heaven puts an end to types; O wondrous thing: the poor, the servant, and the lowly, feed on their Lord!"

"O triune Deity, we beseech Thee, that Thou visit us, as we adore Thee; lead us by Thy ways, whither we direct our steps, to the light wherein Thou dost dwell."

310   At The Name Of Jesus

Tune: KING'S WESTON (65 65D)   Text: Caroline Noel (†1877)

1. At the Name of Je - sus eve - ry knee shall bow,
2. At his voice cre - a - tion sprang at once to sight,

eve - ry tongue con - fess___ him King of glo - ry now;
all the an - gel fac - es, all the hosts of light,

'tis the Fa - ther's pleas - ure we should call him Lord,
Thrones and Dom - i - na - tions, stars up - on their way,

who from the be - gin - ning was the might - y Word.
all the heav'n - ly or - ders, in their great ar - ray.

3. Hum - bled for a sea - son, to re - ceive a Name
4. In your hearts en - throne him; there let him sub - due
5. Know that this Lord Je - sus shall re - turn a - gain,

from the lips of sin - ners, un - to whom he came,
all that is not ho - ly, all that is not true;
with his Fa - ther's glo - ry with his an - gel train;

faith - ful - ly he bore___ it spot - less to the last,
crown him as your Cap - tain in temp - ta - tion's hour;
for all wreaths of em - pire meet up - on his brow,

brought it back vic - to - rious, when from death he passed.
let his will en - fold you in its light and pow'r.
and our hearts con - fess him King of glo - ry now.

I Received The Living God   311

Tune: LIVING GOD (77 77 with refrain)   Text: Anonymous

Refrain: I re-ceived the liv-ing God and my heart is full of joy.____

I re-ceived the liv-ing God and my heart is full of joy.

1. He has said: I am the Bread Knead-ed long to give you life;

You who will par-take of me Need not ev-er fear to die.

2. He has said: I am the Way, And my Fa-ther longs for you;

So I come to bring you home To be one with him a-new.

3. He has said: I am the Truth; If you fol-low close to me,

You will know me in your heart, and my word shall make you free.

4. He has said: I am the Life Far from whom no thing can grow,

But re-ceive this liv-ing bread, And my Spir-it you shall know.

312 Come, Labor On

Tune: ORA LABORA (4 10 10 10 4)   Text: Thomas Noble (†1953)

1. Come, la - bor on! Who dares stand i - dle, on the har - vest
2. Come, la - bor on! Claim the high call - ing an - gels can - not

plain While all a - round him waves the gold - en grain? And
share. To young and old the Gos - pel glad - ness bear; Re

to each ser - vant does the Mas - ter say, "Go work___ to - day."
deem the time; its hours too swift - ly fly. The night___ draws nigh.

3. Come, la - bor on! The en - e - my is watch - ing night and
4. Come, la - bor on! A - way with gloom - y doubts and faith - less

day, To sow the tares, to snatch the seed a - way; While we in
fear! No arm so weak but may do ser - vice here: By feebl - est

sleep our du - ty have for - got, He slum - bered___ not.
a - gents may our God ful - fill His ho - ly___ will.

5. Come, la - bor on! No time for rest, till glows the west - ern
6. Come, la - bor on! The toil is pleas - ant, the re - ward is

sky, Till the long shad - ows o'er our path - way lie, And a glad
sure; Bless - èd are those who to the end en - dure; How full their

sound comes with the set - ting sun, "Well done,___ well___ done!"
joy, how deep their rest shall be, O Lord,___ with___ Thee!

Let Thy Blood In Mercy Poured 313

Tune: LUISE (78 78 77)   Text: John Brownlie (†1925)

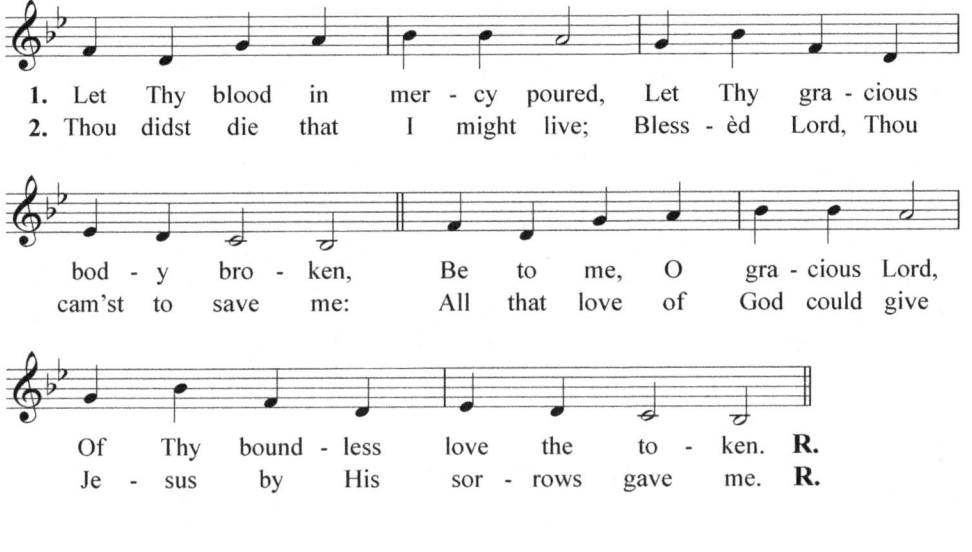

1. Let Thy blood in mer - cy poured, Let Thy gra - cious
2. Thou didst die that I might live; Bless - èd Lord, Thou

bod - y bro - ken, Be to me, O gra - cious Lord,
cam'st to save me: All that love of God could give

Of Thy bound - less love the to - ken. **R.**
Je - sus by His sor - rows gave me. **R.**

Refrain:

Thou didst give Thy - self for me, Now I give my - self to Thee.

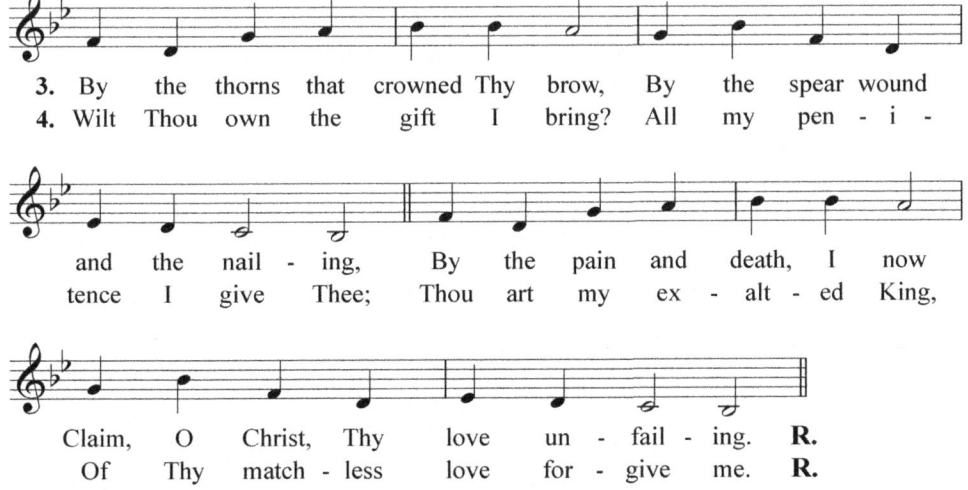

3. By the thorns that crowned Thy brow, By the spear wound
4. Wilt Thou own the gift I bring? All my pen - i -

and the nail - ing, By the pain and death, I now
tence I give Thee; Thou art my ex - alt - ed King,

Claim, O Christ, Thy love un - fail - ing. **R.**
Of Thy match - less love for - give me. **R.**

314 Here, O My Lord, I See Thee Face To Face

Tune: NYACK (10 10 10 10)   Text: Horatius Bonar (†1889)

1. Here, O my Lord, I see thee face to face;
   here would I touch and handle things unseen;
   here grasp with firmer hand eternal grace,
   and all my weariness upon thee lean.

2. This is the hour of banquet and of song;
   this is the heav'nly table spread for me;
   here let me feast, and feasting, still prolong
   the hallowed hour of fellowship with thee.

3. I have no help but thine; nor do I need
   another arm save thine to lean upon;
   it is enough, my Lord, enough indeed;
   my strength is in thy might, thy might alone.

4. Mine is the sin, but thine the righteousness:
   mine is the guilt, but thine the cleansing Blood.
   Here is my robe, my refuge, and my peace;
   thy Blood, thy righteousness, O Lord my God!

5. Feast after feast thus comes and passes by;
   yet, passing, points to the glad feast above,
   giving sweet foretaste of the festal joy,
   the Lamb's great bridal feast of bliss and love.

In Heavenly Love Abiding   315

Tune: NYLAND (76 76D)   Text: Anna Waring (†1910)

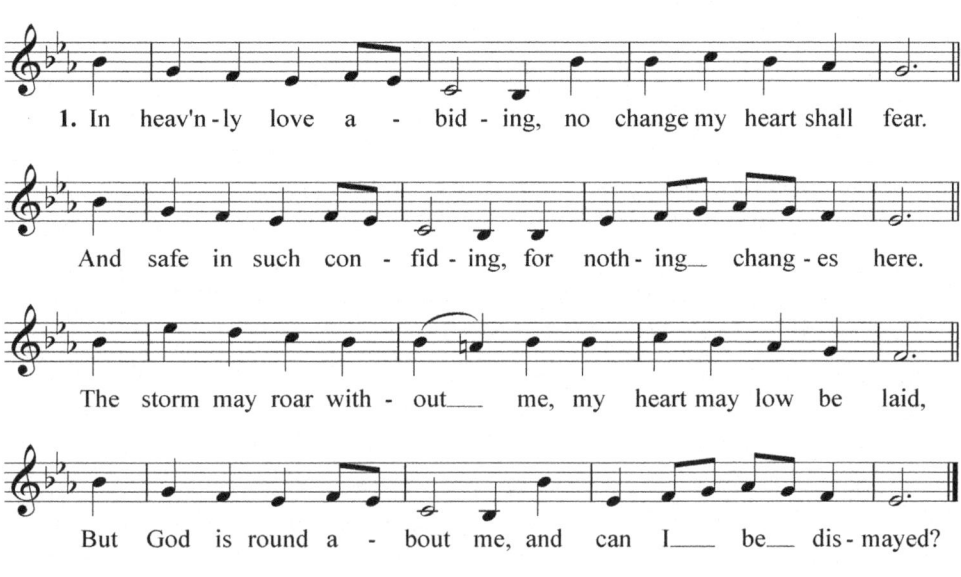

1. In heav'n-ly love a - bid - ing, no change my heart shall fear.

And safe in such con - fid - ing, for noth - ing__ chang - es here.

The storm may roar with - out__ me, my heart may low be laid,

But God is round a - bout me, and can I__ be__ dis - mayed?

2. Wher - ev - er He may_ guide me, no want shall turn me back.
3. Green pas - tures are be - fore me, which yet I have not seen.

My Shep - herd is be - side me, and noth - ing__ can__ I lack.
Bright skies will soon be_ o'er me, where dark - est__ clouds_ have been.

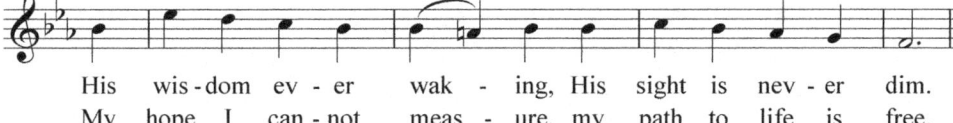

His wis - dom ev - er wak - ing, His sight is nev - er dim.
My hope I can - not meas - ure, my path to life is free.

He knows the way He's_ tak - ing, and I will_ walk_ with Him.
My Sav - ior has my_ treas - ure, and He will_ walk_ with me.

316 Deck Thyself, My Soul, With Gladness

Tune: SCHMÜCKE DICH (88 88D)   Text: Johann Franck (†1677)

1. Deck thy - self, my soul, with glad - ness, Leave the
2. He who craves a pre - cious treas - ure Nei - ther
3. Ah, how hun - gers all my spir - it For the
4. In my heart I find as - cend - ing Ho - ly

1. gloom - y haunts of sad - ness; Come in - to the day - light's
2. cost nor pain will meas - ure; But the price - less gifts of
3. love I do not mer - it! Oft have I, with sighs fast
4. awe, with rap - ture blend - ing, As this mys - ter - y I

1. splen - dor, There with joy thy prais - es ren - der
2. heav - en God to us hath free - ly giv - en.
3. throng - ing, Thought up - on this food with long - ing,
4. pon - der, Fill - ing all my soul with won - der,

1. Un - to Christ Whose grace un - bound - ed Hath this
2. Though the wealth of earth were of - fered, Naught would
3. In the bat - tle well nigh worst - èd, For this
4. Bear - ing wit - ness at this ho - ur Of the

1. won - drous ban - quet found - ed. Higher o'er all the heav'ns He
2. buy the gifts here of - fered: Christ's true bod - y, for thee
3. cup of life have thirst - ed, For the Friend Who here in -
4. great - ness of God's pow - er; Far be - yond all hu - man

1. reign - eth, Yet to dwell with thee He deign - eth.
2. riv - en, And His blood, for thee once giv - en.
3. vites us And to God Him - self u - nites us.
4. tell - ing Is the pow'r with - in Him dwell - ing.

5. Hu - man rea - son, though it pon - der, Can - not
6. Sun, who all my life dost bright - en, Light, who
7. Lord, by love and mer - cy driv - en Thou hast
8. Je - sus, Bread of Life, I pray Thee, Let me

5. fath - om__ this great won - der That Christ's bod - y e'er re -
6. dost my__ soul en - light - en; Joy the best that an - y
7. left Thy__ throne in heav - en On the cross for me to
8. glad - ly__ here o - bey Thee. By Thy love I am in -

5. main - eth Though it count - less__ souls sus - tain - eth
6. know - eth; Fount, whence all my__ be - ing flow - eth;
7. lan - guish And to die in__ bit - ter an - guish,
8. vit - ed, Be Thy love with__ love re - quit - ed;

5. And that He His blood is giv - ing All our
6. At Thy feet I cry, my Mak - er, Let me
7. To fore - go all joy and glad - ness And to
8. From this sup - per let me meas - ure, Lord, how

5. sins, by This, for - giv - ing. These great mys - ter - ies un -
6. be a fit par - tak - er Of this bless - èd food from
7. shed Thy blood in sad - ness. By this blood re - deemed and
8. vast and deep love's treas - ure. Through the gifts Thou here dost

5. sound - ed Are by God a - lone ex - pound - ed.
6. heav - en, For our good, Thy glo - ry, giv - en.
7. liv - ing, Lord, I praise Thee with thanks - giv - ing.
8. give__ me As Thy guest in heav'n re - ceive me.

318   My God, Accept My Heart This Day

Tune: SONG 67 (CM)   Text: Matthew Bridges (†1894)

1. My God, ac - cept my heart this day, and make it al - ways thine,

that I from thee no more may stray, no more from thee de - cline.

2. Be - fore the cross of him who died, be - hold, I pros-trate fall;

let eve - ry sin be cru - ci - fied, and Christ be all in all.

3. A - noint me with thy heav'n-ly grace, and seal me for thine own,

that I may see thy glo -rious face, and wor -ship near thy throne.

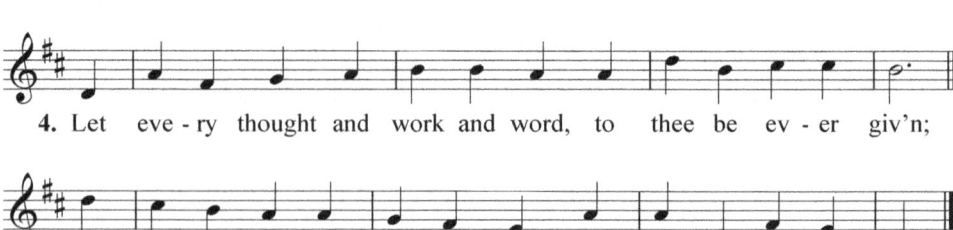

4. Let eve - ry thought and work and word, to thee be ev - er giv'n;

then life shall be thy ser - vice, Lord, and death the gate of heav'n.

I Sought The Lord, And Afterward I Knew 319

Tune: FAITH (10 10 10 6)   Text: Anonymous

1. I sought the Lord, and af - ter - ward I knew he moved my
soul to seek him, seek - ing me; it was not I that____
found, O Sav - ior true; no, I was found of thee.

2. Thou didst reach forth thy hand and mine en - fold; I walked and
sank not on the storm-vexed sea; 'twas not so much that____
I on thee took hold, as thou, dear Lord, on me.

3. I find, I walk, I love, but oh, the whole of love is
but my an - swer, Lord, to thee; for thou wert long be -
fore - hand with my soul, al - ways thou lov - edst me.

320 Blest Are The Pure In Heart

Tune: FRANCONIA (SM)   Text: Keble & Hall (19th century)

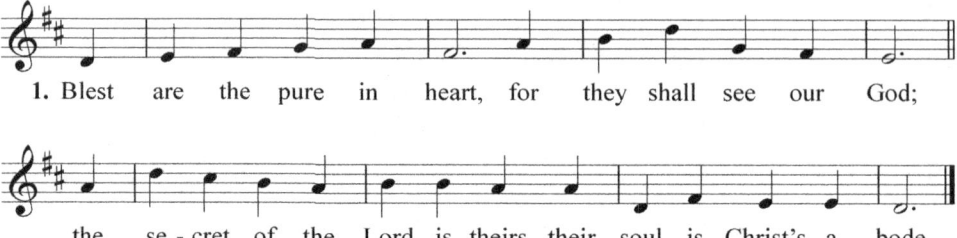

1. Blest are the pure in heart, for they shall see our God;

the se-cret of the Lord is theirs, their soul is Christ's a - bode.

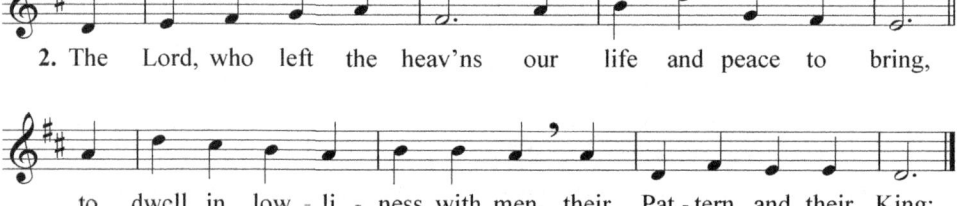

2. The Lord, who left the heav'ns our life and peace to bring,

to dwell in low - li - ness with men, their Pat - tern and their King;

3. Still to the low - ly soul he doth him - self im - part

and for his dwell-ing and his throne choos - eth the pure in heart.

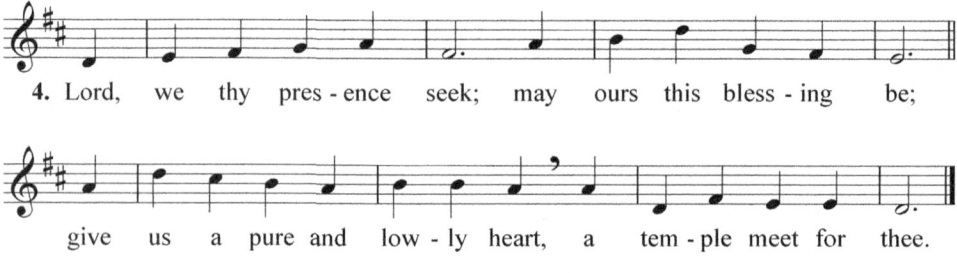

4. Lord, we thy pres - ence seek; may ours this bless - ing be;

give us a pure and low - ly heart, a tem - ple meet for thee.

Fairest Lord Jesus, Ruler Of All Nature 321

Tune: ST. ELIZABETH (568 558)   Text: German Jesuits (17th century)

1. Fair - est Lord Je - sus, Rul - er of all na - ture,
2. Fair are the mead - ows, fair - er still the wood - lands,

O Thou of God and__ man the Son, Thee will I
Robed in the bloom - ing__ garb of spring; Je - sus is

cher - ish, Thee will I hon - or, Thou, my soul's glo - ry,
fair - er, Je - sus is pur - er, Who makes the woe - ful

joy and crown.
heart to sing.

3. Fair is the sun - shine,
4. All fair - est beau - ty,
5. Beau - ti - ful Sav - ior!

Fair - er still the moon - light, And all the twin - kling__
heav - en - ly and earth - ly, Won - drous - ly, Je - sus is
Lord of all the na - tions! Son of__ God and__

star - ry host; Je - sus shines bright - er, Je - sus shines
found in Thee; None can be near - er, fair - er or
Son of Man! Glo - ry and hon - or, praise, ad - o -

pur - er Than all the an - gels heav'n can boast.
dear - er, Than Thou, my Sav - ior, art to me.
ra - tion, Now and for - ev - er more be Thine.

322 Father, We Thank Thee Who Hast Planted

Tune: RENDEZ A DIEU (98 98D)   Text: Based on the *Didache* (Vs. 3 courtesy Vincent Uher)

1. Fa - ther, we thank thee who hast plant - ed Thy ho - ly Name with -
in our hearts. Knowl - edge and faith and life im - mor - tal Je -
sus thy Son to us im - parts. Thou, Lord, didst make all for thy
pleas - ure, Didst give man food for all his days, Giv - ing in
Christ the Bread e - ter - nal; Thine is the pow'r be thine the praise.

2. Watch o'er thy Church, O Lord, in mer - cy, Save it from e - vil,
3. Bread of the world, in mer - cy bro - ken, Wine of the soul, in

guard it still, Strength - en it in thy love, u - nite it, Cleansed and con -
mer - cy shed, By Whom the words of life were spo - ken, And in Whose

formed un - to thy will. As grain once scat - tered on the hill - sides,
death our sins are dead. Oh, see thy Heart by sor - row bro - ken,

Was in this bro - ken bread made one, So from all lands thy
here too the tears by Ma - ry shed; Blest is this Feast more

Church be gath - ered in - to thy king - dom by thy Son.
than mere to - ken, thy Bo - dy bro - ken, thy Blood red.

Hail, True Victim, Life And Light 323

Tune: ST. JOHN DAMASCENE (76 76 D)   Text: Ave Vivens Hostia

1. Hail, true Vic - tim, life and light Un - to sin - ners
2. Je - sus, tru - ly in this place, God and man re -
3. Plead, true Vic - tim, in our stead, To the Fa - ther

lend - ing, Ev - 'ry old - er form and rite
sid - eth; Him no shad - ow doth re - place,
cry - ing, Thou, Thy chil - dren's dai - ly bread,

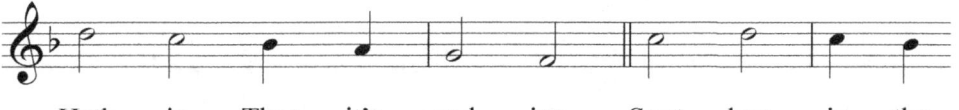

Hath in Thee it's end - ing. Spot - less in the
Him no rent di - vid - eth. Ver - y flesh, al-
Dai - ly health sup - ply - ing; Ban - quet for the

Fa - ther's sight, Ev - er - more as - cend - ing, Ho - ly
though His face, Glo - ri - fied, He hid - eth; Gar-nered
ex - ile spread, Grant us life un - dy - ing: May our

Church in bit - ter fight Ev - er - more be - friend - ing.
in this lit - tle space All of Christ a - bid - eth.
love from Thine be fed, Self and sense de - ny - ing!

324   Jesus, My Lord, My God, My All

Tune: SWEET SACRAMENT (LM with Refrain)   Text: Frederick Faber (†1863)

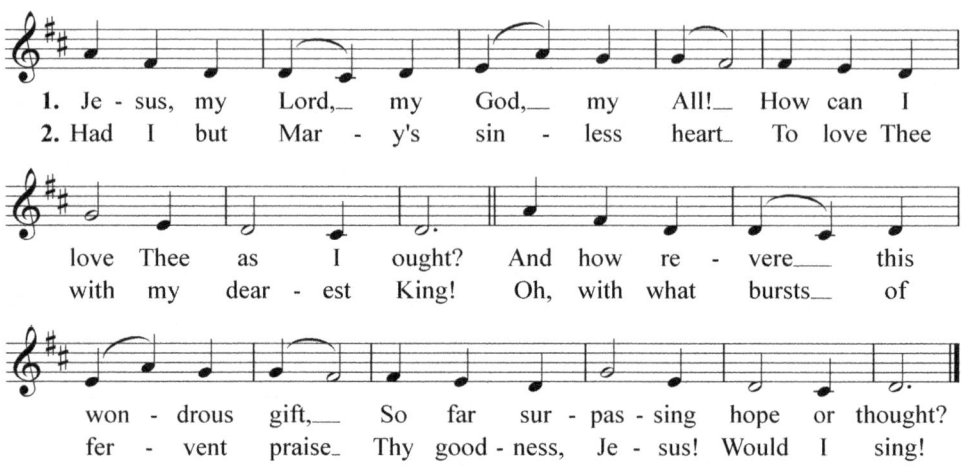

1. Je - sus, my Lord, my God, my All! How can I
2. Had I but Mar - y's sin - less heart To love Thee

love Thee as I ought? And how re - vere this
with my dear - est King! Oh, with what bursts of

won - drous gift, So far sur - pas - sing hope or thought?
fer - vent praise Thy good - ness, Je - sus! Would I sing!

Refrain:

Sweet Sa - cra - ment we Thee a - dore. O make us love Thee

more and more! O make us love Thee more and more!

3. Thy Bod - y, Soul, and God - head all! O mys - ter -
4. Sound, sound His prais - es high - er still, And come, ye

y of love di - vine! I can - not com - pass
an - gels, to our aid; 'Tis God! 'tis God! The

all I have, For all Thou hast and art are mine.
ver - y God, Whose pow'r both man and an - gels made!

God, My King, Thy Might Confessing 325

Tune: STUTTGART (87 87)   Text: Richard Mant (†1848)

1. God, my King, Thy might con-fess-ing, Ev - er will I bless Thy Name;

Day by day Thy throne ad - dress-ing, Still will I Thy praise pro-claim.

2. They shall talk of all Thy glo - ry, On Thy might and great-ness dwell,

Speak of Thy dread acts the sto - ry, And Thy deeds of won - der tell.

3. Nor shall fail from mem-'ry's treas-ure Works by love and mer - cy wrought;

Works of love sur - pas-sing meas-ure, Works of mer - cy pass - ing thought.

4. Full of kind-ness and com-pas - sion, Slow to an - ger, vast in love,

God is good to all cre - a - tion; All His works His good-ness prove.

5. All Thy works, O Lord, shall bless Thee; Thee shall all Thy saints a - dore:

King su-preme shall they con-fess Thee, And pro-claim Thy sov-'reign pow'r.

326   Lo, He Comes with Clouds Descending

Tune: HELMSLEY (87 87 47)   Text: John Cennick (†1755)

1. Lo! he__ comes with__ clouds__ de - scend -ing, Once for
2. Eve - ry__ eye__ shall now____ be - hold__ him Robed in
3. Those dear__ to - kens of_____ his_ pas - sion Still his
4. Yea, A - men! let__ all_____ a - dore__ thee, High on

fa - vored sin - ners__ slain; Thou- sand thou - sand saints___
dread - ful maj - es - ty;__ Those who__ set__ at__ nought__
daz - zling bod - y__ bears; Cause of__ end - less__ ex -
thine e - ter - nal__ throne; Sav - ior,__ take__ the__ pow'r__

at - tend - ing, Swell the tri - umph of__ his__
and__ sold__ him, Pierced and nailed him to__ the__
-ul - ta - tion To his ran - somed wor - ship -
and__ glo - ry, Claim the king - dom for__ thine

train:__ Al - le - lu - ia, Al - le - lu - ia,
tree,__ Deep - ly wail - ing, deep - ly wail - ing,
-ers;__ With__ what rap - ture, with__ what rap - ture,
own;__ O____ come quick - ly! O____ come quick - ly!

Al - le - lu - ia! God ap -pears, on earth to reign.
deep - ly wail - ing, Shall the_ true Mes - si - ah see.
with__ what rap - ture Gaze we_ on those glo - rious scars!
O____ come quick-ly! Al - le - lu - ia! Come, Lord, come!

Creator Of The Stars Of Night   327

Tune: CONDITOR ALME (LM)   Text: Conditor Alme Siderum

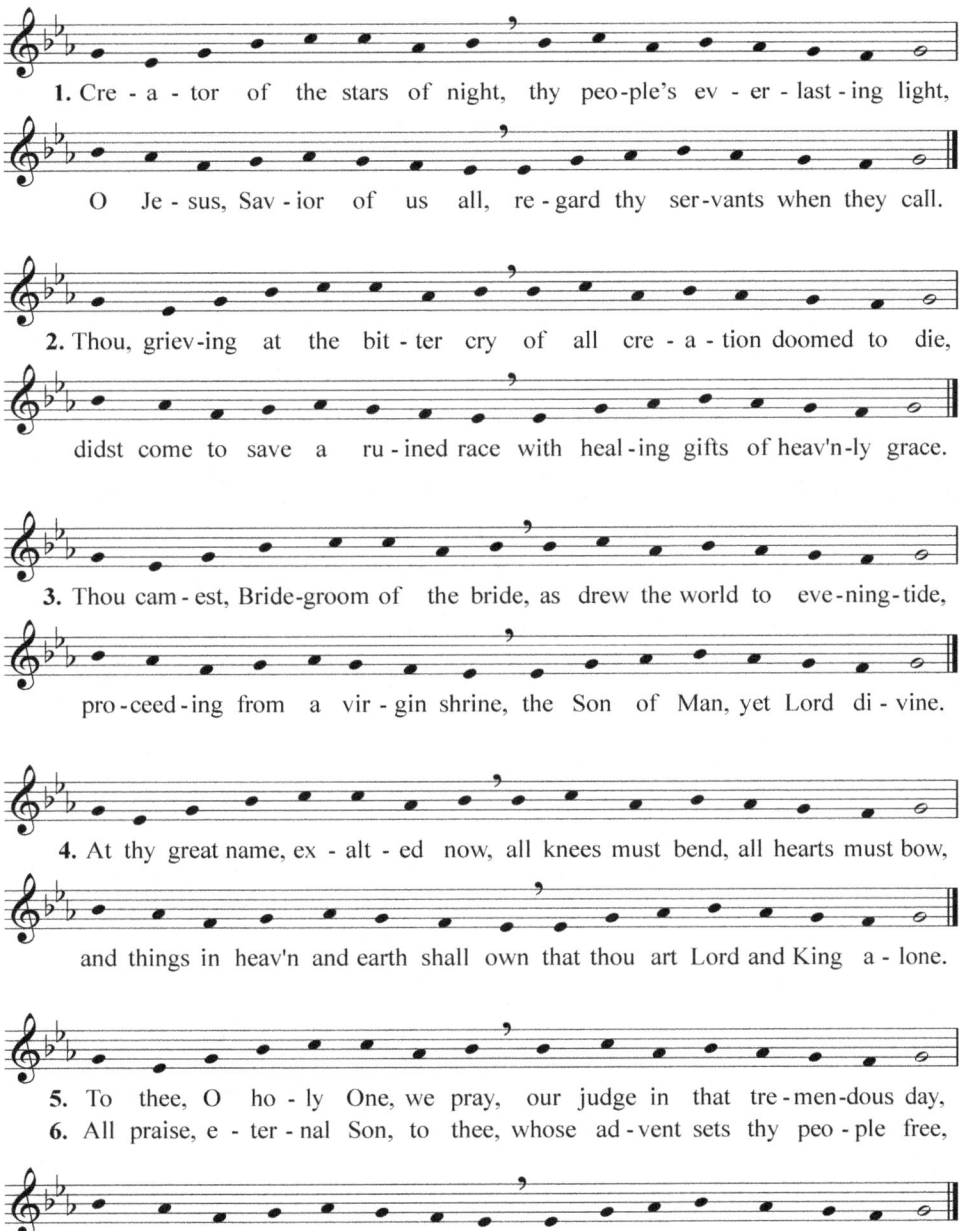

1. Cre - a - tor of the stars of night, thy peo-ple's ev - er - last - ing light,
O Je - sus, Sav - ior of us all, re - gard thy ser-vants when they call.

2. Thou, griev-ing at the bit - ter cry of all cre - a - tion doomed to die,
didst come to save a ru - ined race with heal-ing gifts of heav'n-ly grace.

3. Thou cam - est, Bride-groom of the bride, as drew the world to eve-ning-tide,
pro - ceed - ing from a vir - gin shrine, the Son of Man, yet Lord di - vine.

4. At thy great name, ex - alt - ed now, all knees must bend, all hearts must bow,
and things in heav'n and earth shall own that thou art Lord and King a - lone.

5. To thee, O ho - ly One, we pray, our judge in that tre - men-dous day,
6. All praise, e - ter - nal Son, to thee, whose ad - vent sets thy peo - ple free,
pre - serve us, while we dwell be - low, from eve - ry on - slaught of the foe.
whom with the Fa - ther we a - dore, and Spir - it blest, for ev - er-more.

328   Gabriel's Message Does Away

Tune: GABRIEL'S MESSAGE (777 with refrain)   Text: *Piae Cantiones* (1582)

1. Ga-briel's mes-sage does a-way Sa-tan's curse and
Sa-tan's sway, out of dark-ness brings our Day:
Refrain: so, be-hold, all the gates of heav'n un-fold.

2. He that comes de-spised shall reign; he that can-not
die, be slain; death by death its death shall gain: **R.**

3. Weak-ness shall the strong con-found; by the hands, in
grave clothes wound, A-dam's chains shall be un-bound. **R.**

4. By the sword that was his own, by that sword, and
5. Art by art shall be as-sailed; to the cross shall

that a-lone, shall Go-li-ath be o'er-thrown: **R.**
Life be nailed; from the grave shall hope be hailed: **R.**

Come, Thou Long-Expected Jesus   329

Tune: CROSS OF JESUS (87 87)   Text: Charles Wesley (†1788) alt.

1. Come, thou long-ex-pect-ed Je-sus, born to set_ thy peo-ple free;

from our fears and sins re-lease us, let us find_ our rest in thee.

2. Is-rael's strength and con-so-la-tion, hope of all_ the earth thou art:_

dear de-sire of eve-ry na-tion, joy of eve-ry long-ing heart.

3. Born thy peo-ple to de-liv-er, born a child, and yet a king,

born to reign in us for ev-er, now thy gra-cious king-dom bring.

4. By thine own e-ter-nal Spir-it rule in all_ our hearts a-lone;

by thy grace, help us to mer-it life e-ter-nal at thy throne.

N.B.

This hymn is also often sung to the tune of **STUTTGART**.

330   O Quickly Come, Dread Judge Of All

Tune: VATER UNSER (88 88 88)   Text: Lawrence Tuttiet (†1897) alt

1. O quick-ly come, dread Judge of all, for, aw-ful though thine ad-vent be;

all shad-ows from the truth will fall, and false-hood die, in sight of thee.

O quick-ly come, for doubt and fear like clouds dis-solve when thou art near.

2. O quick-ly come, great King of all; reign all a-round us, and with-in;

let sin no more our souls en-thrall, let pain and sor-row die with sin.

O quick-ly come, for thou a-lone canst make thy scat-tered peo-ple one.

3. O quick-ly come, true Life of all; for death is might-y all a-round;
4. O quick-ly come, sure Light of all; for gloom-y night broods o'er our way;

on eve-ry home his shad-ows fall, on eve-ry heart his mark is found.
and weak-ly souls be-gin to fall with wea-ry watch-ing for the day.

O quick-ly come, for grief and pain can nev-er cloud thy glo-rious reign.
O quick-ly come, for round thy throne no eye is blind, no night is known.

Silent Night, Holy Night   331

Tune: STILLE NACHT (66 89 66)   Text: Joseph Mohr (†1849)

1. Si - lent night, ho - ly night, all is calm, all is bright
2. Si - lent night, ho - ly night, shep - herds quake at the sight,
3. Si - lent night, ho - ly night, Son of God, love's pure light

round yon vir - gin moth-er and child. Ho - ly In - fant, so ten - der and
glo - ries stream from heav - en a - far, heav'n - ly hosts sing al - le - lu
ra - diant beams from thy ho - ly face, with the dawn of re - deem - ing

mild, sleep in heav - en - ly peace. Sleep in heav - en - ly peace.
ia; Christ, the Sav - ior, is born! Christ, the Sav - ior, is born!
grace, Je - sus, Lord at thy birth. Je - sus, Lord at thy birth.

The following verses may be used for EPIPHANY:

1. Si - lent night! peace - ful night! Child of heav'n! O how bright
2. Si - lent night! ho - liest night! Guid - ing Star, lend Thy light!
3. Si - lent night! ho - liest night! Won - drous Star, lend Thy light!

Thou didst smile when Thou wast born; Bless - ed was that hap - py
See the east - ern wise men bring Gifts and hom - age to our
With the an - gels let us sing Al - le - lu - ia to our

morn, Full of heav - en - ly joy. Full of heav - en - ly joy.
King! Christ the Sav - ior is here! Christ the Sav - ior is here!
King! Christ our Sav - ior is here! Christ our Sav - ior is here!

332   Of The Father's Love Begotten

Tune: DIVINUM MYSTERIUM (87 87 87 7)   Text: Corde Natus Ex Parentis

1. Of the Fa-ther's love be-got-ten, ere the worlds be-gan to
2. At his word the worlds were fram-èd; he com-mand-ed; it was

be, he is Al-pha and O-me-ga, he the source, the
done: heav'n and earth and depths of o-cean in their three-fold

end-ing he, of the things that are, that have been,
or-der one; all that grows be-neath the shin-ing

and that fu-ture years shall see, ev-er-more and ev-er-more!
of the moon and burn-ing sun, ev-er-more and ev-er-more!

3. O that birth for ev-er bless-èd, when the Vir-gin, full of
4. This is he whom seers in old time chant-ed of with one ac-

grace, by the Ho-ly Ghost con-ceiv-ing, bare the Sav-ior
cord; whom the voic-es of the proph-ets prom-ised in their

of our race; and the Babe, the world's Re-deem-er,
faith-ful word; now he shines, the long ex-pect-ed,

first re-vealed his sa-cred face, ev-er-more and ev-er-more!
let cre-a-tion praise its Lord, ev-er-more and ev-er-more!

5. O   ye heights of heav'n a - dore_ him; an - gel - hosts, his prais - es
6. Right-eous judge of souls de - part - ed, right-eous King of them_ that

sing; pow'rs, do - min - ions, bow be - fore_ him, and ex - tol our
live, On the Fa - ther's throne ex - alt - ed none in might with

God_ and King; let no tongue on earth be si - - lent,
Thee_ may strive; Who at   last in venge-ance com - - ing

eve - ry voice in con - cert ring, ev - er - more and ev - er - more!
Sin - ners from Thy face shalt drive, ev - er - more and ev - er - more!

7. Thee let old men, thee let young men, thee let boys in   cho - rus
8. Christ, to thee with God the Fa - ther, and, O Ho - ly Ghost, to

sing; ma - trons, vir - gins, lit - tle   maid - ens, with glad voic - es
thee, hymn and chant and high thanks - giv - ing, and un - wea - ried

an - swer - ing: let their guile - less songs re - ech - - o,
prais - es be; hon - or, glo - ry and do - min - - ion,

and the heart its mu - sic bring, ev - er - more and ev - er - more!_
and e - ter - nal vic - to - ry, ev - er - more and ev - er - more!_

334   O Christ, The Ransomer Of Man

Tune: POLISH CAROL (LM)   Text: Jesu Redemptor Omnium

1. O Christ, the Ran - som - er__ of man, Who, ere cre -
2. The Fa - ther's Light__ and Splen - dor Thou, Their end - less

at - ed light__ be - gan, Didst from__ the sov - 'reign
Hope__ to Thee__ that bow; Ac - cept__ the prayers and

Fa - ther spring, His pow'r__ and glo - ry e - qual - ling.
praise__ to - day That through the world__ Thy ser - vants pay.

3. Sal - va - tion's Au - thor, call__ to mind How, tak - ing
4. Thus tes - ti - fies__ the pre - sent day, Through eve - ry

form__ of hu - man - kind, Born of__ a Vir - gin
year__ in long__ ar - ray, That Thou,__ sal - va - tion's

un - de - filed, Thou in__ man's flesh__ be - cam'st a Child.
source a - lone, Pro - ceed - edst from__ the Fa - ther's throne.

5. The heav'ns a - bove, the roll - ing main And all that
6. And we who, by__ Thy pre - cious Blood From sin re -
7. O Lord, the Vir - gin - born,__ to Thee E - ter - nal

earth's__ wide realms con - tain, With joy - ous voice now
deemed, are marked for God, On this__ the day that
praise__ and glo - ry be, Whom with__ the Fa - ther

loud - ly sing The glo - ry of__ their new - born King.
saw__ Thy birth, Sing the__ new song__ of ran - somed earth.
we__ a - dore And Ho - ly Spir - it for - ev - er - more.

From East To West, From Shore To Shore 335

Tune: VOM HIMMEL HOCH (LM)   Text: A Solis Ortus Cardine

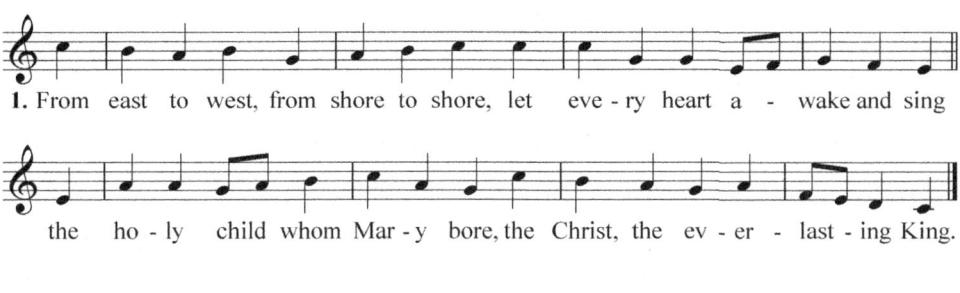

1. From east to west, from shore to shore, let eve-ry heart a-wake and sing
the ho-ly child whom Mar-y bore, the Christ, the ev-er-last-ing King.

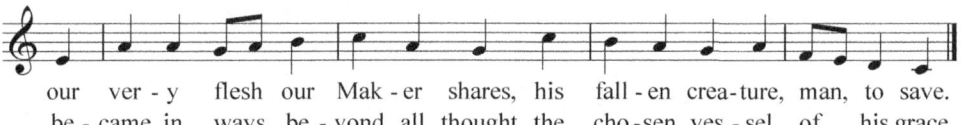

2. Be-hold, the world's Cre-a-tor wears the form and fash-ion_ of a slave;
3. For this how won-drous-ly he wrought! A maid-en, in her_ low-ly place,

our ver-y flesh our Mak-er shares, his fall-en crea-ture, man, to save.
be-came, in ways be-yond all thought, the cho-sen ves-sel of_ his grace.

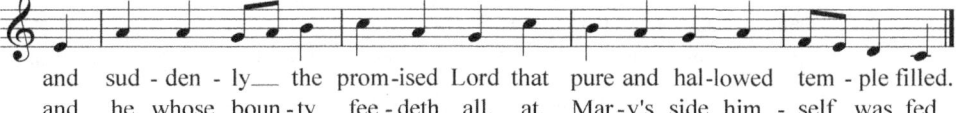

4. She bowed her to the an-gel's word de-clar-ing what the_ Fa-ther willed,
5. He shrank not from the ox-en's stall, he lay with-in the_ man-ger-bed,

and sud-den-ly_ the prom-ised Lord that pure and hal-lowed tem-ple filled.
and he, whose boun-ty fee-deth all, at Mar-y's side him-self_ was fed.

6. And while the an-gels in the sky sang praise a-bove the_ si-lent field,
7. All glo-ry for this bless-ed morn to God the Fa-ther ev-er be;

to shep-herds poor, the Lord Most High, the one great Shep-herd, was_ re-vealed.
all praise to thee, O Vir-gin-born, all praise, O Ho-ly Spir-it to thee.

336   Once In Royal David's City

Tune: IRBY (87 87 77)   Text: Cecil Alexander (†1895)

1. Once in roy - al Da - vid's_ cit - y stood a low - ly
2. He came down to earth_ from_ heav - en, who is God and

cat - tle_ shed, where a moth - er laid_ her_ ba - by in a
Lord of_ all, and his shel - ter was_ a_ sta - ble, and his

man - ger for_ his_ bed: Mar - y was that moth - er mild,
cra - dle was_ a_ stall; with the poor, the scorned, the low - ly,

Je - sus Christ her lit - tle_ child.   3. For he is our
lived on earth our Sav - ior_ ho - ly.   4. And our eyes at
                                            5. Not in that poor

child - hood's pat - tern, day by day like us_ he_ grew; he was
last_ shall_ see him, through his own re - deem - ing_ love; for that
low - ly_ sta - ble, with the ox - en stand - ing_ by, we shall

lit - tle, weak and_ help - less, tears and smiles like us_ he_ knew.
Child who seemed so_ help - less is our Lord in heav'n a - bove;
see him; but_ in_ heav - en, set at God's right hand on_ high;

and he feel - eth for our sad - ness, and he shar - eth in_ our_ glad - ness.
and he leads his chil - dren on_ to the place where he_ is_ gone._
when like stars his chil - dren crowned, all in white shall wait a - round._

Brightest And Best   337

Tune: EPIPHANY (11 10 11 10)   Text: Reginald Heber (†1826)

1. Bright - est and best of the sons of the morn - ing,
2. Cold on His cra - dle the dew - drops are shin - ing;

Dawn on our dark - ness and lend us Thine aid;
Low lies His head with the beasts of the stall;

Star of the East,__ the ho - ri - zon a - dorn - ing,
An - gels a - dore__ Him in slum - ber re - clin - ing,

Guide where our in - fant Re - deem - er is laid.
Mak - er and Mon - arch and Sav - ior of all!

3. Say, shall we yield Him, in cost - ly de - vo - tion,
4. Vain - ly we of - fer each am - ple ob - la - tion,

O - dors of E - dom and of - frings di - vine?
Vain - ly with gifts would His fa - vor se - cure;

Gems of the moun - tain and pearls of the o - cean,
Rich - er by far__ is the heart's ad - o - ra - tion,

Myrrh from the for - est, or gold from the mine?
Dear - er to God are the prayers of the poor.

338   What Child Is This?

Tune: GREENSLEEVES (87 87 68 67)   Text: William Dix (†1898)

1. What Child is this_____ who, laid to rest_____ On
2. Why lies He in_____ such mean es - tate,_____ Where
3. So bring Him in - cense, gold and myrrh,_____ Come

Mar - y's lap_____ is sleep - ing? Whom an - gels
ox and ass_____ are feed - ing? Good Chris - tians,
peas - ant, king_____ to own_____ Him; The King of

greet___ with an - thems sweet,__While shep - herds watch___ are
fear,___ for sin - ners here___ The si - lent Word___ is
kings___ sal - va - tion brings,__ Let lov - ing hearts___ en -

keep - ing? This, this_____ is Christ the King,_____ Whom
plead - ing. *Nails, spear___ shall pierce Him through, ___ The*
throne Him. *Raise, raise___ a song on high, _____ The*

shep - herds guard___ and an - gels sing; Haste, haste,___ to
cross be borne ___ for me, for you. Hail, hail ___ the
vir - gin sings___ her lull - a - by. Joy, joy___ for

bring Him laud,_____ The Babe,___ the Son_____ of Mar - y.
Word made flesh, ___ The Babe, ___ the Son ___ of Mar - y.
Christ is born, ___ The Babe, ___ the Son ___ of Mar - y.

* This note is sung as C-sharp in some editions.

Bethlehem, Of Noblest Cities   339

Tune: STUTTGART (87 87)   Text: O Sola Magnarum Urbium

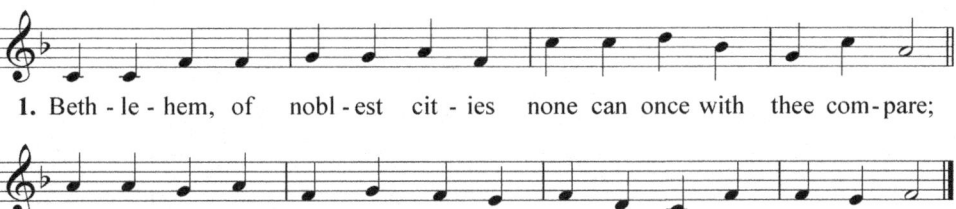

1. Beth - le - hem, of nobl - est cit - ies none can once with thee com - pare;

thou a - lone the Lord from heav - en didst for us in - car - nate bear.

2. Fair - er than the sun at morn - ing was the star that told his birth;

to the lands their God an - nounc - ing, seen in flesh - ly form on earth.

3. By its lam - bent beau - ty guid - ed see the east - ern kings ap - pear;

see them bend, their gifts to of - fer, gifts of in - cense, gold and myrrh.

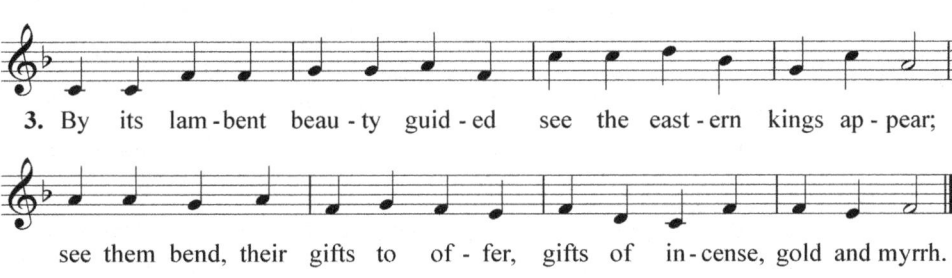

4. Sol - emn things of mys - tic mean - ing: in - cense doth the God dis - close,
5. Ho - ly Je - sus, in thy bright - ness to the Gen - tile world dis - played,

gold a roy - al child pro - claim - eth, myrrh a fu - ture tomb fore - shows.
with the Fa - ther and the Spir - it end - less praise to thee be paid.

340   Man To Christ's Sacred Wound

Tune: ROCKINGHAM (LM)   Text: Saint Robert Southwell (†1595)

1. O   pleas - ant spot! O place of rest! O
2. I   lie___ la - ment - ing at Thy gate, Yet
3. Dis - charge me of this heav - y load, That

roy - al rift! O wor - thy wound!
dare I not ad - ven - ture in:___
eas - ier pas - sage I___ may find,___

Come har - bour me, a wea - ry guest, That
I bear with me a trou - blous mate, And
With - in this bow'r to make_ a - bode, And

in the world no ease___ have found!
cum - ber'd am with heaps___ of sin.
in this glo - rious tomb___ be shrined.

4. Here must I live, here must I die, / Here would I utter all my grief;
   Here would I all those pains descry, / Which here did meet for my relief.

5. Here would I view the bloody sore, / Which dint of spiteful spear did breed:
   The bloody wounds laid there in store, / Would force a stony heart to bleed.

6. Here is the spring of trickling tears, / The mirror of all mourning wights,
   With doleful tunes for dumpish ears, / And solemn shows for sorrow'd sights.

7. Oh, happy soul, that flies so high / As to attain this sacred cave!
   Lord, send me wings, that I may fly, / And in this harbour quiet have!

When I Survey The Wondrous Cross 341

Tune: ROCKINGHAM (LM)   Text: Isaac Watts (†1748)

1. When I___ sur - vey the won - drous cross On which the
Prince of glo - ry died,___ My rich - est gain I
count_ but loss, And pour con - tempt on all___ my pride.

2. For - bid_ it, Lord, that I should boast, Save in the
3. See from_ His head, His hands, His feet, Sor - row and
death of Christ_ my God!_ All the vain things that
love flow min - gled down! Did e'er such love and
charm me most, I sac - ri - fice them to___ His blood.
sor - row meet, Or thorns com - pose so rich___ a crown?

4. His dy - ing crim - son, like a robe, Spreads o'er His
5. Were the___ whole realm of na - ture mine, That were a
bod - y on___ the tree;_ Then I am dead to
pre - sent far___ too small;_ Love so a - maz - ing,
all___ the globe, And all the globe is dead___ to me.
so___ di - vine, De - mands my soul, my life,___ my all.

342   At The Cross Her Station Keeping

Tune: COUTURE (887)   Text: Stabat Mater Dolorosa

1. At the Cross__ her sta - tion keep-ing, stood the mourn-ful
2. Through her heart,__ His sor - row shar-ing, all His bit - ter

Moth - er weep - ing, close to Je - sus to the last.
an - guish bear - ing, now at length__ the sword has passed.

3. O how sad__ and sore__ dis - tressed was that Moth - er,
4. Christ a - bove__ in tor - ment hangs, she be - neath be -

high - ly blest,_____ of the sole - be - got - ten One.
holds the pangs_____ of her dy - ing glo - rious Son.

5. Is there one__ who would__ not weep,__ whelmed in mis - er -
6. Can the hu - man heart__ re - frain__ from par - tak - ing

ies so deep,_____ Christ's dear Moth - er to be - hold?
in her pain,_____ in that Moth - er's pain un - told?

7. Bruised, de - rid - ed, cursed, de - filed,__ she be - held her
8. For the sins__ of His__ own na - tion, saw Him hang in

ten - der Child_____ All with blood - y scourg - es rent;
des - o - la - tion, Till His spir - it forth He sent.

9. O thou Moth - er! fount_ of love!_ Touch my spir - it
10. Make me feel_ as thou_ hast felt;_ make my soul to

from a - bove,_ make my heart_ with thine ac - cord:
glow and melt_ with the love_ of Christ my Lord.

11. Ho - ly Moth - er! pierce_ me through, in my heart each
12. Let me share_ with thee_ His pain,_ who for all my

wound re - new_ of my Sav - ior cru - ci - fied:
sins was slain,_ who for me_ in tor - ments died.

13. Let me min - gle tears_ with thee, mourn-ing Him who
14. By the Cross_ with thee_ to stay,_ there with thee to

mourned for me,_ all the days_ that I may live:
weep and pray,_ is all I ask_ of thee to give.

15. Vir - gin of_ all vir - gins blest!_ Lis - ten to my
16. Let me, to_ my lat - est breath, in my bod - y

fond re - quest:_ let me share_ thy grief di - vine;
bear the death_ of that dy - ing Son of thine.

17. Wound-ed with His eve - ry wound, steep my soul till
18. Be to me, O vir - gin, nigh, lest in flames I

it hath swooned, in His ver - y Blood a - way;
burn and die, in His aw - ful Judg-ment Day.

19. Christ, when Thou shalt call me hence, be Thy Moth - er

my de - fense, be Thy Cross my vic - to - ry;

20. While my bod - y here de - cays, may my soul Thy good-ness

praise, safe in par - a - dise with Thee. A - men.

All Ye Who Seek A Comfort Sure   345

Tune: ST. BERNARD (CM)   Text: Edward Caswall (†1878)

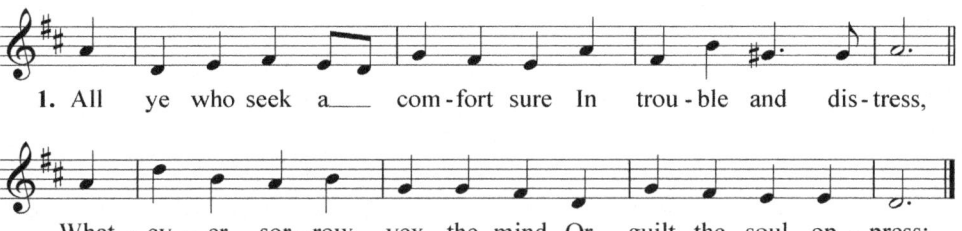

1. All ye who seek a___ com-fort sure In trou-ble and dis-tress,

What - ev - er sor - row vex the mind, Or guilt the soul op - press:

2. Our Lord, who gave Him - self for you Up - on the Cross to die,

O - pens to you His sa - cred Heart; O to that Heart draw nigh.

3. Ye hear how kind - ly___ he in - vites; Ye hear His words so blest:
4. What meek - er than the___ Sav-iour's Heart? As on the Cross He lay,

"All ye that la - bor come to Me, And I will give you rest."
It did His mur - der - ers for - give, And for their par - don pray.

5. O Heart, Thou joy of___ Saints on high, Thou hope of sin - ners here,
6. Wash thou my wounds in___ that dear Blood, Which forth from Thee doth flow;

At - tract - ed by those lov - ing words To Thee I life my prayer.
New grace, new hope in - spire, a new And bet - ter heart be - stow.

346 Ah, Holy Jesus, How Hast Thou Offended?

Tune: HERZLIEBSTER JESU (11 11 11 5)   Text: Johann Heermann (†1647)

1. Ah, ho-ly Je-sus, how hast thou of-fend-ed,
that man to judge thee hath in hate pre-tend-ed? By foes de-rid-ed, by thine own re-ject-ed, O most af-flict-ed.

2. Who was the guilt-y? Who brought this up-on thee?
A-las, my trea-son, Je-sus, hath un-done thee. 'Twas I, Lord Je-sus, I it was de-nied thee: I cru-ci-fied thee.

3. Lo, the Good Shep-herd for the sheep is of-fered;
the slave hath sin-nèd, and the Son hath suf-fered; for our a-tone-ment, while we noth-ing heed-eth, God in-ter-ced-eth.

4. For me, kind Je-sus, was thy in-car-na-tion,
thy mor-tal sor-row, and thy life's ob-la-tion; thy death of an-guish and thy bit-ter pas-sion, for my sal-va-tion.

5. There-fore, kind Je-sus, since I can-not pay thee,
I do a-dore thee, and will ev-er pray thee, think on thy pit-y and thy love un-swerv-ing, not my de-serv-ing.

Jesus, Meek And Lowly   347

Tune: LALANDE (66 66)   Text: Henry Collins (†1919)

1. Je - sus, meek and low - ly, Sav - ior, pure and ho - ly,
On Thy love re - ly - ing Hear me hum - bly cry - ing.

2. Prince of life__ and pow - er, My sal - va-tion's tow - er,
On the cross I view__ Thee Call -ing sin - ners to__ Thee.

3. There be - hold__ me gaz - ing At the sight a - maz - ing;
Bend-ing low be - fore__ Thee, Help-less I__ a - dore__ Thee.

4. By Thy red__wounds stream - ing, With Thy life blood gleam - ing,
Blood for sin -ners flow - ing Par - don free__ be - stow - ing;

5. By that fount of bless - ing, Thy dear love ex - press - ing,
6. Lord, in mer - cy guide me, Be Thou e'er be - side__ me;
All my ach -ing sad - ness Turn Thou in - to glad - ness.
In Thy ways di - rect__ me; 'Neath Thy wings pro - tect__ me.

348 O Love, How Deep, How Broad, How High

Tune: DEO GRACIAS (LM)   Text: Benjamin Webb (†1885)

1. O love, how deep, how broad, how high, it fills__ the heart__ with__ ec-sta - sy, that God, the Son__ of God, should take our mor - tal form for mor-tals' sake!

2. He sent no an - gel to our race of high - er or__ of__ low - er place, but wore the robe__ of hu-man frame him - self, and to this lost world came.

3. For us bap - tized, for us he bore his ho - ly fast__ and__ hun-gered sore, for us temp - ta - tion sharp he knew; for us the tempt - er o - ver - threw.

4. For us he prayed; for us he taught; for us___ his
dai - ly___ works he wrought; by words and signs___ and
ac-tions thus still seek - ing not him - self, but us.

5. For us to wick - ed men be - trayed, scourged, mocked, in
pur - ple___ robe ar - rayed, he bore the shame - ful
cross and death, for us at length gave up his breath.

6. For us he rose from death a - gain; for us___ he
7. To him whose bound - less love has won sal - va - tion

went___ on___ high to reign; for us he sent___ his
for___ us___ through his Son, to God the Fa - ther,

Spir - it here, to guide, to strength - en and to cheer.
glo - ry be both now and through e - ter - ni - ty.

350 Thou Loving Maker Of Mankind

Tune: SONG 5 (LM)   Text: Audi Benigne Conditor

1. Thou lov-ing Mak-er of man-kind, Be-fore Thy throne we pray and weep! Oh, strength-en us with grace di-vine Du-ly this sa-cred Lent to keep.

2. Search-er of hearts! Thou dost our ills Dis-cern, and all our weak-ness know; A-gain to Thee with tears we turn, A-gain to us Thy mer-cy show.

3. Much have we sinned; but we con-fess Our guilt, and all our faults de-plore: Oh, for the praise of Thy great name Our faint-ing souls to health re-store!

4. And grant us, while by fasts we strive This mor-tal bod-y to con-trol, To fast from all the food of sin, And so to pu-ri-fy the soul.

5. Hear us, O Trin-i-ty thrice blest! Sole U-ni-ty! to Thee we cry: Vouch-safe us from these fasts be-low To reap im-mor-tal fruit on high.

Sweet The Moments, Rich In Blessing 351

Tune: Based on BATTY (87 87)　　　Text: William Shirley (†1786)

1. Sweet the mo-ments, rich in bless-ing, Which be - fore the cross we spend,
2. Here I stay, for - ev - er view-ing Mer - cy stream-ing in His blood;

Life and health and peace pos-sess-ing From the sin - ner's dy - ing Friend.
Pre-cious drops, my soul be-dew-ing, Plead and claim my peace with God.

3. Tru - ly bless-èd is the sta - tion, Low be - fore His cross to lie,
4. Here we find our hope of Heav - en, While up - on the Lamb we gaze;

While I see di - vine com-pas-sion Float-ing in His lan-guid eye.
Lov - ing much, and much for - giv - en, Let our hearts o'er - flow with praise.

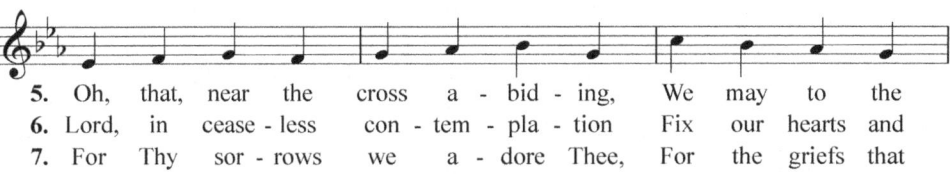

5. Oh, that, near the cross a - bid - ing, We may to the
6. Lord, in cease - less con - tem - pla - tion Fix our hearts and
7. For Thy sor - rows we a - dore Thee, For the griefs that

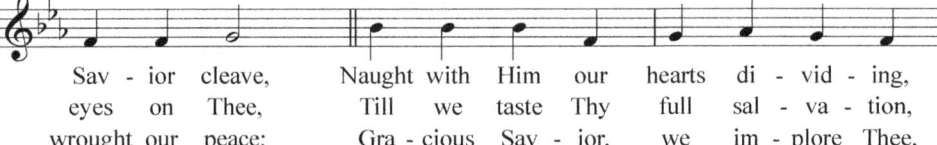

Sav - ior cleave, Naught with Him our hearts di - vid - ing,
eyes on Thee, Till we taste Thy full sal - va - tion,
wrought our peace; Gra - cious Sav - ior, we im - plore Thee,

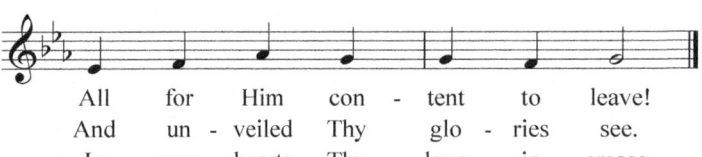

All for Him con - tent to leave!
And un - veiled Thy glo - ries see.
In our hearts Thy love in - crease.

352   O Kind Creator, Bow Thine Ear

Tune: Based on ST. BOTOLPH (LM)   Text: Audi Benigne Conditor

1. O Kind Cre - a - tor, bow_ thine ear to mark the cry,_ to
know the tear be - fore thy throne of mer - cy
spent_ in this thy ho - ly fast_ of Lent.

2. Our hearts are o - pen, Lord,_ to thee: thou know - est
3. Our sins are man - y, this_ we know; spare us, good

our_ in - fir - mi - ty; pour out on all_ who
Lord,_ thy mer - cy show; and for the hon - or

seek_ thy face_ a - bun - dance of_ thy par - d'ning grace.
of_ thy name_ our faint - ing souls_ to life_ re - claim.

4. Give us the self - con - trol_ that springs from dis - ci -
5. We pray thee, Ho - ly Trin - i - ty, one God, un -

pline_ of out - ward things, that fast - ing in - ward
chang - ing U - ni - ty, that we from this_ our

se - cret - ly_ the soul may pure - ly dwell_ with thee.
ab - sti - nence may reap the fruits_ of pen - i - tence.

At The Lamb's High Feast We Sing   353

Tune: SALZBURG (77 77D)   Text: Ad Regias Agni Dapes

1. At the Lamb's high feast we sing praise to our vic - to - rious King,
2. Where the Pas - chal blood is poured, death's dark an-gel sheathes his sword;

who hath washed us in the tide flow - ing from his wound -ed side;
Is - rael's hosts tri - um - phant go through the wave that drowns the foe.

praise we him,__ whose love di - vine gives his sa -cred Blood for wine,
Praise we Christ, whose blood was shed, Pas - chal vic-tim, Pas - chal bread;

gives his Bod - y for the feast, Christ the vic-tim, Christ the priest.
with sin - cer - i - ty and love eat we man - na from a - bove.

3. Might - y vic - tim from the sky, Pow'rs of hell be - neath Thee lie;
4. Pas - chal tri - umph, pas - chal joy, On - ly sin can this de - stroy;

Death is con -quered in the fight; Thou hast brought us life and light;
From the death of sin set free Souls re - born, dear Lord, in Thee.

Now thy ban - ner thou dost wave; Van-quished Sa - tan and the grave;
Hymns of glo - ry songs of praise, Fa - ther, un - to Thee we raise.

An - gels join his praise to tell: See o'er -thrown the prince of hell.
Ris - en Lord, all praise to Thee, Ev - er with the Spir - it be.

354   Ye Sons And Daughters Of The King

Tune: O FILII ET FILIAE (888 with Refrain)   Text: Jean Tisserand (†1494)

Refrain: *Repeat Ad Libitum*

Al - le - lu - ia!__ Al - le - lu - ia! Al - le - lu - ia!

1. Ye sons and daugh - ters of__ the King, whom heav'n- ly hosts in
2. That East - er morn, at break of day, The faith - ful wom - en
3. An an - gel clad in white they see, Who sat, and spoke un -

4. That night th'a -pos - tles met__ in fear; A - midst them came their
5. When Thom - as first the tid - ings heard, How they had seen the
6. "My pierc - èd side, O Thom -as, see; My hands, My feet, I

7. No long - er Thom - as then__ de - nied; He saw the feet, the
8. How blest are they who have__ not seen, And yet whose faith has
9. On this most ho - ly day__ of days Our hearts and voic - es,

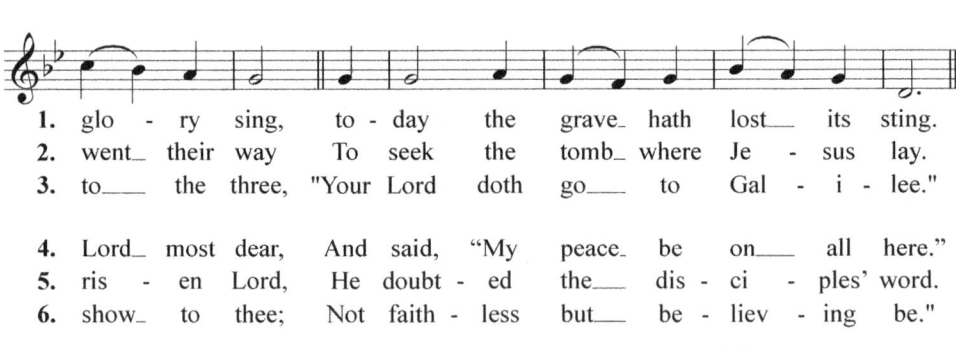

1. glo - ry sing, to - day the grave__ hath lost__ its sting.
2. went__ their way To seek the tomb__ where Je - sus lay.
3. to__ the three, "Your Lord doth go__ to Gal - i - lee."

4. Lord__ most dear, And said, "My peace__ be on__ all here."
5. ris - en Lord, He doubt - ed the__ dis - ci - ples' word.
6. show__ to thee; Not faith - less but__ be - liev - ing be."

7. hands, the side; "Thou art my Lord__ and God," he cried.
8. con - stant been; For they e - ter - nal life__ shall win.
9. Lord,__ we raise To Thee, in ju - bi - lee__ and praise.

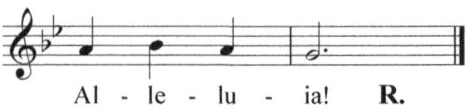

Al - le - lu - ia!   **R.**

I Know That My Redeemer Lives 355

Tune: DUKE STREET (LM)   Text: Samuel Medley (†1799)

1. I know that my Re - deem - er lives; What joy the
   blest as - sur - ance gives! He lives, he lives, who
   once was dead; he lives, my ev - er liv - ing Head.

2. He lives tri - um - phant from the grave, he lives e -
   ter - nal - ly to save, he lives all - glo - rious
   in the sky, he lives ex - alt - ed there on high.

3. He lives to bless us with his love, he lives to
   plead for us a - bove. He lives our hun - gry
   souls to feed, he lives to help in time of need.

4. He lives to si - lence all our fears, he lives to
   wipe a - way our tears he lives to calm the
   trou - bled heart, he lives all bless - ings to im - part.

5. He lives and grants me dai - ly breath; he lives, and
   I shall con - quer death: he lives my man - sion
   to pre - pare; he lives to bring me safe - ly there.

6. He lives, all glo - ry to his Name! he lives, my
   Je - sus, still the same. oh, the sweet joy this
   sen - tence gives, I know that my Re - deem - er lives!

356 Love's Redeeming Work Is Done

Tune: SAVANNAH (77 77)   Text: Charles Wesley (†1788)

1. Love's re - deem-ing work is done, fought the— fight, the bat - tle won.

Lo, our Sun's e - clipse is o'er! Lo, he sets in— blood no more!

2. Vain the— stone, the watch, the seal! Christ has— burst the gates of hell;

death in vain for - bids him rise; Christ has o - pened par - a - dise.

3. Lives a - gain our glo - rious King; where, O— death, is now— thy sting?

Dy - ing once, he— all doth save; where thy vic - to - ry, O grave?

4. Soar we— now where Christ has led, fol - low-ing our ex - alt - ed Head;

made like him, like— him we rise, ours the cross, the— grave, the skies.

5. Hail the— Lord of earth and heav'n! Praise to— thee by both be giv'n:

thee we greet tri - um-phant now; hail, the Res - ur - rec - tion thou!

O Thou, The Heavens' Eternal King   357

Tune: Based on ST. BOTOLPH (LM)   Text: Rex Sempiterne Coelitum

1. O Thou, the heav'ns' e - ter - nal King, Cre - a - tor,
2. Re - deem - er, Thou for us__ didst deign To hang up -

un - to Thee we sing, With God the Fa - ther ev - er
on__ the Cross of pain, And give for us__ the lav - ish

One,__ Co - e - qual, co - e - ter - nal Son.
price__ Of thine own blood__ in sac - ri - fice.

3. Grant, Lord, in Thee each faith - ful mind Un -
4. With Christ we died, with Christ__ we rose, When

ceas - ing Pas - chal joy may find; And from the death of
at the font__ His name we chose; Oh, let not sin__ our

sin__ set free__ Souls new - ly born__ to life__ by Thee.
robes__ de - face,__ And turn to grief__ the Pas - chal grace.

5. Let hymns of joy to grief__ suc - ceed, We know that
6. To Thee, once dead, who now__ dost live, All glo - ry,

Christ__ is ris'n in - deed; We hear His white - robed
Lord,__ Thy peo - ple give, Whom, with the Fa - ther,

An - gel's voice, And in our ris - en Lord__ re - joice.
we__ a - dore,__ And Ho - ly Ghost for - ev - er - more.

358 The Eternal Gates Lift Up Their Heads

Tune: Based on CRUCIS VICTORIA (CM)   Text: Cecil Alexander (†1895)

1. The e - ter - nal gates lift up their heads, the doors are o - pened wide,

the King of glo - ry is gone up un - to his_ Fa - ther's side.

2. And ev - er on our earth - ly path a gleam of glo - ry lies,

a light still breaks be - hind the cloud that veils thee_ from the eyes.

3. Lift up our hearts, lift up our minds, and let thy grace be giv'n,

that, while we live on earth be - low, our treas - ure_ be in heav'n;

4. That, where thou art at God's right hand, our hope, our love may be:

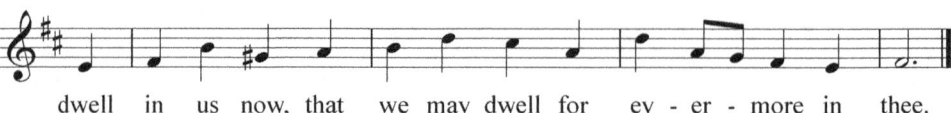

dwell in us now, that we may dwell for ev - er - more in thee.

A Hymn Of Glory Let Us Sing   359

Tune: Based on ST. BOTOLPH (LM)   Text: Hymnum Canamus Domino

1. A hymn of glo - ry let__ us sing New songs through
2. The ho - ly ap - os - tol - ic band Up - on the

out__ the world shall ring Christ, by a road__ be - fore__ un -
Mount of Ol - ives stand And with His fol - low - ers__ they

trod__ As - cend - eth to__ the throne__ of God.
see__ our Lord's re - splend - ent maj - es - ty.

3. To Whom the an - gels draw - ing nigh, "Why
4. "A - gain ye shall be - hold__ Him so, As

stand and gaze__ up - on the sky? This is the Sav - ior,"
ye have to - day seen Him go. In glo - rious pomp as -

thus__ they say.__ "This is His no - ble tri - umph day."
cend - ing high__ Up to the por - tals of__ the sky."

5. Be Thou our Joy and strong De - fense, Who art our
6. O ris - en Christ, as - cend - ed Lord, All praise to

fu - ture Rec - om - pense, So shall the light__ that
Thee__ let earth ac - cord, Who art, while end - less

springs from Thee__ Be ours through all__ e - ter - ni - ty,
ag - es run,__ With Fa - ther and__ with Spir - it One.

360   Eternal Monarch, King Most High

Tune: WAREHAM (LM)   Text: Aeterne Rex Altissime

1. E - ter - nal Mon - arch, King_ most high, whose blood hath
brought re - demp - tion nigh, by whom the_ death of
Death was wrought, and_ con-quer-ing Gra - ce's bat - tle fought.

2. As - cend - ing to the throne of might, and seat - ed
3. Yea, an - gels trem - ble when they see how changed is
at___ the Fa - ther's right, all pow'r_ in__ heav'n is
our__ hu - man - i - ty; that flesh_ hath_ purged what
Je - sus' own, that_ here_ his man - hood had__ not known.
flesh had stained, and_ God,_ the flesh_ of God,_ hath reigned.

4. Be thou_ our joy and strong de - fense, who art__ our
5. O ris - en Christ, as - cend - ed Lord, all praise to
fu - ture rec - om - pense: so shall_ the_ light that
thee__ let earth_ ac - cord, who art,__ while end - less
springs from thee be__ ours_ through all__ e - ter - ni - ty.
ag - es run, with Fa - ther and__ with Spir - it one.

Come, Holy Ghost, Our Souls Inspire   361

Tune: VENI CREATOR (MECHLIN)   Text: John Cosin (†1672)

1. Come, Ho - ly Ghost, our souls_ in - spire, and light - en
2. Thy bless - èd unc - tion from_ a - bove is com - fort,

with_ ce - les - tial fire. Thou the_ a - noint - ing
life,_ and fire_ of love. En - a - ble with_ per -

Spir - it art, who dost thy sev'n - fold gifts_ im - part.
pet - ual light the dull - ness of_ our blind - ed sight.

3. A - noint_ and cheer_ our soil - èd face with the a -
4. Teach us_ to know_ the Fa - ther, Son, and thee, of

bun - dance of_ thy grace. Keep far_ from foes,_ give
both,_ to be_ but One, that through the ag - es

peace_ at home: where thou art Guide, no ill_ can come.
all_ a - long, this_ may be_ our end - less song:

Ending: Praise_ to thy_ e - ter - nal mer - it,

Fa - ther, Son,_ and Ho - ly Spir - it. A - men.

362   Come, Thou Holy Spirit, Come!

Tune: VENI SANCTE SPIRITUS (777D)   Text: Archbishop Langton (†1228)

1. Come, Thou Ho - ly Spir - it, come! And from Thy ce - les - tial home

Shed thy light and bril - lian-cy: Fa - ther of the__ poor, draw near;

Giv - er of all gifts, be here; Come, the soul's true ra - dian - cy:

2. Come, of com - fort - ers the best, Of the soul the sweet - est guest,
3. O most bless - èd Light di-vine, Shine with - in these hearts of Thine,

Come in toil re - fresh - ing - ly: Thou in la - bor__ rest most sweet,
And our in - most be - ing fill! Where Thou art not,_ man hath naught,

Thou art shad - ow from the heat, Com - fort in ad - ver - si - ty.
Noth - ing good in deed or thought, Noth - ing free from taint of ill.

4. Sin - ful hearts do thou make whole, Bring to life the ar - id soul,
5. On the faith - ful, who a - dore And con - fess Thee, ev - er - more

Guide the feet that go a - stray. Make the stub - born_ heart un - bend,
In Thy sev'n - fold gift de-scend; Give them vir - tue's_ sure re - ward

To the faint, new hope ex - tend, Wound-ed souls, their hurt al - lay.
Give them Thy sal - va - tion, Lord; Give them joys that nev - er end.

Come, Holy Ghost, Creator Blest 363

Tune: EISENACH (LM)   Text: Veni Creator Spiritus

1. Come, Ho - ly Ghost, Cre - a - tor blest, vouch -
safe with - in our souls to rest; come with thy grace and
heav'n - ly aid, and fill the hearts— which thou hast made.

2. To— thee, the Com - fort - er, we cry, to
3. The— sev'n - fold gifts of grace are thine; O

thee, the Gift of God most high, the Fount of life, the
Fin - ger of the Hand Di - vine, true prom - ise of the

Fire of love, the soul's a - noint - ing from a - bove.
Fa - ther thou, who dost the tongue— with pow'r en - dow.

4. Thy— light to eve - ry sense im - part, and
5. Praise we the Fa - ther and the Son and

shed thy love in eve - ry heart; thine own un - fail - ing
Ho - ly Spir - it with them One; and may the Son on

might sup - ply to strength - en our— in - fir - mi - ty.
us be - stow the gifts that from— the Spir - it flow.

364   Come Down, O Love Divine

Tune: DOWN AMPNEY (66 11D)   Text: Bianco da Sienna (†1434)

1. Come down, O love di-vine, seek Thou this soul of mine, And vis-it it with Thine own ar-dor glow-ing. O Com-fort-er, draw near, with-in my heart ap-pear, And kin-dle it, Thy ho-ly flame be-stow-ing.

2. O let it free-ly burn, til earth-ly pas-sions turn To dust and ash-es in its heat con-sum-ing; And let Thy glo-rious light shine ev-er on my sight, And clothe me round, the while my path il-lum-ing.

3. Let ho-ly char-i-ty mine out-ward ves-ture be, And low-li-ness be-come mine in-ner cloth-ing; True low-li-ness of heart, which takes the hum-bler part, And o'er its own short-com-ings weeps with loath-ing.

4. And so the yearn-ing strong, with which the soul will long, Shall far out-pass the pow'r of hu-man tell-ing; For none can guess its grace, till he be-come the place Where-in the Ho-ly Spir-it makes His dwell-ing.

O God Almighty Father   365

Tune: GOTT VATER (76 76 with Refrain)   Text: Based on John Rothensteiner (†1434)

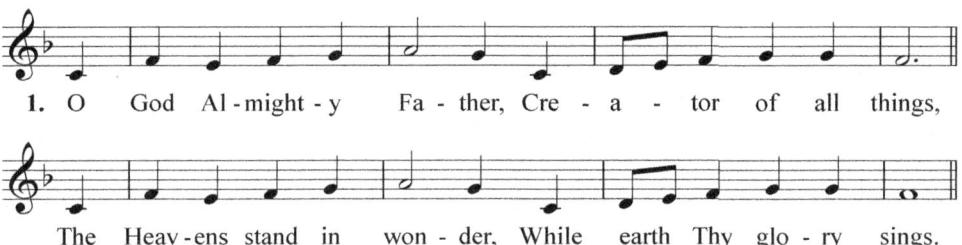

1. O God Al-might-y Fa-ther, Cre-a-tor of all things,

The Heav-ens stand in won-der, While earth Thy glo-ry sings.

Refrain:

O most Ho-ly Trin-i-ty, Un-di-vid-ed— U-ni-ty;

Ho-ly God, Might-y God, God Im-mor-tal, be a-dored.

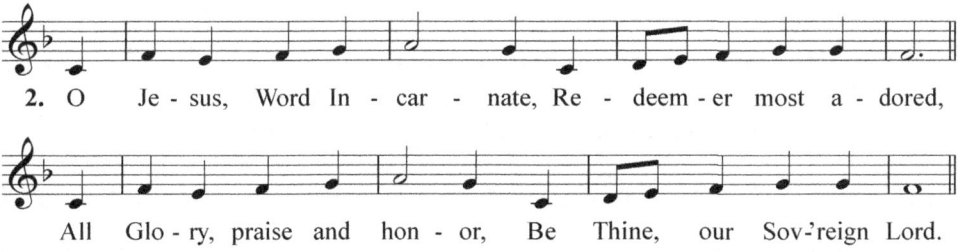

2. O Je-sus, Word In-car-nate, Re-deem-er most a-dored,

All Glo-ry, praise and hon-or, Be Thine, our Sov-'reign Lord.

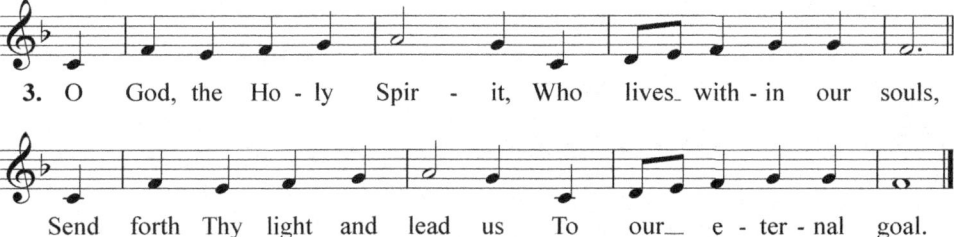

3. O God, the Ho-ly Spir-it, Who lives— with-in our souls,

Send forth Thy light and lead us To our— e-ter-nal goal.

366   Hail, O Star That Pointest

Tune: LALANDE (66 66)   Text: Athelstan Riley (†1945)

1. Hail, O star__ that point-est T'ward the port of Heav-en,
Thou to whom as maid-en God for Son__ was giv-en.

2. Tak-ing that__ sweet A - VE Erst by Ga-briel spo-ken,
E - VA's name re - vers-ing, Be of peace__ the to - ken.

3. Bound by Sa-tan's fet-ters, Health and vi-sion need-ing,
God will aid and light__ us At thy gen - tle plead-ing.

4. Show thy - self__ a moth-er, In thy sup - pli - ca - tion
5. That, O match-less maid - en, Pass-ing meek and low - ly,
He will hear who chose__ thee At His in - car - na - tion.
Thy dear Son may make__ us Blame-less, chaste and ho - ly.

6. So, as now__ we jour-ney Aid our weak en - deav - or,
7. Fa-ther, Son__ and Spir - it, Three in One con - fess-ing,
Till we gaze on Je - sus, And re - joice__ for - ev - er.
Give we e - qual glo - ry, E - qual praise and bless - ing.

Maiden, Yet A Mother 367

Tune: UNE VAINE CRAINTE (65 65D)   Text: Dante Alighieri (✝1321)

1. Maid - en, yet a moth - er, Daugh - ter of thy Son,
2. Thus His place pre - par - èd, He Who all things made

High be - yond all oth - er, Low - li - er is none;
'Mid His crea - tures tar - ried, In thy bos - om laid;

Thou the con - sum - ma - tion Planned by God's de - cree,
There His love He nour - ished Warmth that gave in - crease

When our lost cre - a - tion No - bler rose in thee!
To the root whence flour - ished Our e - ter - nal peace.

3. Noon on Zi - on's moun - tain Is thy char - i - ty;
4. Nor a - lone thou hear - est When thy name we hail;
5. La - dy, lest our vi - sion, Striv - ing heav'n-ward, fail,

Hope its liv - ing foun - tain Finds on earth in thee.
Of - ten thou art near - est When our voic - es fail;
Still let thy pe - ti - tion With thy Son pre - vail,

La - dy, such thy pow - er, He who grace would buy
Mir - rored in thy fash - ion All cre - a - tion's good
Un - to Whom all mer - it, Pow'r and maj - es - ty

Not as of thy dow - er, With - out wings would fly.
Mer - cy might, com - pas - sion Grace they wom - an - hood.
With the Ho - ly Spir - it And the Fa - ther be.

368   The God Whom Earth And Sea And Sky

Tune: EISENACH (LM)   Text: Quem Terra Pontus Sidera

1. The__ God Whom earth, and sea, and sky, A-dore, and laud, and mag-ni-fy, Who o'er their three-fold fab-ric reigns, The vir-gin's spot-less womb con-tains.

2. The__ Lord whom sun and moon o-bey, whom all things serve from day to day, was by the Ho-ly Ghost con-ceived of her who through his grace be-lieved.

3. How__ blest that Moth-er, in whose shrine the world's Cre-a-tor, Lord di-vine, whose hand con-tains the earth and sky, once deigned, as in__ his ark, to lie.

4. Blest,_ in the mes-sage Ga-briel brought; Blest, by the work the Spir-it wrought: From whom the Great De-sire of earth Took hu-man flesh_ and hu-man birth.

5. All__ hon-or, laud, and glo-ry be, O Je-sus, vir-gin-born, to Thee! All glo-ry, as is ev-er meet, To Fa-ther and__ to Par-a-clete.

O Sanctissima / O Most Holy One 369

Tune: O DU FRÖHLICHE (55 7 55 7)   Text: Traditional

1. O most ho - ly one,___ O most low - ly one,___
2. *O san - ctís - si - ma, ___ O pi - ís - si - ma,___*

Lov - ing Vir - gin, Ma - ri - a! Moth - er, Maid of
Dul - cis Vir - go Ma - ri - a! Ma - ter a -

fair - est love, La - dy, Queen of all a - bove,
ma - ta, in - te - me - rá - ta.

O - ra,___ o - ra pro no - bis!
O - ra, ___ o - ra pro no - bis!

3. Vir - gin ev - er fair.___ Moth - er, hear our prayer,__
4. *Vir - go, ré - spi - ce; ___ Ma - ter, ád - spi - ce.___*

Look up - on us, Ma - ri - a! Bring to us your
Au - di nos, O Ma - rí - a! Tu___ me - di -

treas - ure, grace be - yond all meas - ure;
cí - nam por - tas di - ví - nam.

O - ra,___ o - ra pro no - bis!
O - ra, ___ o - ra pro no - bis!

370 Concordi Laetitia / Sounds Of Joy

Tune: CONCORDI LAETITIA (77 77 5)   Text: Traditional (13th century)

1. Sounds of joy have put to flight   All the sad-ness of the night:
1. *Con-cór-di læ - tí - ti - a,   Pro-púl-sa mœ - stí - ti - a,*

2. Who is she whom an-gels sing,   Mak-ing all cre - a - tion ring?
2. *Quam con-cén - tu pá - ri - li   Cho-ri lau-dant caé - li - ci,*

1. Now a maid be-yond com-pare   Hears her prais-es fill the air:
1. *Ma - rí - æ præ - có - ni - a   Ré - co - lat Ec - clé - si - a:*

2. She it is who wins our praise,   As on earth our voice we raise:
2. *Et nos cum cæ - lé - sti-bus,   No-vum me-los pán - gi - mus;*

Vir - go Ma - rí - a.

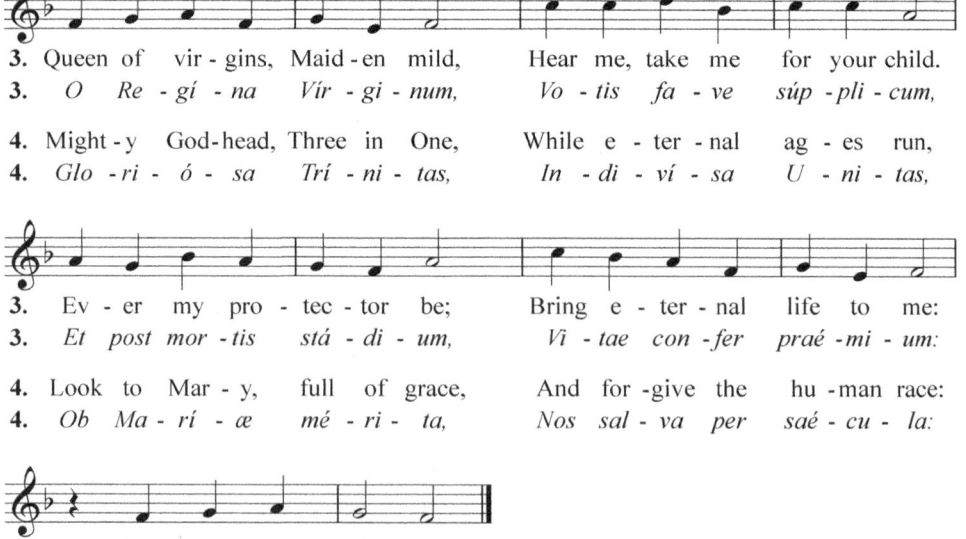

3. Queen of vir-gins, Maid-en mild,   Hear me, take me for your child.
3. *O Re-gí - na Vír-gi-num,   Vo - tis fa - ve súp-pli - cum,*

4. Might-y God-head, Three in One,   While e - ter - nal ag - es run,
4. *Glo-ri - ó - sa Trí - ni - tas,   In - di - ví - sa U - ni - tas,*

3. Ev - er my pro - tec - tor be;   Bring e - ter - nal life to me:
3. *Et post mor-tis stá - di - um,   Ví - tae con-fer praé-mi - um:*

4. Look to Mar - y, full of grace,   And for-give the hu-man race:
4. *Ob Ma - rí - æ mé - ri - ta,   Nos sal - va per saé-cu - la:*

Vir - go Ma - rí - a.

Salve Regina / Hail, Holy Queen   371

Tune: MODE V   Text: Hermanus Contractus (†1054)

1. Sal - ve, Re - gí - na, ma - ter mi - se - ri - cór - di - ae: Vi - ta, dul
2. *Hail, O ho - ly Queen! Hail, O Moth - er all mer - ci - ful, our life, our*

cé - do, et spes no - stra, sal - ve. Ad te cla - má - mus,
sweet - ness, and our hope, we hail___ thee! To thee do we cry,

éx - su - les fí - li - i He - vae. Ad te su - spi - rá - mus,
poor ban - ished chil - dren of Eve. To thee we send our sighs

ge - mén - tes et flen - tes in hac la - cri - má - rum val - le.
while mourn - ing and weep - ing in this low - ly val - ley of tears.

E - ia er - go, Ad - vo - cá - ta no - stra, il - los tu - os
Turn then thine eyes, most gra - cious Ad - vo - cate, O turn thine eyes,

mi - se - ri - cór - des ó - cu - los ad nos con - ver - te.
so lov - ing and com - pas - sion - ate, up - on us sin - ners.

Et Je - sum, be - ne - dí - ctum fru - ctum ven - tris tu - i,
And Je - sus, the most bless - èd fruit of thy vir - gin womb,

no - bis post hoc ex - sí - li - um os - tén - de. O_____ cle - mens,
show us when this earth - ly ex - ile is end - ed. O_____ clem - ent,

O_____ pi - a, O_____ dul - cis Vir - go Ma - rí - a.
O_____ lov - ing, O_____ most _ sweet Vir - gin Mar - y.

372 Regina Caeli / Queen Of Heaven, Rejoice

Tune: MODE VI   Text: Traditional (14th century)

1. Re - gí - na cae - li lae - tá - re, al - le - lú - ia:
2. *O Queen of heav - en, be joy - ful, Al - le - lu - ia.*

Qui - a quem me - ru - í - sti por - tá - re, al - le - lú - ia:
For He Whom thou hast mer - i - ted to bear, Al - le - lu - ia.

Re - sur - ré - xit, sic - ut di - xit, al - le - lú - ia:
Rose in splen - dor as he prom - ised, Al - le - lu - ia.

O - ra pro no - bis De - um, al - le - lú - ia.
Pour for us to God thy prayer, Al - le - lu - ia.

Jesus, Son Of Mary   373

Tune: WARUM SIND DIE THRÄNEN   Text: Edmund Palmer (†1931)

1. Je - sus, Son of Mar - y, fount of life a - lone,
2. Think, O Lord, in mer - cy on the souls of those

here we hail thee pre - sent on thine al - tar - throne.
Who, in faith gone from us, now in death re - pose.

Hum - bly we a - dore thee, Lord of end - less might,
Here 'mid stress and con - flict toils can nev - er cease;

in our tab - er - nac - les veiled from earth - ly sight.
There, the war - fare end - ed, bid them rest in peace.

3. Of - ten were they wound - ed in the dead - ly strife;
4. Rest e - ter - nal grant them, af - ter wea - ry fight;

Heal them, Good Phy - si - cian, with the balm of life.
Shed on them the ra - diance of Thy heav'n - ly light.

Eve - ry taint of e - vil, frail - ty and de - cay,
Lead them on - ward, up - ward, to the ho - ly place,

Good and gra - cious Sav - ior, cleanse and purge a - way.
Where Thy saints, made per - fect, gaze up - on Thy face.

DURING EASTERTIDE.

VI-di a-quam * egre- di- én-tem de tem-

plo, a lá- te-re dex- tro, alle- lú- ia:

et omnes, ad quos pervénit a- qua i-sta,

sal- vi fa- cti sunt, et di- cent, alle-lú- ia,

al- le- lú- ia. *Ps. 117* Confi-témi-ni Dómino quó-

ni- am bonus: * quó-ni- am in saécu-lum mi-

se-ri-cór-di- a e-jus. Gló-ri- a Patri, et Fí-li- o,

et Spi-rí-tu- i Sancto. * Si-cut e-rat in princí-pi- o,

et nunc, et semper, et in saécu-la saecu- ló-rum.

Amen.

I SAW WATER flowing from the Temple, | from its right-hand side, alleluia: | and all to whom this water came | were saved and shall say: Alleluia, alleluia.

In the Extraordinary Form, the prayers on the following page are then sung, with "alleluia" added to each.

SUNDAYS OUTSIDE OF EASTERTIDE.

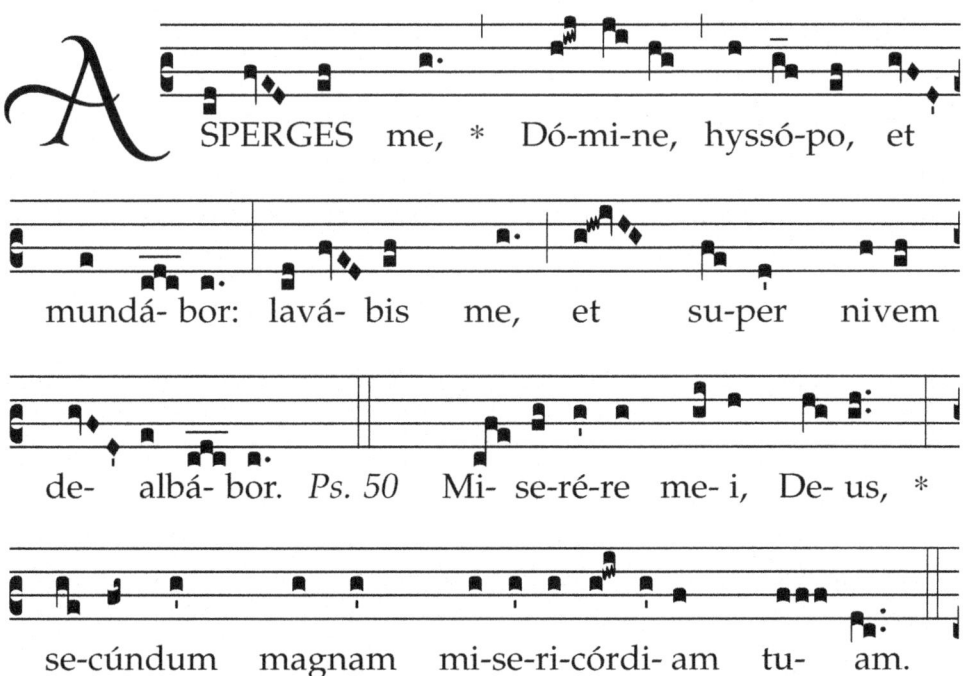

ASPERGES me, * Dó-mi-ne, hyssó-po, et mundá-bor: lavá-bis me, et su-per nivem de- albá-bor. *Ps. 50* Mi-se-ré-re me-i, De-us, * se-cúndum magnam mi-se-ri-córdi-am tu- am.

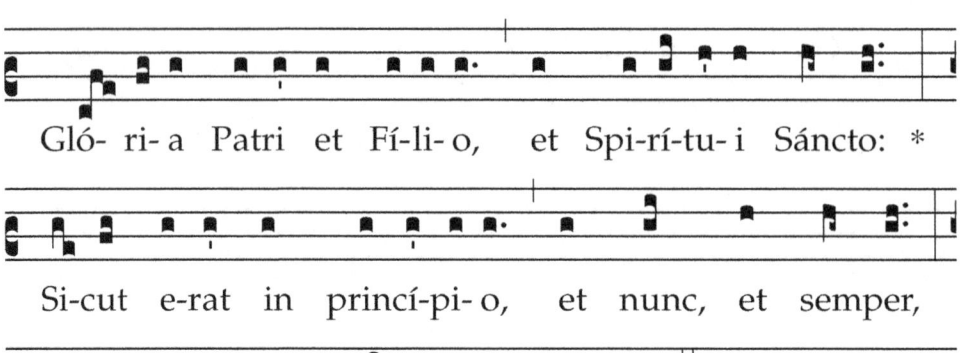

Gló- ri- a Patri et Fí-li- o, et Spi-rí-tu- i Sáncto: *

Si-cut e-rat in princí-pi- o, et nunc, et semper,

et in saécu-la saecu-lórum. A- men.

SPRINKLE ME with hyssop, O Lord, and I shall be cleansed; | wash me and I shall be whiter than snow.

These prayers may follow:

℣. Osténde nobis, Dómine, misericórdiam tuam.

℣. Show us, O Lord, Thy mercy.

℟. Et salutáre tuum da nobis.

℟. And grant us Thy salvation.

℣. Dómine, exáudi oratiónem meam.

℣. O Lord, hear my prayer.

℟. Et clamor meus ad te véniat.

℟. And let my cry come unto Thee.

℣. Dóminus vobíscum.

℣. The Lord be with you.

℟. Et cum spíritu tuo.

℟. And with thy spirit.

Orémus.

Let us pray.

EXÁUDI NOS, Dómine sancte, Pater omnípotens, ætérne Deus, et míttere dignéris sanctum ángelum tuum de cælis, qui custódiat, fóveat, prótegat, vísitet, atque deféndat omnes habitántes in hoc habitáculo. Per Christum Dóminum nostrum.

GRACIOUSLY hear us, O Holy Lord, Father Almighty, Eternal God; and vouchsafe to send down from heaven Thy holy Angel, to guard, cherish, protect, visit and defend all who dwell in this house. Through Christ our Lord.

℟. AMEN.

℟. AMEN.

I. – *Lux et origo.*

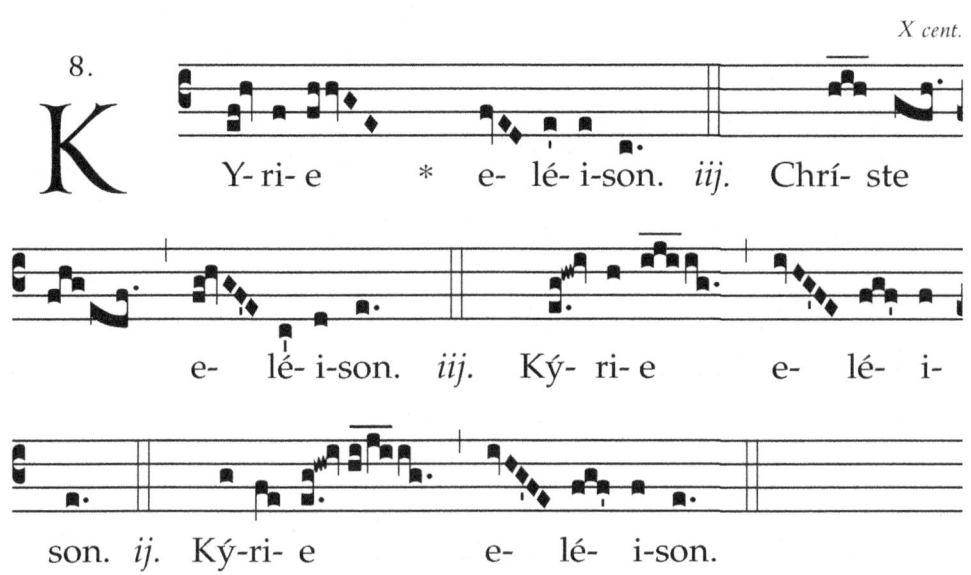

KYRIE
Y- ri- e * e- lé- i-son. *iij.* Chrí- ste
e- lé- i-son. *iij.* Ký- ri- e e- lé- i-
son. *ij.* Ký-ri- e e- lé- i-son.

X cent.
8.

G
4.
Lóri- a in excél-sis Dé- o. Et in tér- ra
pax ho-mí-nibus bónae vo-luntá- tis. Laudámus te.
Benedí-ci- mus te. Adorámus te. Glo-ri-fi-cá-mus
te. Grá-ti- as ágimus tí- bi propter mágnam

X cent.

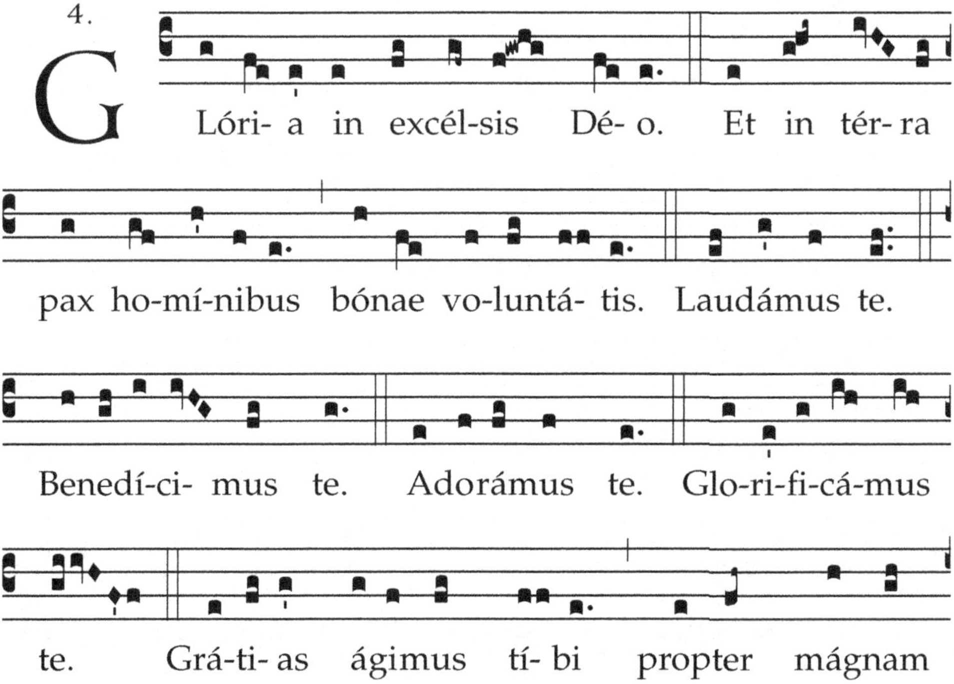

gló-ri-am tú- am. Dó-mine Dé- us, Rex cae-lé-stis,

Dé- us Pá- ter omní-po-tens. Dómine Fí- li unigéni-

te Jé-su Chrí-ste. Dó- mi-ne Dé- us, A-gnus Dé-

i, Fí- li- us Pá-tris. Qui tóllis peccá-ta múndi,

mi-se-ré-re nó- bis. Qui tóllis peccá-ta múndi,

súscipe depreca-ti- ónem nóstram. Qui sédes ad

déx- teram Pá-tris, mi-se-ré-re nó- bis. Quóni- am tu

só-lus sánctus. Tu só-lus Dó- minus. Tu só-lus

Altíssimus, Jé-su Chrí-ste. Cum Sáncto Spí-ri-tu,

in gló-ri- a Dé- i Pá-tris. A- men.

X cent.

4.

S Anctus, Sánctus, Sánctus Dóminus Dé- us

Sába- oth. Plé-ni sunt caé- li et térra gló- ri-

a tú- a. Hosánna in ex-cél-sis. Be-ne-díctus qui

vé-nit in nó- mine Dó-mi-ni. Ho- sánna in

excél- sis.

X cent.

4. Agnus Dé- i, * qui tóllis peccá-ta mún-di: mi-se-ré- re nó- bis. Agnus Dé- i, * qui tóllis peccá-ta mún-di: mi-se-ré- re nó- bis. Agnus Dé- i, * qui tóllis peccá-ta mún-di: dóna nó- bis pá- cem.

8. -te, missa est, alle-lú-ia, alle- lú- ia.
De-o grá-ti- as, alle- lú- ia, alle- lú- ia.

7. - te, mis-sa est.
De- o grá- ti- as.

II. – *Kyrie fons bonitatis.*

X cent.

3.

KY-ri- e, * e-lé- i-son. *iij.*

Chrí-ste, e-lé- i-son. *iij.*

Ký-ri- e, e-lé- i-son. *ij.* Ký-ri-

e * ** e-lé- i-son.

XIII cent.

1.

GLóri- a in excélsis Dé-o. Et in térra pax

ho-mí- ni- bus bónae vo-luntá- tis. Laudámus te.

Benedí-cimus te. Ado-rámus te. Glo-ri-fi-cá- mus

te. Grá-ti- as   ágimus   tí-bi   propter   má- gnam

gló- ri- am tú- am.   Dómine Dé-us,   Rex cae-léstis,

Dé-us Pá-ter   omnípot- ens.   Dó-   mine Fí-li u-

ni-gé-ni-te   Jé-su   Chrís-te.   Dómine   Dé-us,   Agnus

Dé- i,   Fí- li- us   Pá-tris.   Qui   tól- lis   peccá-ta

múndi,   mi-se-ré-re   nó-bis.   Qui   tól- lis   peccá-ta

múndi,   súscipe   depreca-ti- ó-nem   nóstram.   Qui

sédes   ad déx- te-ram Pá- tris,   mi-se-ré-re   nó-bis.

Quóni- am tu só- lus sánctus. Tu só-lus Dó-minus.

Tu só-lus Al- tíssimus, Jé- su Chrís-te. Cum Sáncto

Spí-ri-tu, in gló- ri- a Dé- i Pá- tris. A- men.

XII-XIII cent.

1. S An- ctus, * Sán- ctus, Sán- ctus

Dóminus Dé- us Sába-oth. Plé-ni sunt caéli et tér-

ra gló- ri- a tú-a. Hosánna in ex-cél-sis.

Be-ne-díctus qui vé- nit in nó- mine Dómi-ni.

Hosánna in ex-cél-sis.

X cent.

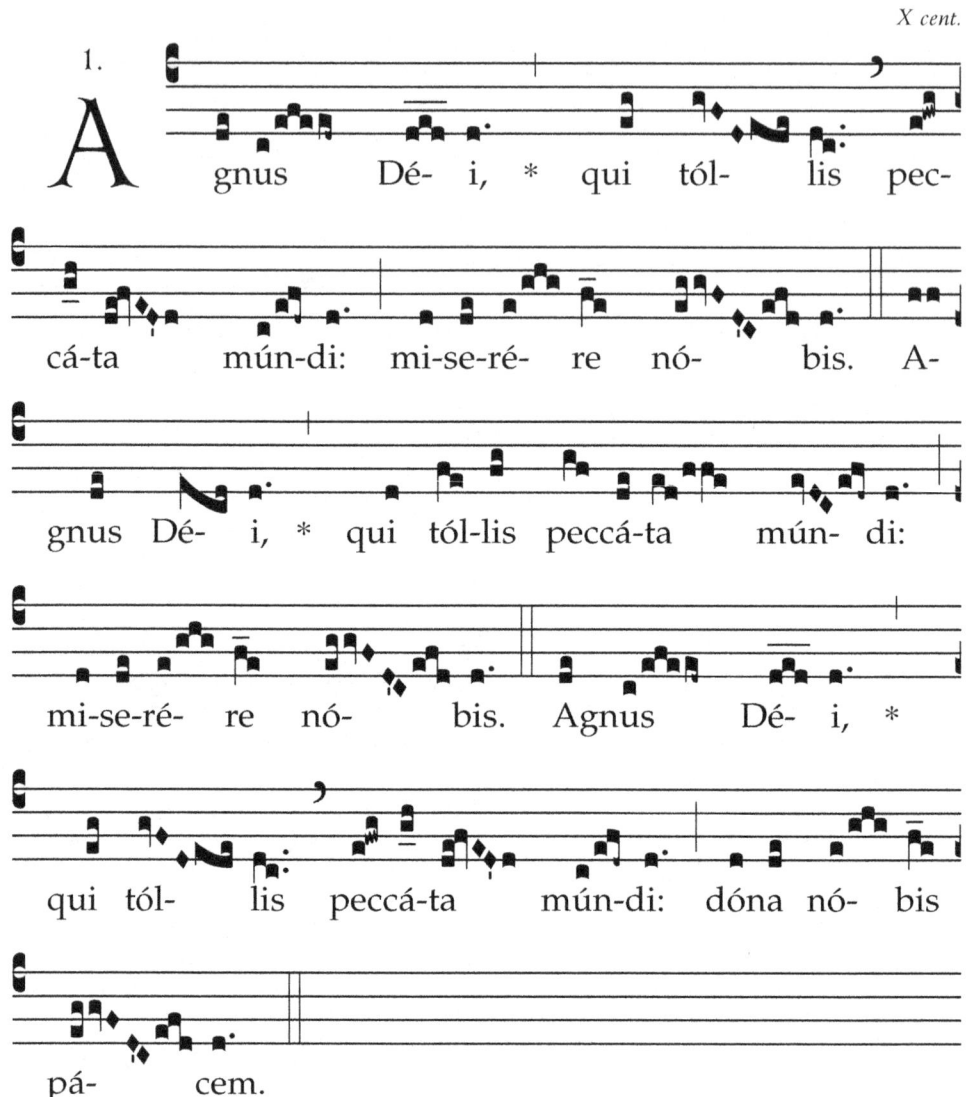

1.

Agnus Dé- i, * qui tól- lis pec-

cá-ta mún-di: mi-se-ré- re nó- bis. A-

gnus Dé- i, * qui tól-lis peccá-ta mún- di:

mi-se-ré- re nó- bis. Agnus Dé- i, *

qui tól- lis peccá-ta mún-di: dóna nó- bis

pá- cem.

3.

I - te, mis-sa est.

℟. De- o grá- ti- as.

Or, more usually:

5.

I — te, mis- sa est.

℟. De- o grá- ti- as.

Ad libitum:

4.

I —te, mis-sa est. ℟. De–o grá–ti–as.

III. – *Kyrie Deus sempiterne.*

XI cent.

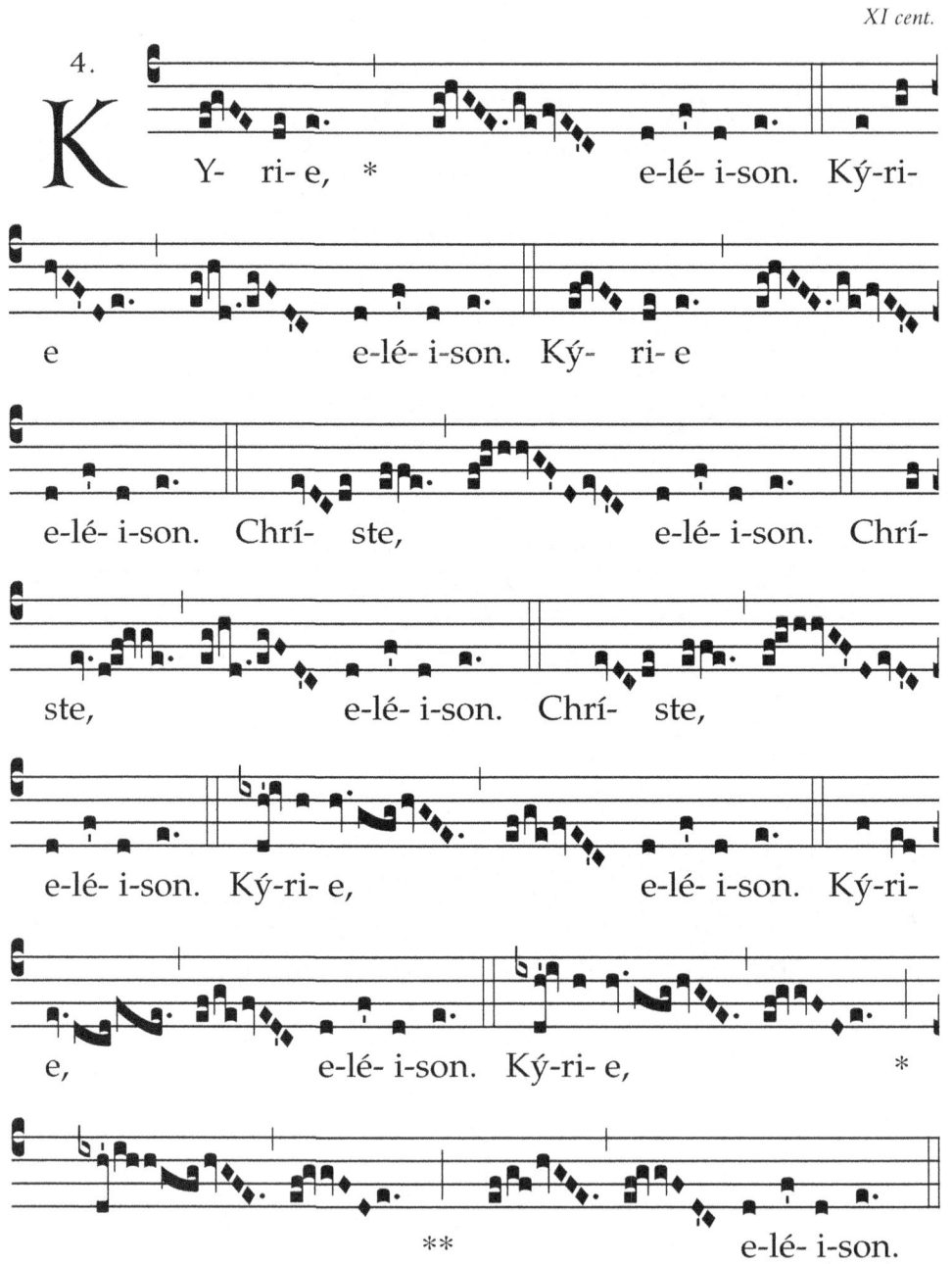

4.

KY- ri- e, * e-lé- i-son. Ký-ri- e e-lé- i-son. Ký- ri- e e-lé- i-son. Chrí- ste, e-lé- i-son. Chrí- ste, e-lé- i-son. Chrí- ste, e-lé- i-son. Ký-ri- e, e-lé- i-son. Ký-ri- e, e-lé- i-son. Ký-ri- e, * ** e-lé- i-son.

XI cent.

8.

Glóri- a in excél-sis Dé- o. Et in térra

pax homí-nibus bó- nae vo-luntá- tis. Lau-dá-mus

te. Bene-dí-ci- mus te. Ado-rá-mus te. Glo-

ri- fi-cá- mus te. Grá-ti- as ágimus tí-bi propter

má- gnam gló-ri- am tú- am. Dómine Dé-us, Rex

cae-léstis, Dé-us Pá- ter o- mní-pot-ens. Dómine Fí-

li u-ni-géni-te Jé-su Chrí-ste. Dómine Dé-us,

Agnus Dé- i, Fí-li- us Pátris. Qui tóllis pec- cá-ta

mún-di, mi-se-ré-re nó-bis. Qui tóllis pec- cá-ta

mún-di, súscipe depre-ca- ti- ónem nóstram. Qui sé-

des ad déxteram Pá- tris, mi-se- ré-re nó-bis.

Quóni- am tu só-lus sánctus. Tu só-lus Dóminus.

Tu só-lus Altíssimus, Jé- su Chrí- ste. Cum Sáncto

Spí-ri-tu, in gló-ri- a Dé- i Pá- tris. A- men.

(XI) XII cent.

4.

S An- ctus, * Sánctus, Sán- ctus Dó-mi-

nus Dé-us Sá-ba-oth. Pléni sunt caé-li et tér-

ra gló- ri- a tú- a. Ho- sánna in excél-sis.

Bene-díctus qui vénit in nó-mine Dó-mi-ni.

Ho- sánna in excél-sis.

XI-XII cent.

4.

A - gnus Dé- i, * qui tól- lis peccá-

ta mún- di: mi- se-ré-re nó-bis. Agnus Dé-

i, * qui tól- lis peccá- ta mún- di: mi-

se-ré-re nó-bis. A- gnus Dé- i, * qui tól- lis

peccá- ta   mún- di: dó- na   nóbis   pá-cem.

5. I – te,   mis- sa est.

℟. De- o   grá- ti- as.

IV. – *Cunctipotens Genitor Deus.*

X cent.

1.

Ky-ri- e   *   e- lé- i-son. *iij.*

Chríste   e- lé- i-son. *iij.* Ký-ri- e

e- lé- i-son. *ij.* Ký-ri- e   *   **

e- lé- i-son.

X cent.

4.

Lóri- a in excélsis Dé- o. Et in térra pax

ho-mí-ni-bus bónae vo-luntá- tis. Laudámus te.

Be-ne-dí-cimus te. Ado-rá- mus te. Glo-ri-fi-cá-

mus te. Grá-ti- as ágimus tí-bi propter

mágnam gló-ri-am tú- am. Dómi-ne Dé-us, Rex

cae-léstis, Dé- us Pá- ter omní-pot-ens. Dómi-ne

Fí-li u-ni-gé-ni-te Jé- su Chrí- ste. Dómi-ne

Dé-us, Agnus Dé- i, Fí- li-us Pá- tris. Qui

tóllis peccá-ta múndi, mi-se-ré-re nó-bis. Qui tóllis

peccá-ta múndi, súscipe depreca-ti- ónem nóstram.

Qui sé-des ad déxte-ram Pátris, mi-se-ré-re nó-bis.

Quó-ni- am tu só-lus sánctus. Tu só-lus Dó-minus.

Tu só-lus Altíssimus, Jé- su Chrí- ste. Cum

Sán-cto Spí- ri- tu, in gló-ri- a Dé- i Pá- tris.

A- men.

XI cent.

8.

S An- ctus, * Sánctus, Sán- ctus Dóminus

Dé-us Sá- ba-oth. Pléni sunt caéli et térra gló- ri- a

tú- a. Ho- sánna in ex- cél- sis. Benedíctus qui

vé-nit in nómine Dó- mi-ni. Ho- sánna

in ex- cél- sis.

(XII) XIII cent.

6. **A**gnus Dé- i, * qui tóllis peccá-ta

múndi: mi-se-ré- re nó- bis. Agnus Dé-i, * qui

tóllis peccá-ta múndi: mi-se-ré- re nó- bis. Agnus

Dé- i, * qui tóllis peccá-ta múndi: dóna nó- bis

pá- cem.

1. **I**-te, missa est.

℟. De-o grá-ti- as.

V. – *Kyrie magnæ Deus potentiæ.*

XIII cent.

8.

K Y-ri- e * e- lé- i-son. *iij.*

Chrí- ste e- lé- i-son. *iij.* Ký-ri- e

* e- lé- i-son. *iij.*

XII cent.

8.

G Lóri- a in excél-sis Dé- o. Et in térra pax

ho- mí-ni-bus bónae vo-lun-tá- tis. Laudámus te.

Bene-dí-cimus te. Adorámus te. Glo-ri- fi- cá-mus

te. Grá- ti- as á-gimus tí-bi propter mágnam

gló- ri- am tú- am. Dó- mi-ne Dé-us, Rex cae-

lé-stis, Dé-us Pá-ter o- mní-pot-ens. Dó- mi-ne

Fí-li unigéni-te Jé-su Chrí-ste. Dómine Dé-us,

A- gnus Dé- i, Fí- li- us Pá- tris. Qui tól-lis peccá-

ta múndi, mi-se- ré- re nó-bis. Qui tól-lis

peccá- ta múndi, súscipe depre- ca-ti- ónem nós-

tram. Qui sé-des ad déxte-ram Pá-tris, mi-se-

ré- re nó-bis. Quó- ni- am tu só-lus sánctus.

Tu só-lus Dóminus. Tu só-lus Al- tíssi-mus, Jé- su

Chrí- ste. Cum Sáncto Spí-ri-tu, in gló-ri- a Dé- i

Pá- tris. A- men.

XII cent.

4.

S An- ctus, * Sán- ctus, Sán- ctus Dóminus

Dé-us Sá- ba- oth. Pléni sunt caéli et térra

gló-ri- a tú- a. Ho- sánna in excél- sis.

Benedíctus qui vé-nit in nó-mi-ne Dómi-ni.

Ho- sánna in excél- sis.

XII cent.

4. A - gnus Dé- i, * qui tól- lis pec-

cá- ta mún-di: mi-se-ré- re nó- bis. A-

gnus Dé- i, * qui tól- lis pec-cá- ta mún-di:

mi-se-ré- re nó- bis. A- gnus Dé- i, *

qui tól- lis pec-cá- ta mún-di: dóna nó- bis

pá- cem.

8. I —te,   missa est.
     De-o   *grá- ti- as.*

VI. – *Kyrie Rex Genitor.*

X cent.

Kyrie * eleison. Kyrie eleison. Kyrie eleison. Christe eleison. Christe eleison. Christe eleison. Kyrie eleison. Kyrie eleison. Kyrie * ** eleison.

X cent.

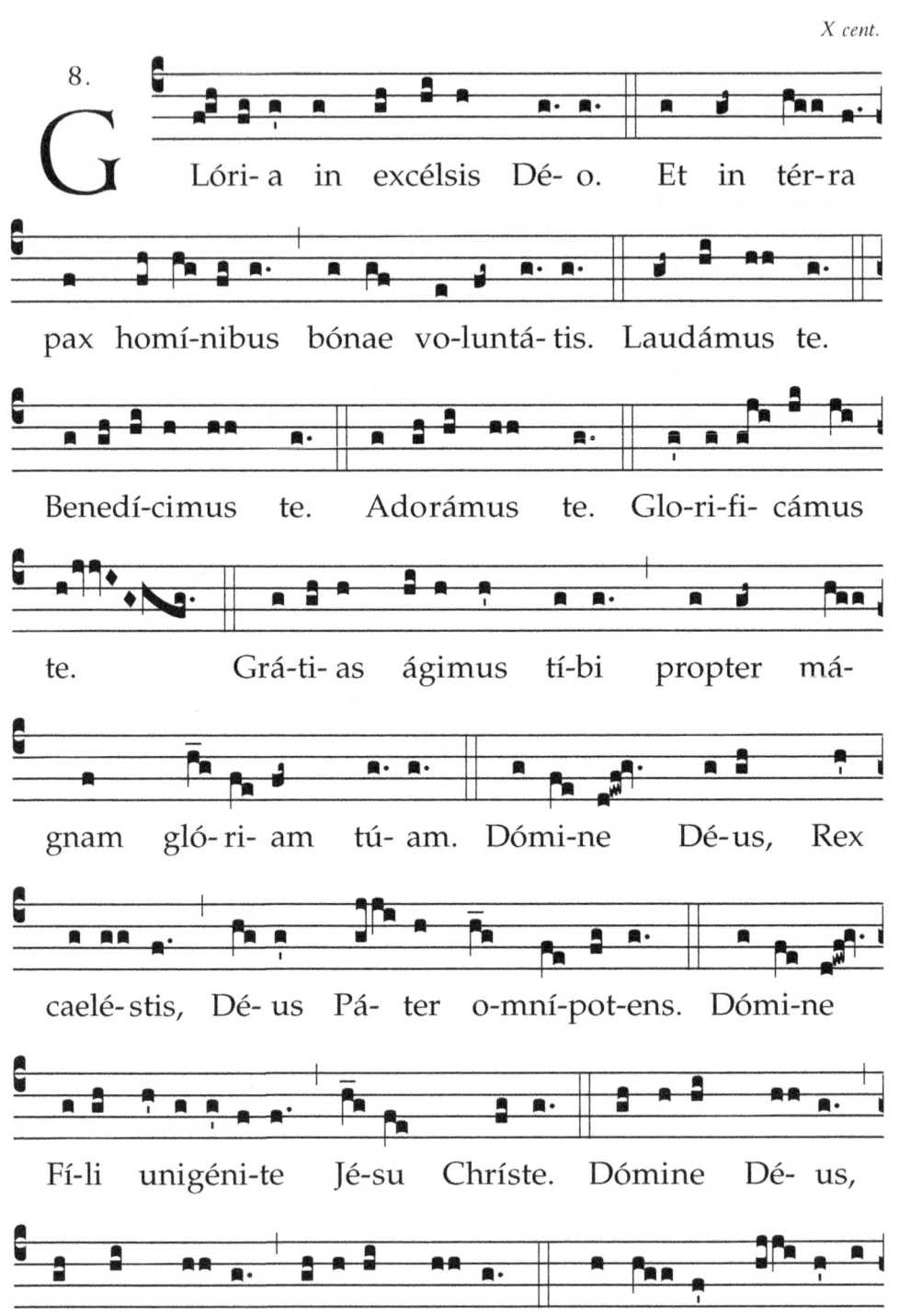

8.

Glóri- a in excélsis Dé- o. Et in tér-ra

pax homí-nibus bónae vo-luntá- tis. Laudámus te.

Benedí-cimus te. Adorámus te. Glo-ri-fi- cámus

te. Grá-ti- as ágimus tí-bi propter má-

gnam gló- ri- am tú- am. Dómi-ne Dé-us, Rex

caelé-stis, Dé- us Pá- ter o-mní-pot-ens. Dómi-ne

Fí-li unigéni-te Jé-su Chríste. Dómine Dé- us,

Agnus Dé- i, Fí-li- us Pá-tris. Qui tól- lis pec-cá-ta

múndi, mi-se-ré-re nó-bis. Qui tól- lis peccá-ta

mún-di, sú- scipe depreca-ti- ónem nóstram. Qui

sé- des ad déxte-ram Pá- tris, mi-se-ré-re nó-bis.

Quóni- am tu só-lus sánctus. Tu só-lus Dó-minus.

Tu só-lus Altíssimus, Jé-su Chrí-ste. Cum Sán-cto

Spí-ri-tu, in gló- ri- a Dé- i Pá-tris. A- men.

XI cent.

3. Anctus, Sánctus, Sánctus Dóminus Dé-us

Sá-ba- oth. Pléni sunt caé- li et tér-ra gló-ri- a

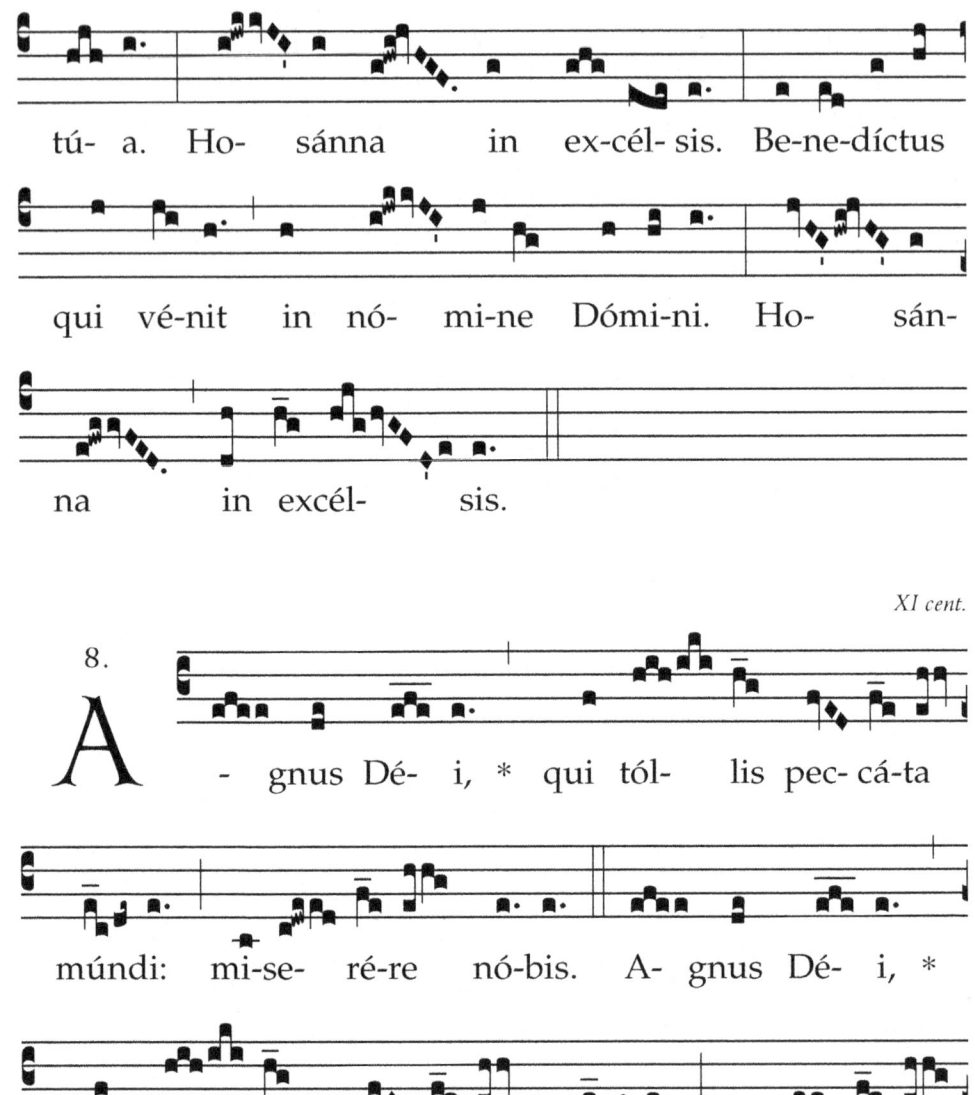

tú- a. Ho- sánna   in   ex-cél- sis.   Be-ne-díctus

qui vé-nit in nó- mi-ne Dómi-ni.   Ho-   sán-

na   in excél-   sis.

XI cent.

8.

A - gnus Dé- i, * qui tól-   lis pec- cá-ta

múndi: mi-se- ré-re nó-bis.   A- gnus Dé- i, *

qui tól- lis pec-cá-ta múndi: mi-se- ré-re

nó-bis.   A- gnus Dé- i, * qui tól-   lis pec- cá-ta

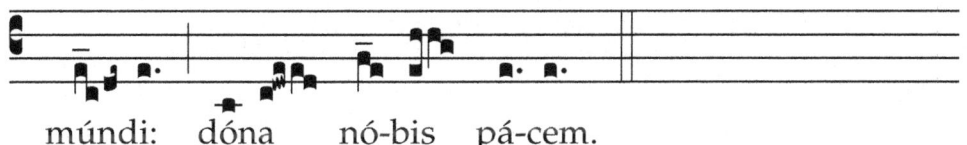

múndi: dóna nó-bis pá-cem.

8.

– te, missa est.

De- o *grá- ti- as.*

VII. – *Kyrie Rex splendens.*

X cent.

8.

KY-ri- e   *   e- lé- i-son. *iij.*

Chríste   e- lé-

i-son. *iij.* Ký-ri- e   *

e- lé- i-son. *iij.*

XII cent.

6.

GLóri- a in excél-sis Dé- o. Et in térra

pax ho-mí-nibus bónae voluntá- tis. Laudámus te.

Bene-dí-cimus te. Ado-rámus te. Glo-ri- fi-cámus

te. Grá-ti- as á-gimus tí-bi propter mágnam gló-ri-

am tú- am. Dómine Dé-us, Rex cae-lé-stis, Dé- us

Pá-ter o-mní-pot-ens. Dómine Fí- li u-ni-gé-ni- te

Jé-su Chrí-ste. Dómine Dé- us, Agnus Dé- i,

Fí- li- us Pá-tris. Qui tóllis peccá-ta múndi,

mi-se-ré-re nóbis. Qui tóllis peccá-ta múndi,

súscipe depreca-ti- ónem nóstram. Qui sédes ad

déxte-ram Pá-tris, mi-se-ré-re nó- bis. Quóni- am tu

só-lus sánctus. Tu só-lus Dóminus. Tu só-lus

Altíssimus, Jésu Chrí- ste. Cum Sán- cto Spí- ri-tu,

in gló-ri- a Dé- i Pá-tris. A- men.

XI cent.

8.

S An- ctus, * Sán- ctus, Sán- ctus

Dóminus Dé- us Sá- ba- oth. Plé-ni sunt caé-li

et tér- ra gló-ri- a tú- a. Ho- sánna

in ex-cél- sis. Be- nedí- ctus qui vé-

nit in nómine Dómi-ni. Ho- sánna in ex-cél-

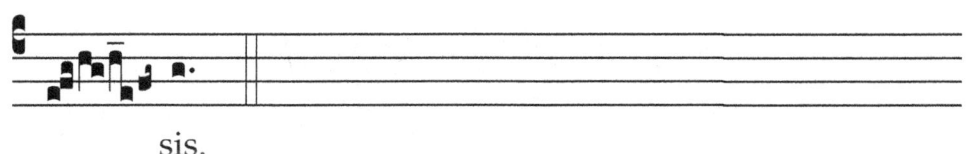

sis.

XV cent.

8. A - gnus Dé- i, * qui tól- lis peccá-ta

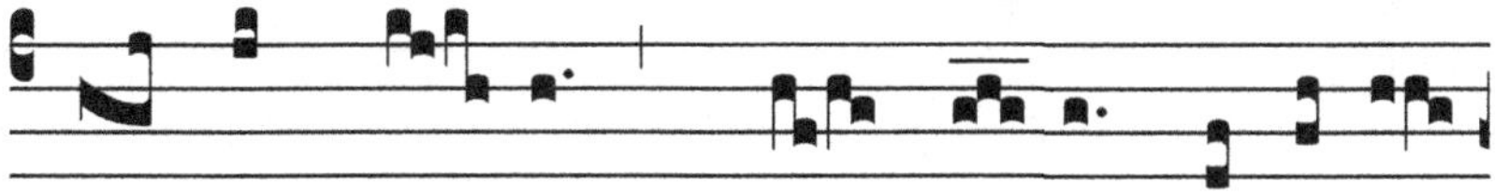

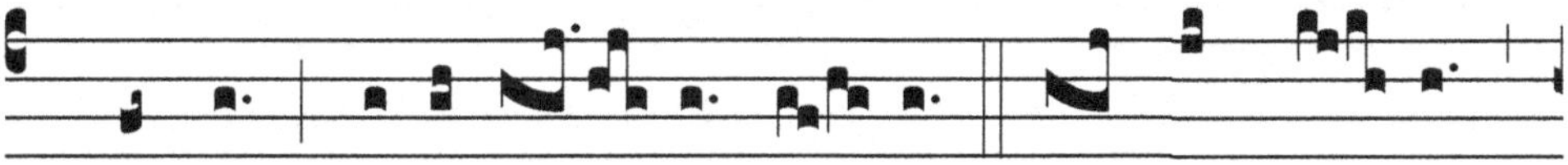

múndi: mi-se-ré- re nó- bis. A- gnus Dé- i, *

qui tól- lis peccá-ta múndi: mi-se-ré- re nó-

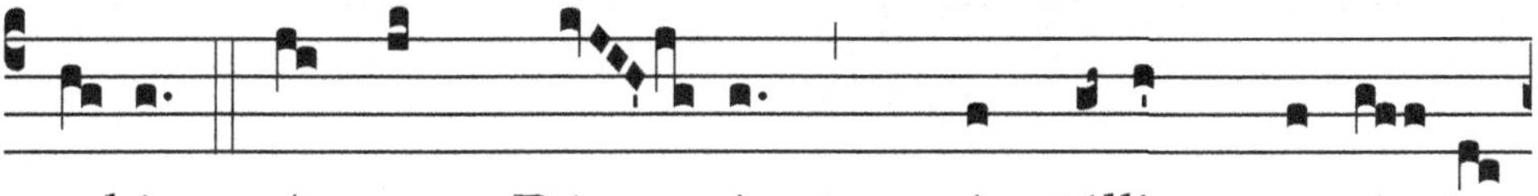

bis. Agnus Dé- i, * qui tóllis peccá- ta

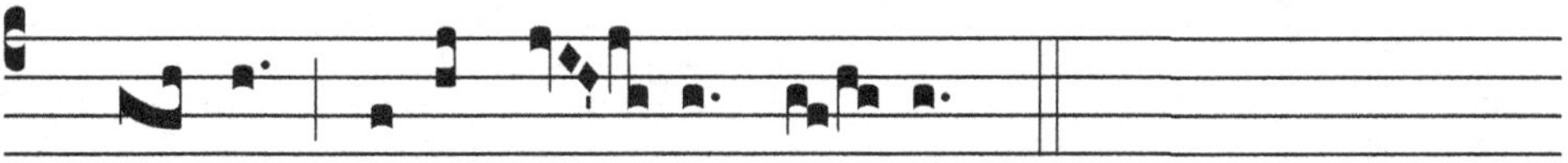

mún-di: dóna nó- bis pá- cem.

8. I -te, missa est.

De- o *grá- ti- as.*

VIII. – *De Angelis.*

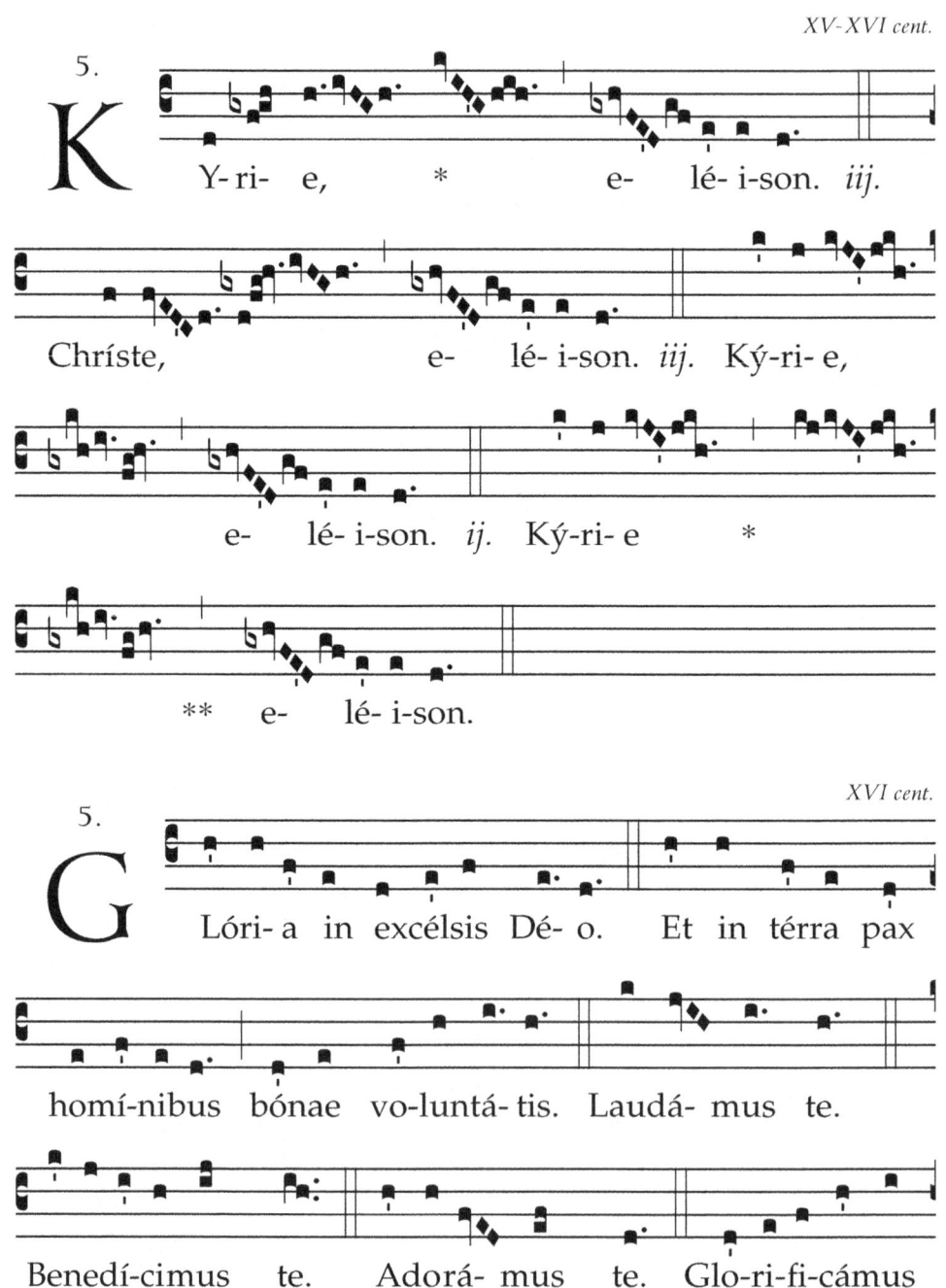

XV-XVI cent.

5.

K Y- ri- e,   *   e- lé- i-son. *iij.*

Chríste,   e- lé- i-son. *iij.* Ký-ri- e,

e- lé- i-son. *ij.* Ký-ri- e   *

** e- lé- i-son.

XVI cent.

5.

G Lóri- a in excélsis Dé- o.   Et in térra pax

homí-nibus bónae vo-luntá- tis. Laudá- mus te.

Benedí-cimus te.   Adorá- mus te.   Glo-ri-fi-cámus

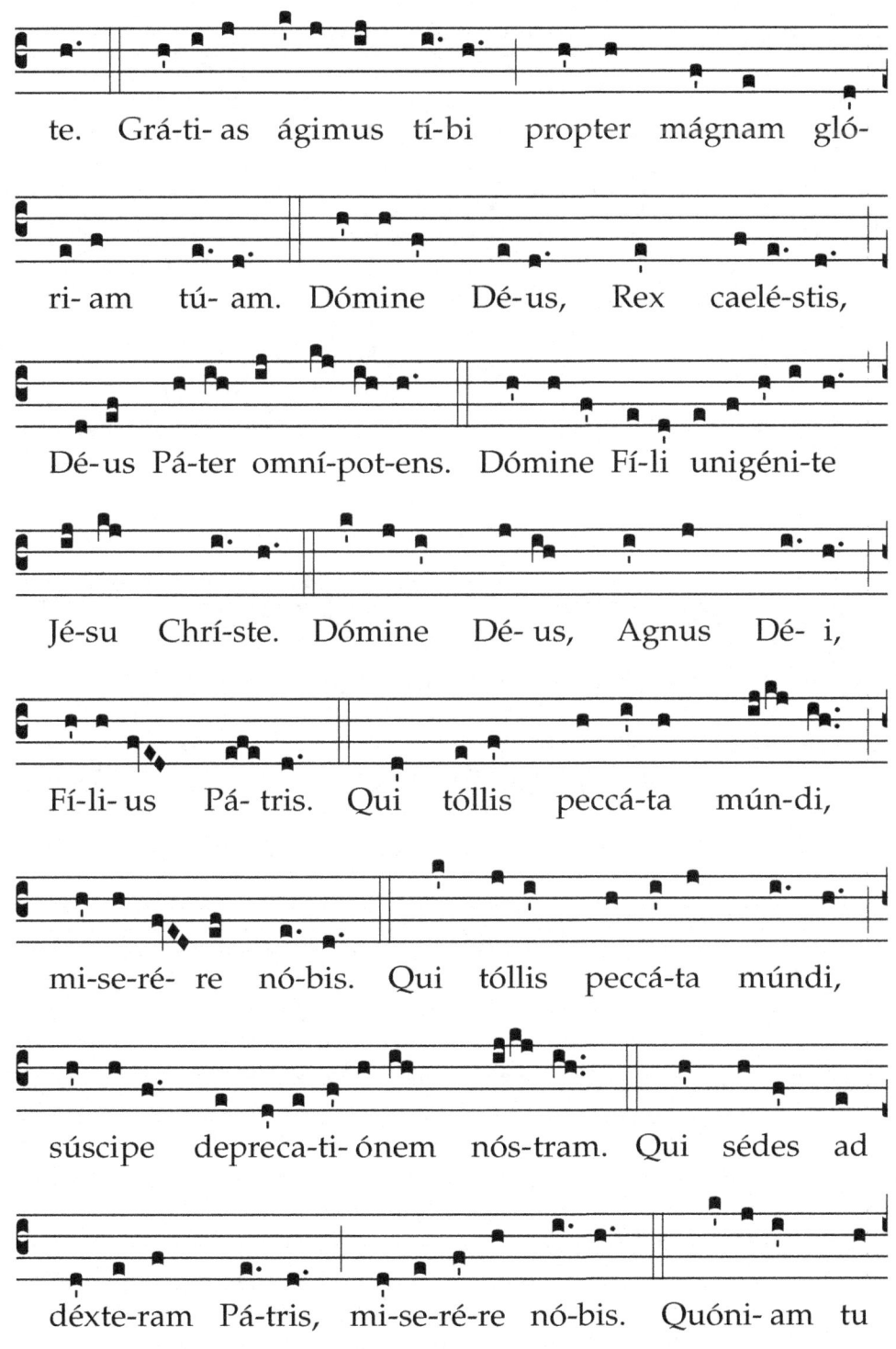

te. Grá-ti- as ágimus tí-bi propter mágnam gló-

ri- am tú- am. Dómine Dé-us, Rex caelé-stis,

Dé-us Pá-ter omní-pot-ens. Dómine Fí-li unigéni-te

Jé-su Chrí-ste. Dómine Dé- us, Agnus Dé- i,

Fí-li- us Pá- tris. Qui tóllis peccá-ta mún-di,

mi-se-ré- re nó-bis. Qui tóllis peccá-ta múndi,

súscipe depreca-ti- ónem nós-tram. Qui sédes ad

déxte-ram Pá-tris, mi-se-ré-re nó-bis. Quóni- am tu

só-lus sánctus. Tu só-lus Dómi-nus. Tu só-lus

Altíssimus, Jé-su Chrí-ste. Cum Sáncto Spí-ri-

tu, in gló-ri- a Dé- i Pá- tris. A- men.

(XI) XII cent.

6.

S An- ctus, * Sánctus, Sán- ctus Dó- mi-

nus Dé- us Sá- ba- oth. Pléni sunt caé- li

et tér- ra gló- ri- a tú- a. Hosánna in ex-

cél- sis. Benedí- ctus qui vé- nit in nómine

Dó-mi-ni. Ho-sán- na in excél- sis.

XV cent.

6. A - gnus Dé- i, * qui tól-lis peccá-ta

múndi: mi-se-ré-re nó- bis. Agnus Dé- i, *

qui tól- lis peccá-ta múndi: mi-se-ré-re nó- bis.

A- gnus Dé- i, * qui tól-lis peccá-ta múndi: dóna

nó-bis pá- cem.

5. I - te, * missa est.
De- o grá- ti- as.

IX. – *Cum jubilo.*

XII cent.

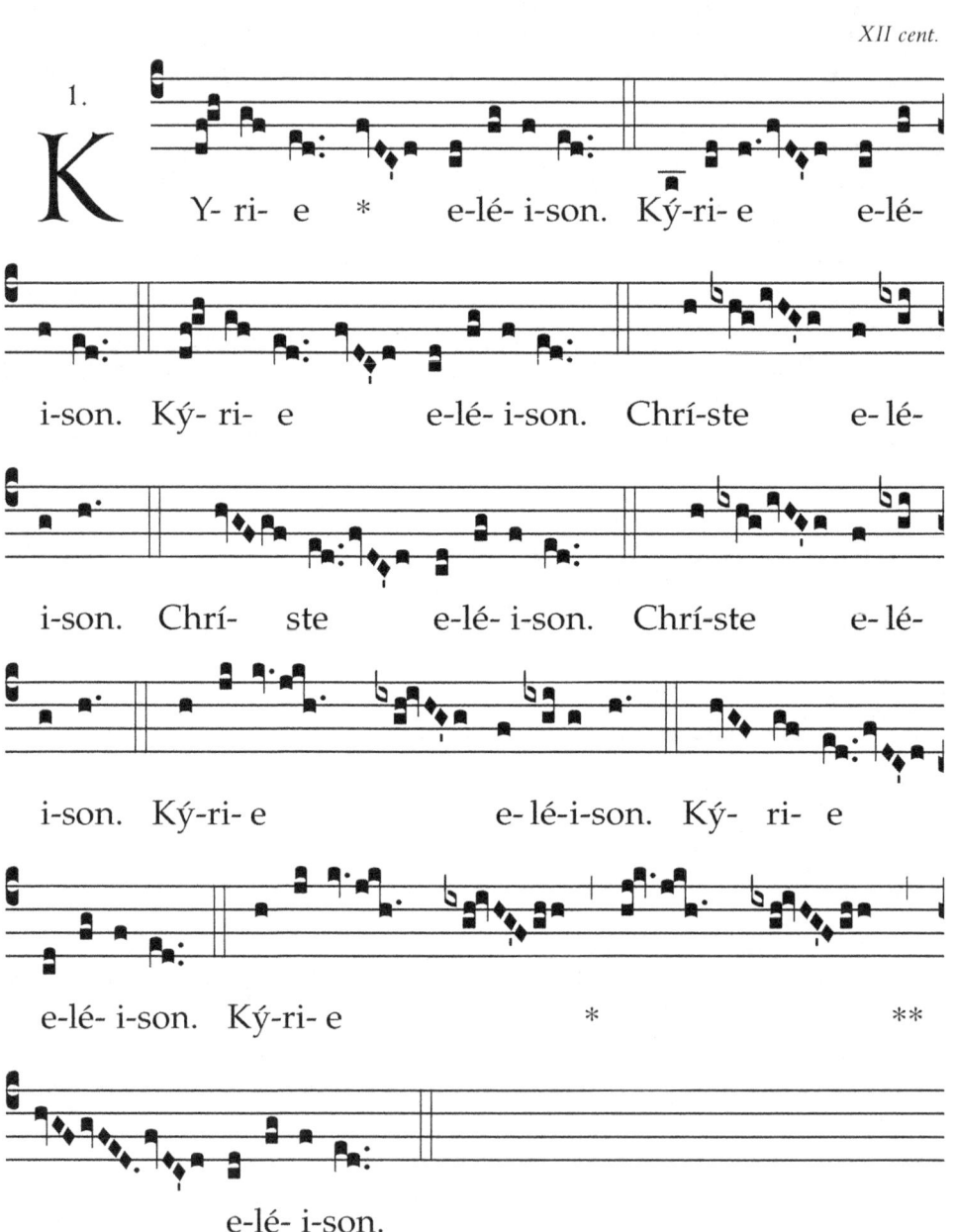

1.

K Y- ri- e   *   e-lé- i-son. Ký-ri- e   e-lé-

i-son. Ký- ri- e   e-lé- i-son. Chrí-ste   e-lé-

i-son. Chrí- ste   e-lé- i-son. Chrí-ste   e-lé-

i-son. Ký-ri- e   e-lé-i-son. Ký- ri- e

e-lé- i-son. Ký-ri- e   *   **

e-lé- i-son.

XI cent.

7.

G Ló-ri- a in excél-sis Dé- o.   Et in térra pax

homí- ni-bus bónae vo-luntá- tis. Laudá- mus te.

Bene- dí-cimus te.   Ado- rá- mus te.   Glo-ri-fi-cá-

mus te. Grá-ti- as ágimus tí-bi   propter mágnam

gló- ri- am tú- am. Dómine Dé- us, Rex cae-

léstis, Dé- us Pá-ter o-mní-pot-ens. Dómine Fí-li

uni-gé-ni-te Jésu Chrí- ste. Dó- mine Dé-us, Agnus

Dé- i, Fí-li- us Pá-tris. Qui tóllis peccá-ta múndi,

mi-se-ré-re nóbis. Qui tól-lis peccá-ta múndi,

sú- scipe depreca-ti- ó-nem nóstram. Qui sédes ad

déxte-ram Pátris, mi-se-ré-re nóbis. Quóni- am tu

só-lus sánctus. Tu só-lus Dóminus. Tu só-lus

Altíssimus, Jésu Chrí- ste. Cum Sáncto Spí-ri-tu,

in gló-ri- a Dé- i Pá- tris. A- men.

XIV cent.

5.

S An- ctus, * Sán-ctus, Sán- ctus Dómi-

nus Dé- us Sá- ba- oth. Plé-ni sunt caéli et

tér- ra gló-ri- a tú- a. Hosán-na in excél- sis.

Be- nedíctus qui vé- nit in nó- mi-ne Dó- mi-

ni. Ho- sánna in ex-cél- sis.

(X) XIII cent.

5.

A gnus Dé- i * qui tól- lis peccá-ta

mún- di: mi-se- ré-re nó- bis. Agnus Dé- i *

qui tól-lis peccá-ta múndi: mi-se- ré-re nó- bis.

Agnus Dé- i * qui tól- lis peccá-ta mún- di:

dó-na nó-bis pá- cem.

1.

I - te, missa est.

R̸. De- o grá-ti- as.

Ad libitum:

4.

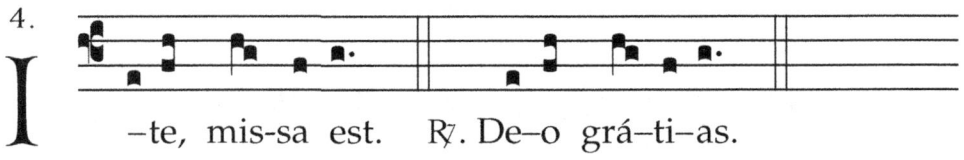

I -te, mis-sa est. R̸. De-o grá-ti-as.

X. – *Alme Pater.*

XI cent.

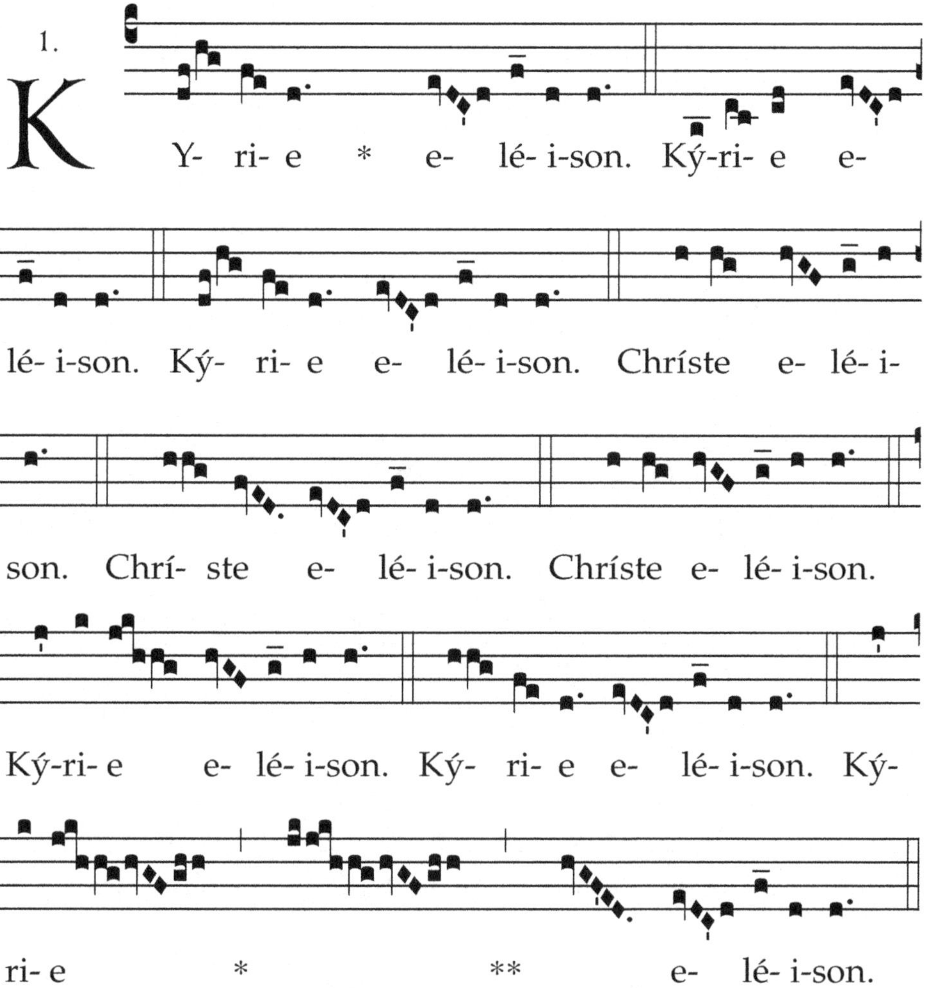

1.

K Y- ri- e   *   e- lé- i-son. Ký-ri- e e-

lé- i-son. Ký- ri- e e- lé- i-son. Chríste e- lé- i-

son. Chrí- ste e- lé- i-son. Chríste e- lé- i-son.

Ký-ri- e e- lé- i-son. Ký- ri- e e- lé- i-son. Ký-

ri- e   *   **   e- lé- i-son.

XV cent.

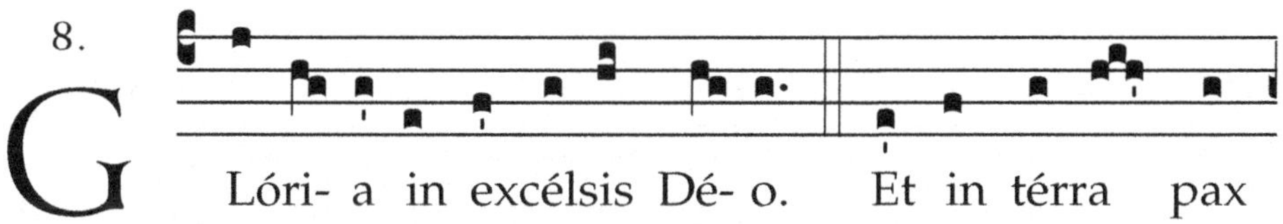

8.

G Lóri- a in excélsis Dé- o. Et in térra pax

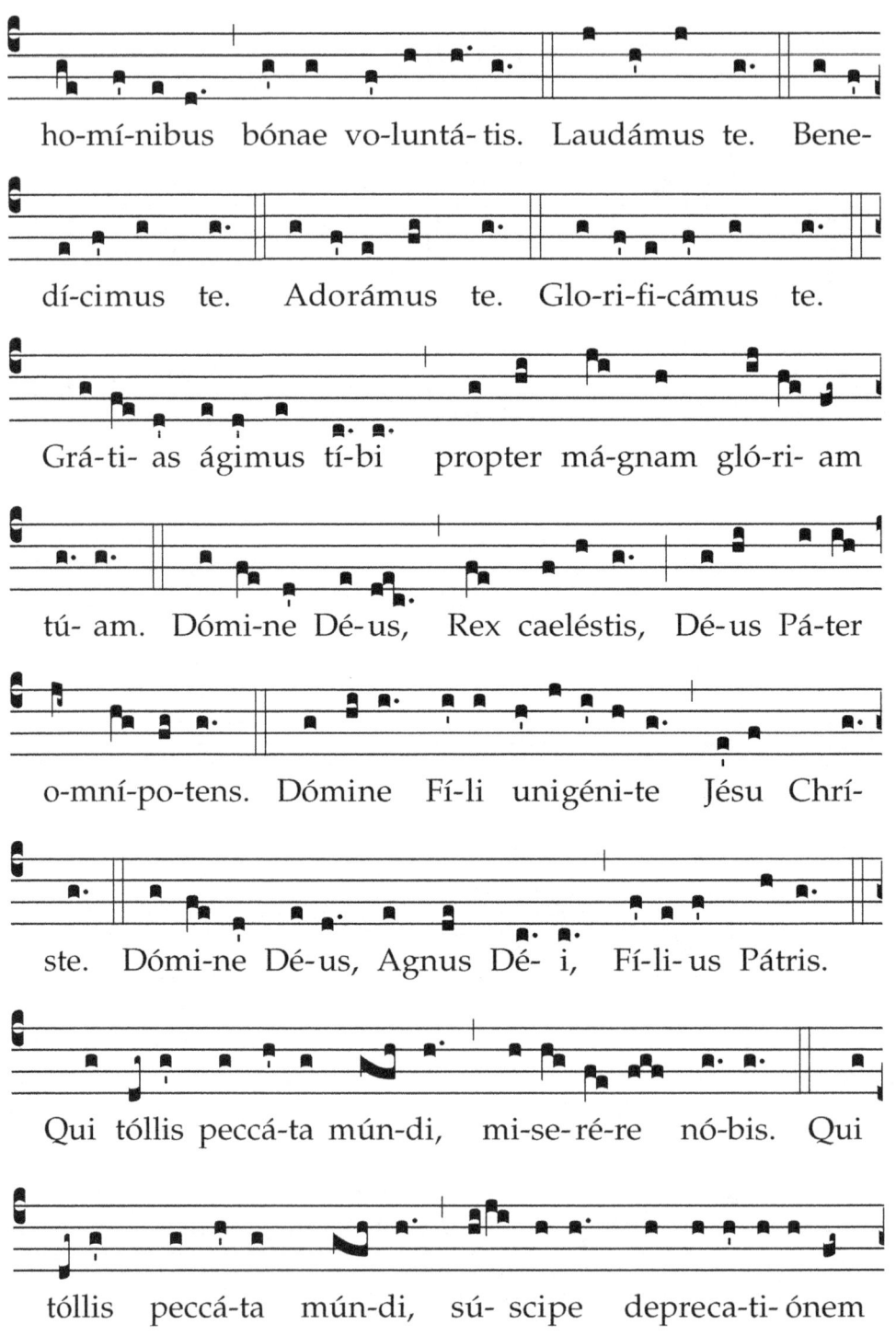

ho-mí-nibus bónae vo-luntá-tis. Laudámus te. Bene-

dí-cimus te. Adorámus te. Glo-ri-fi-cámus te.

Grá-ti- as ágimus tí-bi   propter má-gnam gló-ri- am

tú- am. Dómi-ne Dé-us,   Rex caeléstis, Dé-us Pá-ter

o-mní-po-tens. Dómine Fí-li unigéni-te Jésu Chrí-

ste. Dómi-ne Dé-us, Agnus Dé- i, Fí-li- us Pátris.

Qui tóllis peccá-ta mún-di, mi-se-ré-re nó-bis. Qui

tóllis peccá-ta mún-di, sú- scipe depreca-ti- ónem

nóstram. Qui sédes ad déxte-ram Pátris, mi-se-ré-re

nó-bis. Quó-ni- am tu só-lus sánctus. Tu só-lus

Dó-mi-nus. Tu só-lus Altíssimus, Jésu Chrí-ste.

Cum Sáncto Spí-ri-tu, in gló- ri- a Dé- i Pá-tris.

A- men.

4.

S Anctus, * Sán-ctus, Sánctus Dóminus Dé- us

Sá-ba- oth. Pléni sunt caéli et térra gló-ri- a tú- a.

Hosánna in excél-sis. Benedíctus qui vé- nit in

nómine Dómi-ni.   Hosánna in excél-sis.

XII cent.

4.

A gnus Dé- i, * qui tóllis peccá-ta múndi:

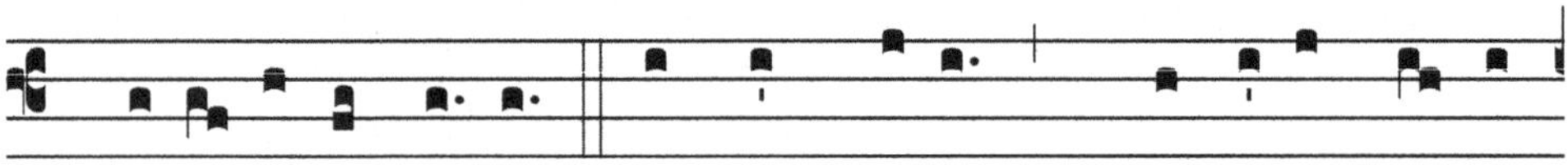

mi-se-ré-re nó-bis.   Agnus Dé- i, * qui tóllis peccá-

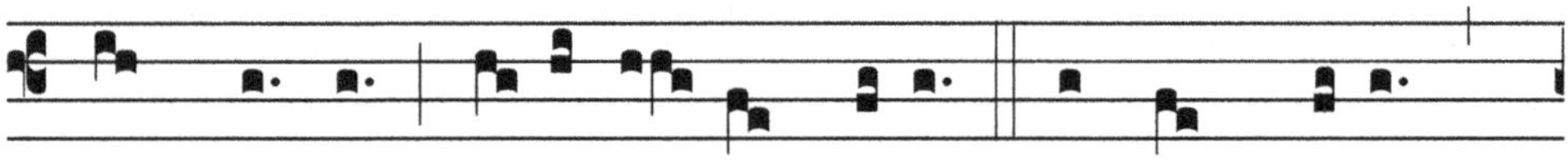

ta múndi: mi-se-ré- re nóbis.   Agnus Dé- i, *

qui tóllis peccá-ta múndi: dóna nóbis pá-cem.

1.

I - te,   missa est.

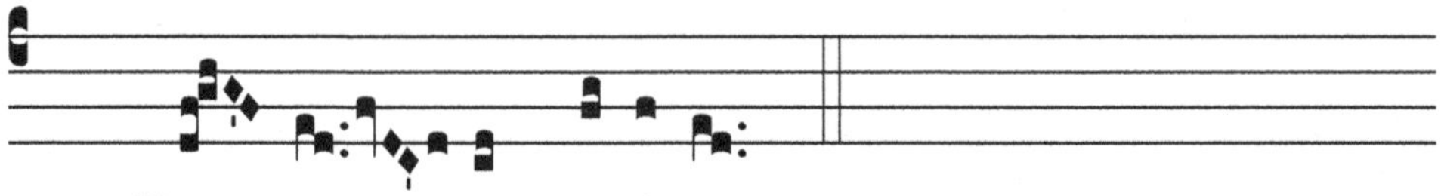

℟. De- o   grá-ti- as.

XI. – *Orbis factor.*

(X) XIV–XVI cent.

1.

KY-ri- e　*　e- lé- i-son. *iij.* Chrí-

ste　e- lé- i-son. *iij.* Ký-ri- e　e-

lé- i-son. *ij.* Ký- ri- e　*　e- lé- i-son.

X cent.

2.

GLó-ri- a in excélsis Dé- o.　Et in térra pax

homí-ni-bus bó-nae　vo-luntá- tis. Laudámus　te.

Bene-dí-cimus　te.　Adorámus　te. Glo-ri-fi-cámus

te.　Grá-ti- as ágimus tí-bi　propter mágnam

gló-ri- am tú- am. Dómi-ne Dé- us, Rex caelé-stis,

Dé-us Pá-ter omní-pot-ens. Dómi-ne Fí- li uni-

géni-te Jé-su Chrí-ste. Dómi-ne Dé- us, Agnus

Dé- i, Fí- li- us Pá-tris. Qui tóllis peccá-ta múndi,

mi-se-ré-re nó-bis. Qui tóllis peccá-ta múndi,

súscipe depreca-ti- ónem nóstram. Qui sé-des ad

déx- te-ram Pá-tris, mi-se-ré-re nó-bis. Quó-ni- am

tu só-lus sánctus. Tu só-lus Dóminus. Tu só-lus

Altíssimus, Jé-su Chrí-ste. Cum Sáncto Spí-ri-

tu, in gló-ri- a Dé- i Pá- tris. A- men.

XI cent.

2.

S Anctus, * Sán- ctus, Sánctus Dó-minus Dé-

us Sá-ba-oth. Plé-ni sunt caé- li et tér- ra

gló- ri- a tú- a. Hosánna in ex- célsis. Bene-

díctus qui vé-nit in nó- mine Dó-mi-ni.

Hosánna in ex- célsis.

XIV cent.

1.

A - gnus Dé- i, * qui tóllis peccá- ta

múndi: mi-se-ré-re nóbis. Agnus Dé-i, * qui

tól- lis peccá-ta mún-di: mi-se-ré- re nóbis. Agnus

Dé- i, * qui tóllis pec-cá- ta múndi: dóna nóbis

pácem.

1.

I -te, mis- sa est.

℞. De-o grá- ti- as.

Ad libitum:

4.

I -te, mis-sa est. ℞. De-o grá–ti–as.

XII. – *Pater cuncta.*

XII cent.

8.

KY-ri- e * e-lé- i-son. *iij.* Chríste

e-lé- i-son. *iij.* Ký-ri- e e-lé- i-son. *ij.* Ký-ri-

e * e-lé- i-son.

XII cent.

4.

GLóri- a in excélsis Dé- o. Et in tér-

ra pax homí-nibus bónae vo-luntá- tis. Laudá-mus

te. Benedí-cimus te. Adorámus te. Glo-ri-fi-cámus

te. Grá-ti- as ágimus tí-bi propter mágnam gló-

ri- am tú- am. Dómine Dé- us, Rex caeléstis, Dé- us

Pá-ter omní-pot-ens. Dómine Fí-li unigéni-te Jésu

Chrí-ste. Dómine Dé- us, Agnus Dé- i, Fí- li- us Pá-

tris. Qui tóllis peccá-ta múndi, mi-se-ré-re nó-bis.

Qui tóllis peccá-ta múndi, súscipe depreca-ti- ónem

nóstram. Qui sédes ad déxte-ram Pátris, mi-se-ré-re

nó-bis. Quóni- am tu só-lus sánctus. Tu só-lus

Dóminus. Tu só-lus Altíssi-mus, Jésu Chríste.

Cum Sáncto Spí- ri-tu, in gló-ri- a Dé- i Pátris.

A- men.

XIII cent.

2.

SAn- ctus, * Sán-ctus, Sán- ctus Dómi-

nus Dé- us Sába-oth. Pléni sunt caéli et térra

gló-ri- a tú- a. Hosánna in excél- sis. Benedí-

ctus qui vé-nit in nó-mi-ne Dómi-ni. Hosánna

in excél- sis.

XI cent.

2.

Agnus Dé- i, * qui tól- lis peccá- ta

múndi: mi-se- ré-re nó-bis. Agnus Dé- i, *

qui tóllis peccá-ta múndi: mi-se-ré-re nó-bis.

Agnus Dé- i, * qui tól- lis peccá- ta múndi:

dóna nó-bis pá-cem.

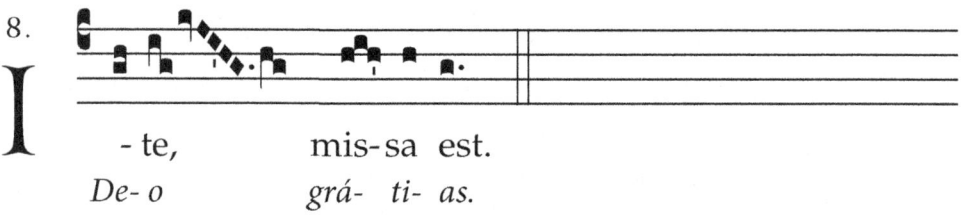

8.

     - te,   mis-sa est.
     De- o   *grá- ti- as.*

XIII. – *Stelliferi Conditor orbis.*

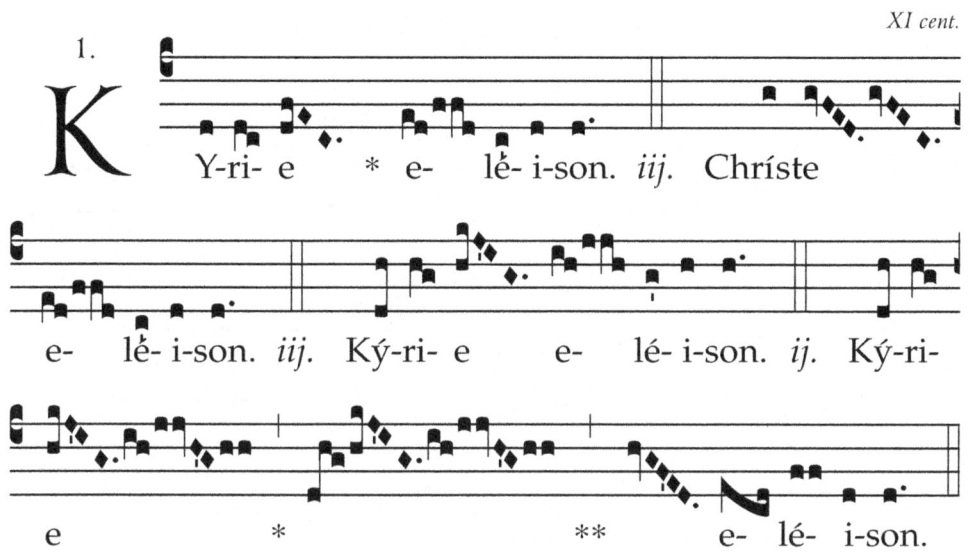

XI cent.

1. KY-ri- e * e- lé- i-son. *iij.* Chríste

e- lé- i-son. *iij.* Ký-ri- e e- lé- i-son. *ij.* Ký-ri-

e * ** e- lé- i-son.

XII cent.

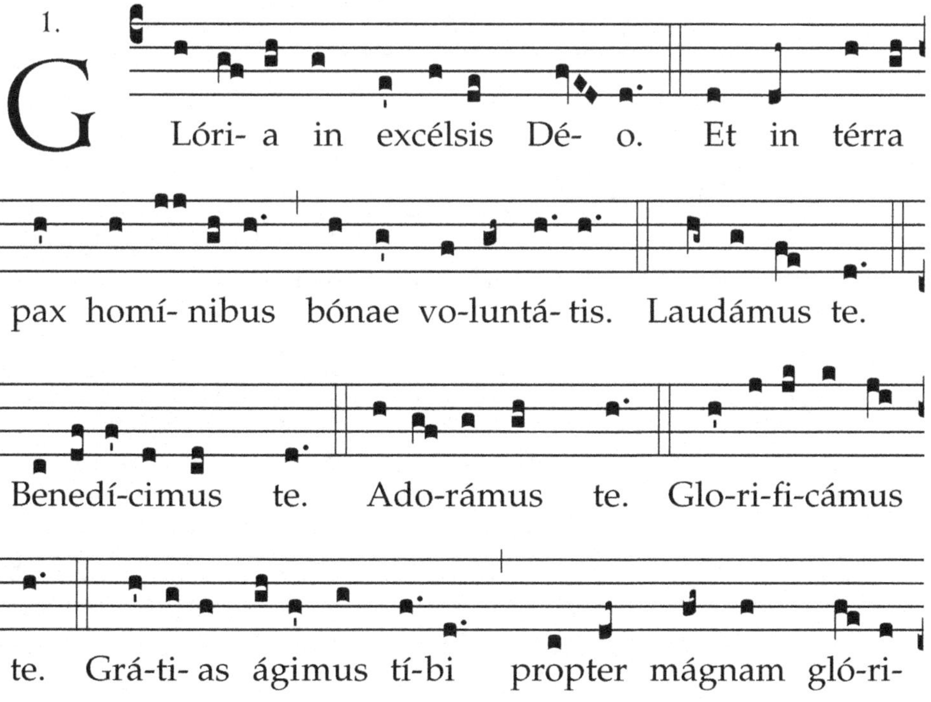

1. G Lóri- a in excélsis Dé- o. Et in térra

pax homí- nibus bónae vo-luntá- tis. Laudámus te.

Benedí-cimus te. Ado-rámus te. Glo-ri-fi-cámus

te. Grá-ti- as ágimus tí-bi propter mágnam gló-ri-

am tú- am. Dómine Dé-us, Rex cae-lé-stis, Dé-us

Pá-ter o-mnípot-ens. Dómine Fí-li u-ni-gé-ni-te

Jé- su Chrí-ste. Dómine Dé-us, Agnus Dé- i,

Fí-li- us Pátris. Qui tóllis peccá-ta múndi,

mi-se-ré- re nó-bis. Qui tóllis peccá-ta múndi,

súscipe depreca-ti- ónem nóstram. Qui sédes ad

déxte-ram Pá-tris, mi-se-ré-re nó-bis. Quóni- am tu

só-lus sánctus. Tu só-lus Dóminus. Tu só-lus

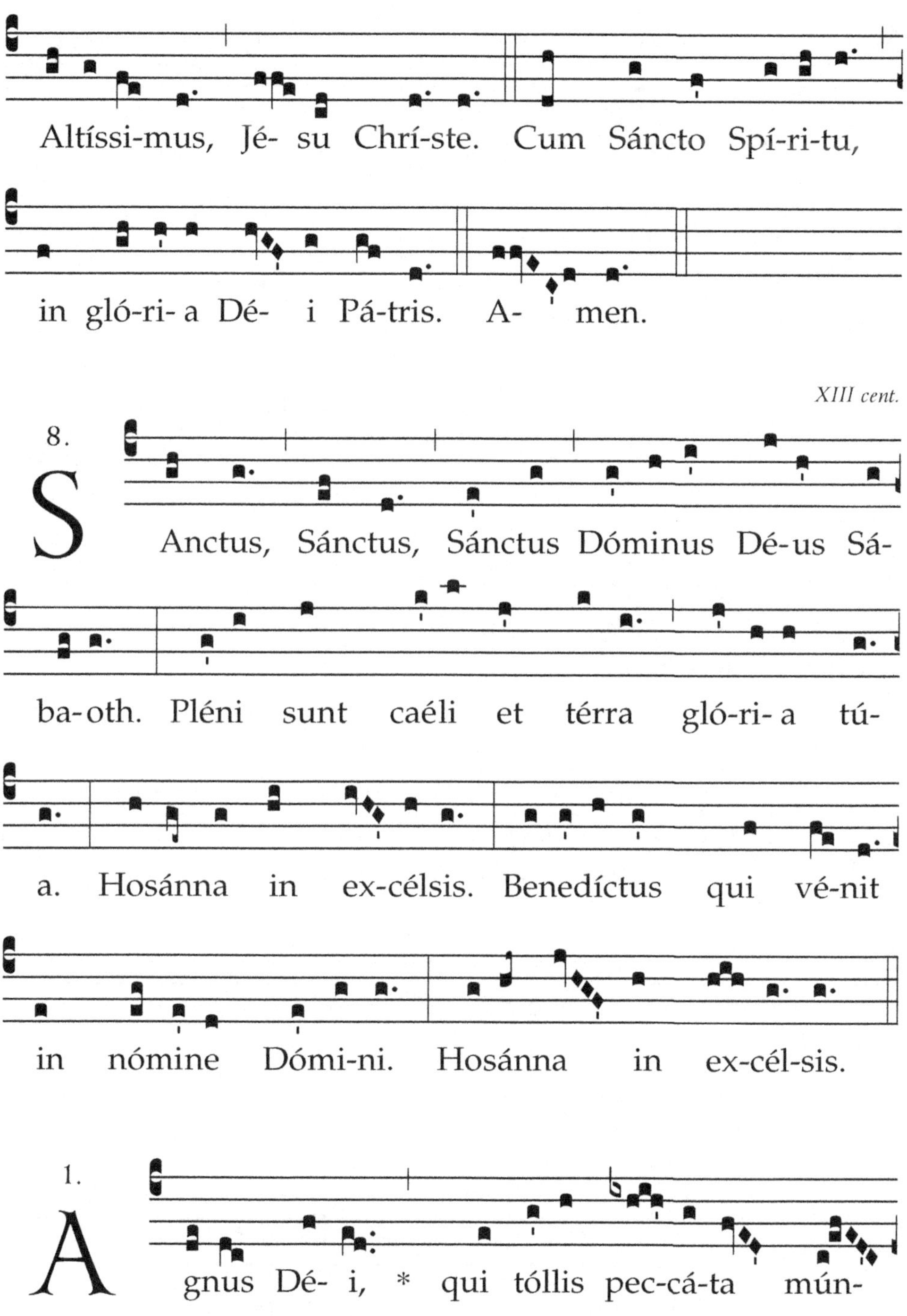

Altíssi-mus, Jé- su Chrí-ste. Cum Sáncto Spí-ri-tu,

in gló-ri- a Dé- i Pá-tris. A- men.

XIII cent.

8.

Sanctus, Sánctus, Sánctus Dóminus Dé-us Sá-

ba-oth. Pléni sunt caéli et térra gló-ri- a tú-

a. Hosánna in ex-célsis. Benedíctus qui vé-nit

in nómine Dómi-ni. Hosánna in ex-cél-sis.

1.

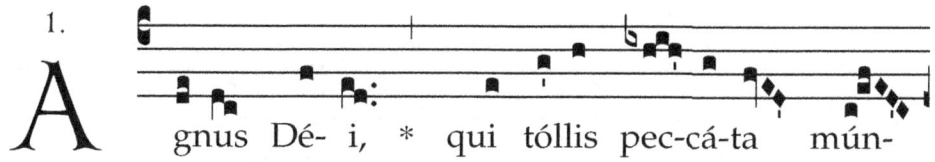

Agnus Dé- i, * qui tóllis pec-cá-ta mún-

di: mi-se-ré-re nó-bis. Agnus Dé- i, * qui

tól- lis peccá-ta múndi: mi-se-ré- re nó-

bis. Agnus Dé- i, * qui tóllis pec-cá-ta mún-

di: dóna nóbis pá-cem.

1.

I -te, mis- sa est.

℞. De- o grá- ti- as.

Ad libitum:

4.

I —te, mis-sa est. ℞. De—o grá–ti–as.

XIV. – *Jesu Redemptor.*

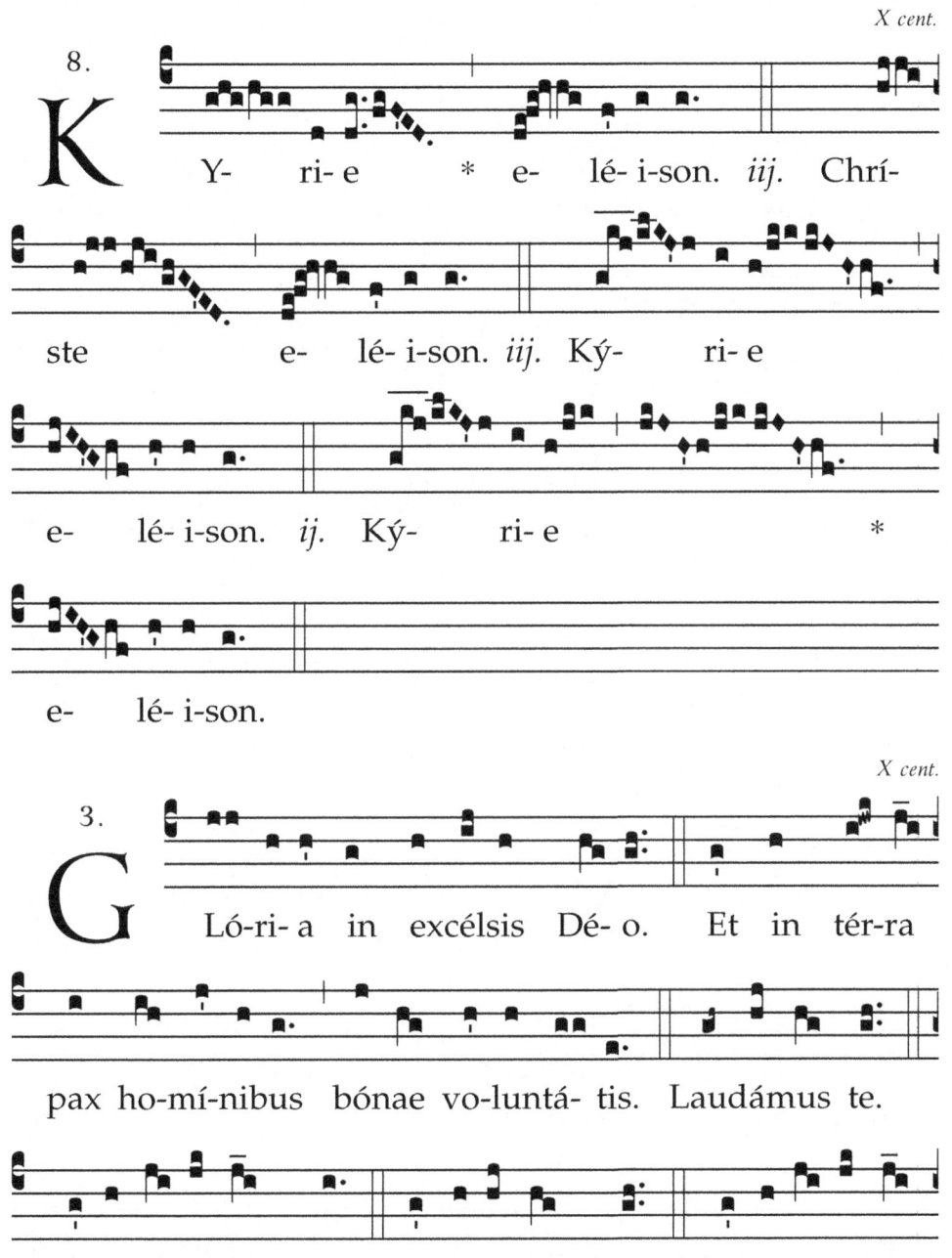

X cent.

8.

KY- ri- e * e- lé- i-son. *iij.* Chrí-

ste e- lé- i-son. *iij.* Ký- ri- e

e- lé- i-son. *ij.* Ký- ri- e *

e- lé- i-son.

X cent.

3.

GLó-ri- a in excélsis Dé- o. Et in tér-ra

pax ho-mí-nibus bónae vo-luntá- tis. Laudámus te.

Bene-dí-cimus te. Adorámus te. Glo-ri- fi-cámus

te. Grá-ti- as ágimus tí- bi propter mágnam gló-ri-

am tú-am. Dómine Dé- us, Rex cae- lé- stis, Dé-us

Pá-ter o-mní-po-tens. Dómi-ne Fí-li unigé-ni- te

Jésu Chrí- ste. Dómine Dé- us, Agnus Dé- i,

Fí-li- us Pá- tris. Qui tóllis peccá-ta múndi,

mi-se- ré-re nóbis. Qui tóllis peccá-ta múndi,

sú-scipe depreca-ti- ónem nós-tram. Qui sédes ad

déxte-ram Pá- tris, mi-se- ré-re nóbis. Quóni-

am tu só-lus sánctus. Tu só-lus Dómi-nus.

Tu só-lus Altíssi-mus, Jésu Chrí- ste. Cum Sáncto

Spí-ri-tu, in gló-ri- a Dé- i Pá- tris. A- men.

XII cent.

1. S An- ctus, Sán- ctus, Sán- ctus Dómi-

nus Dé- us Sá- ba- oth. Pléni sunt caé- li

et térra gló-ri- a tú- a. Ho- sánna in ex-

cél- sis. Be- nedí- ctus qui vé-nit in

nómine Dó- mi-ni. Ho- sánna in excél- sis.

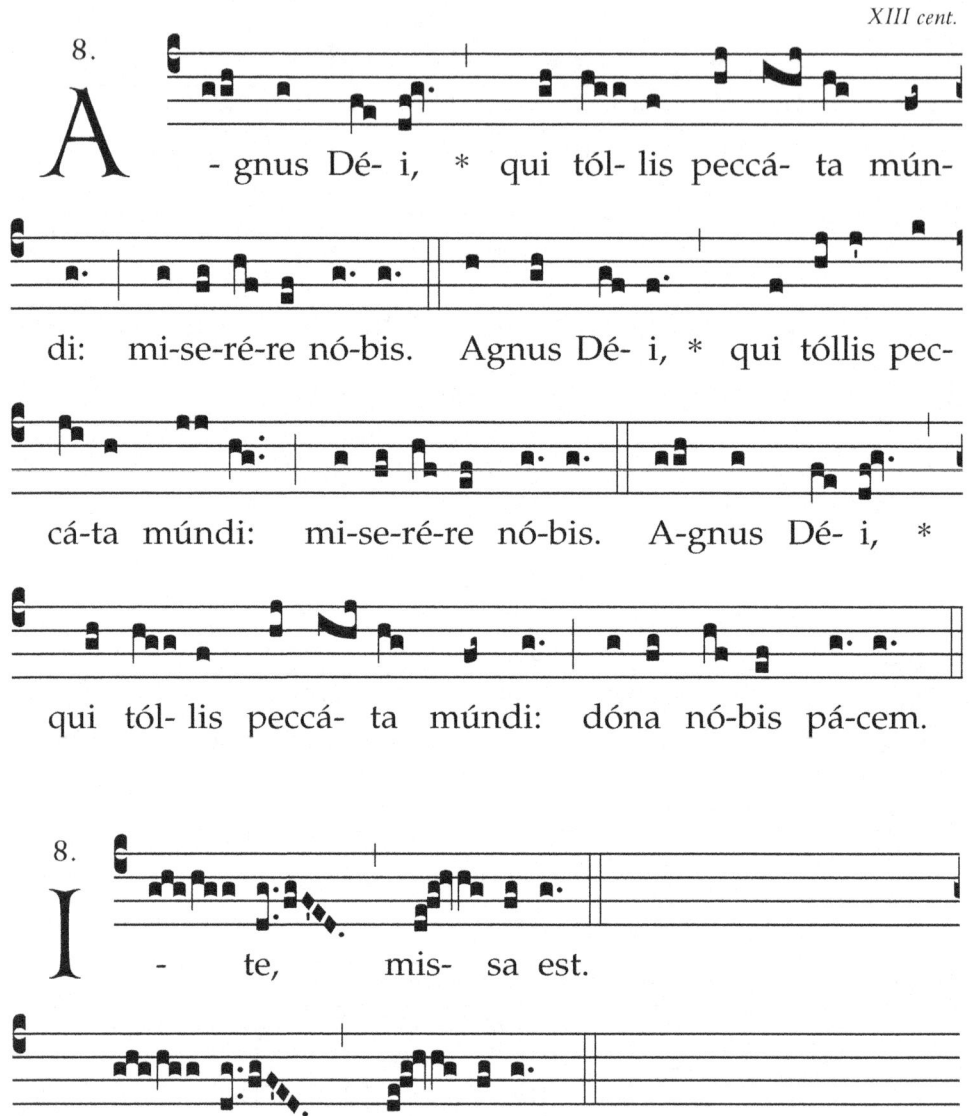

XIII *cent.*

8.

A - gnus Dé- i, * qui tól- lis peccá- ta mún-

di: mi-se-ré-re nó-bis. Agnus Dé- i, * qui tóllis pec-

cá-ta múndi: mi-se-ré-re nó-bis. A-gnus Dé- i, *

qui tól- lis peccá- ta múndi: dóna nó-bis pá-cem.

8.

I - te, mis- sa est.

℟. De- o, grá- ti- as.

XV. – *Dominator Deus.*

XI-XIII *cent.*

4.

KYri-e * e-lé-i-son. Ky-ri-e e-lé-i-son. Ky-ri-e e-lé-i-son. Chríste e-lé-i-son.

Chrí-ste e-lé-i-son. Chríste e-lé-i-son. Ký-ri-e e-lé-i-son. Ký-ri-e e-lé-i-son. Ký-ri-e * e-lé-i-son.

X *cent.*

4.

GLóri-a in excélsis Dé-o. Et in térra pax homí-nibus bónae vo-luntá-tis. Laudámus te. Bene-

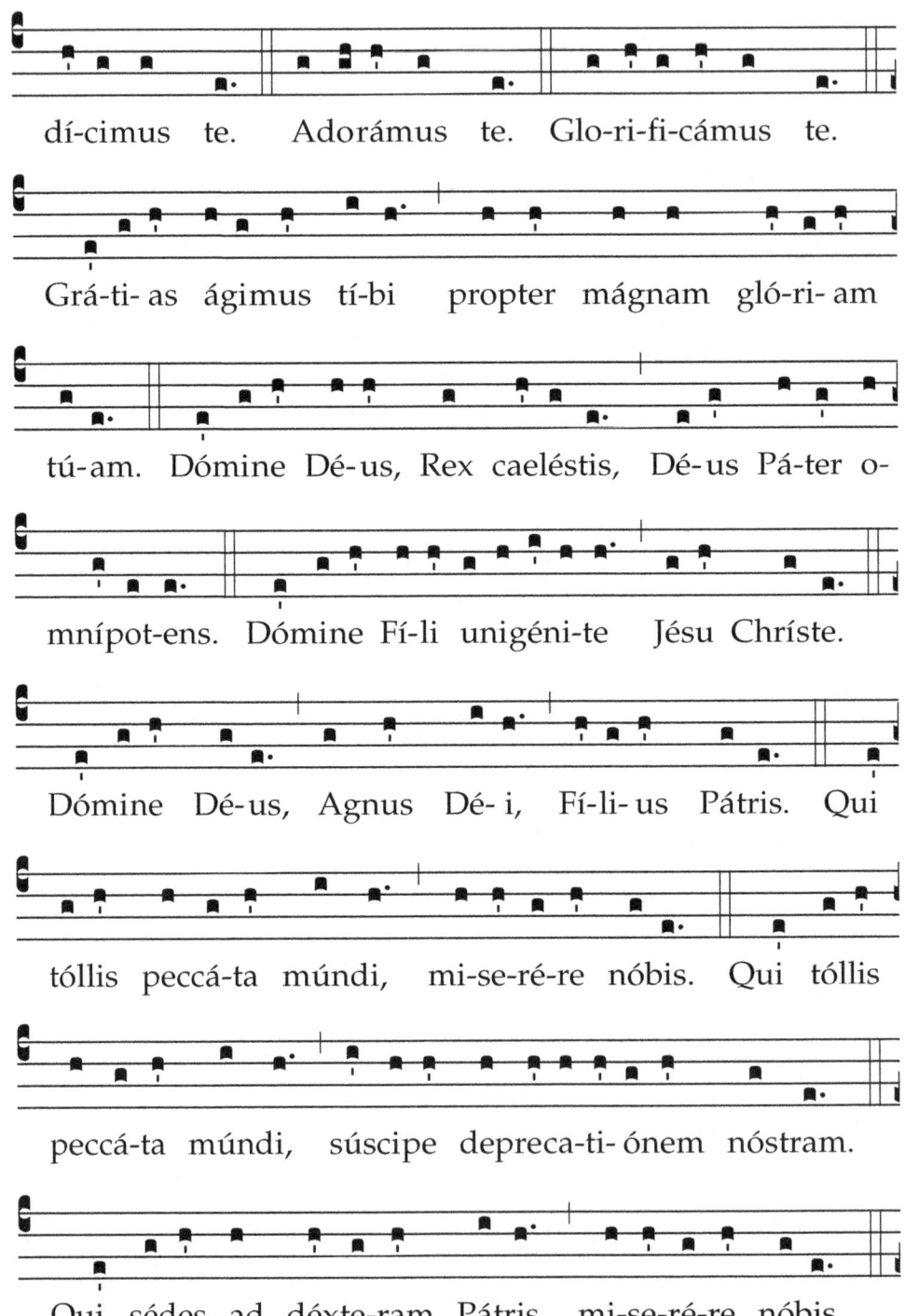

dí-cimus te.   Adorámus te.   Glo-ri-fi-cámus te.

Grá-ti- as ágimus tí-bi   propter mágnam gló-ri- am

tú-am.   Dómine Dé-us, Rex caeléstis,   Dé-us Pá-ter o-

mnípot-ens.   Dómine Fí-li unigéni-te   Jésu Chríste.

Dómine Dé-us, Agnus Dé- i,   Fí-li- us Pátris.   Qui

tóllis peccá-ta múndi,   mi-se-ré-re nóbis.   Qui tóllis

peccá-ta múndi,   súscipe depreca-ti- ónem nóstram.

Qui sédes ad déxte-ram Pátris, mi-se-ré-re nóbis.

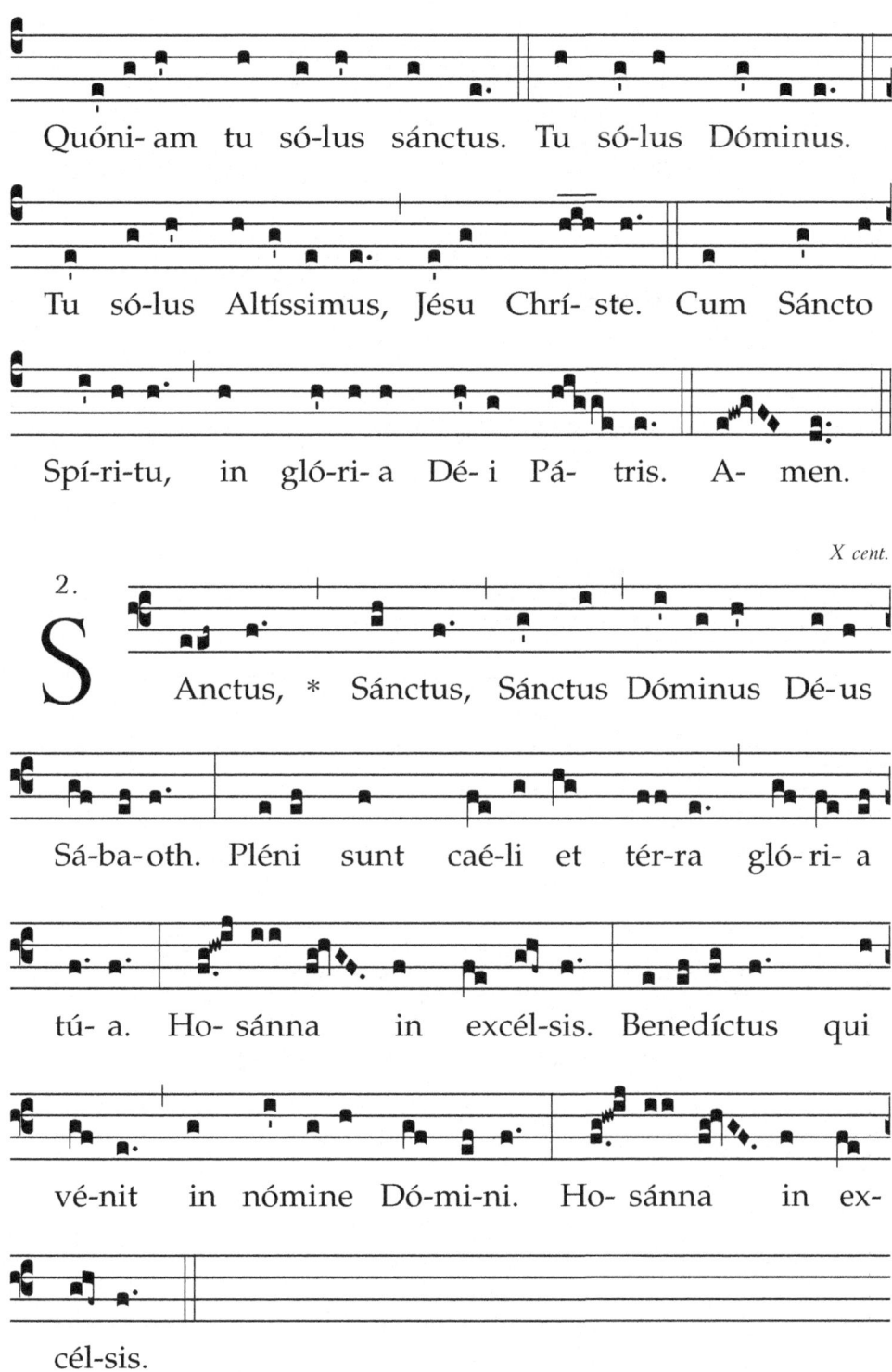

Quóni- am tu só-lus sánctus. Tu só-lus Dóminus.

Tu só-lus Altíssimus, Jésu Chrí- ste. Cum Sáncto

Spí-ri-tu, in gló-ri- a Dé- i Pá- tris. A- men.

X cent.

2.

S Anctus, * Sánctus, Sánctus Dóminus Dé-us

Sá-ba- oth. Pléni sunt caé-li et tér-ra gló- ri- a

tú- a. Ho- sánna in excél-sis. Benedíctus qui

vé-nit in nómine Dó-mi-ni. Ho- sánna in ex-

cél-sis.

(XII) XIV cent.

1.

Agnus Dé- i, * qui tóllis peccá-ta múndi:

mi-se-ré-re nó- bis.   Agnus Dé- i, * qui tól- lis pec-

cá-ta múndi: mi-se-ré- re nó- bis.   Agnus

Dé- i, * qui tóllis peccá-ta múndi: dóna nó-bis

pá- cem.

4.

I-te, mis-sa est.   ℟. De-o grá-ti-as.

This tone may be used ad libitum *for all Masses where* Ite, missa est *is sung without* allelúja.

XVI. – *In feriis per annum.*

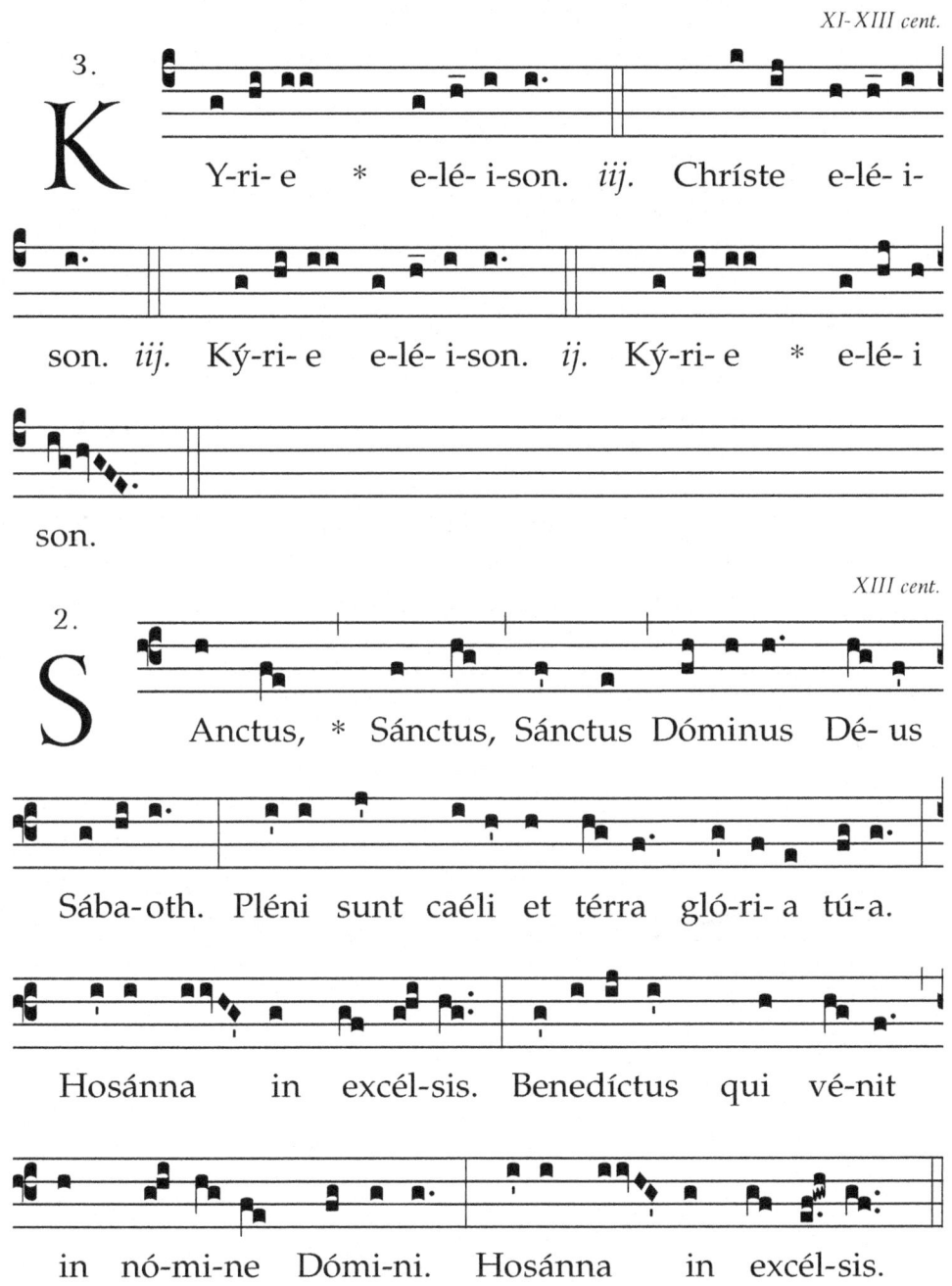

XI-XIII cent.

3.

KY-ri- e * e-lé- i-son. *iij.* Chríste e-lé- i-

son. *iij.* Ký-ri- e e-lé- i-son. *ij.* Ký-ri- e * e-lé- i

son.

XIII cent.

2.

SAnctus, * Sánctus, Sánctus Dóminus Dé- us

Sába-oth. Pléni sunt caéli et térra gló-ri- a tú-a.

Hosánna in excél-sis. Benedíctus qui vé-nit

in nó-mi-ne Dómi-ni. Hosánna in excél-sis.

X-XI cent.

1. Agnus Dé- i, * qui tóllis peccá-ta mún-di: mi-se-ré-re nó- bis. Agnus Dé- i, * qui tóllis peccá-ta múndi: mi-se-ré-re nó-bis. Agnus Dé-i, * qui tóllis peccá-ta mún- di: dóna nó-bis pá- cem.

4. —te, mis-sa est. ℞. De–o grá–ti–as.

XVII. – *In dominicis Adventus et Quadragesimæ.*

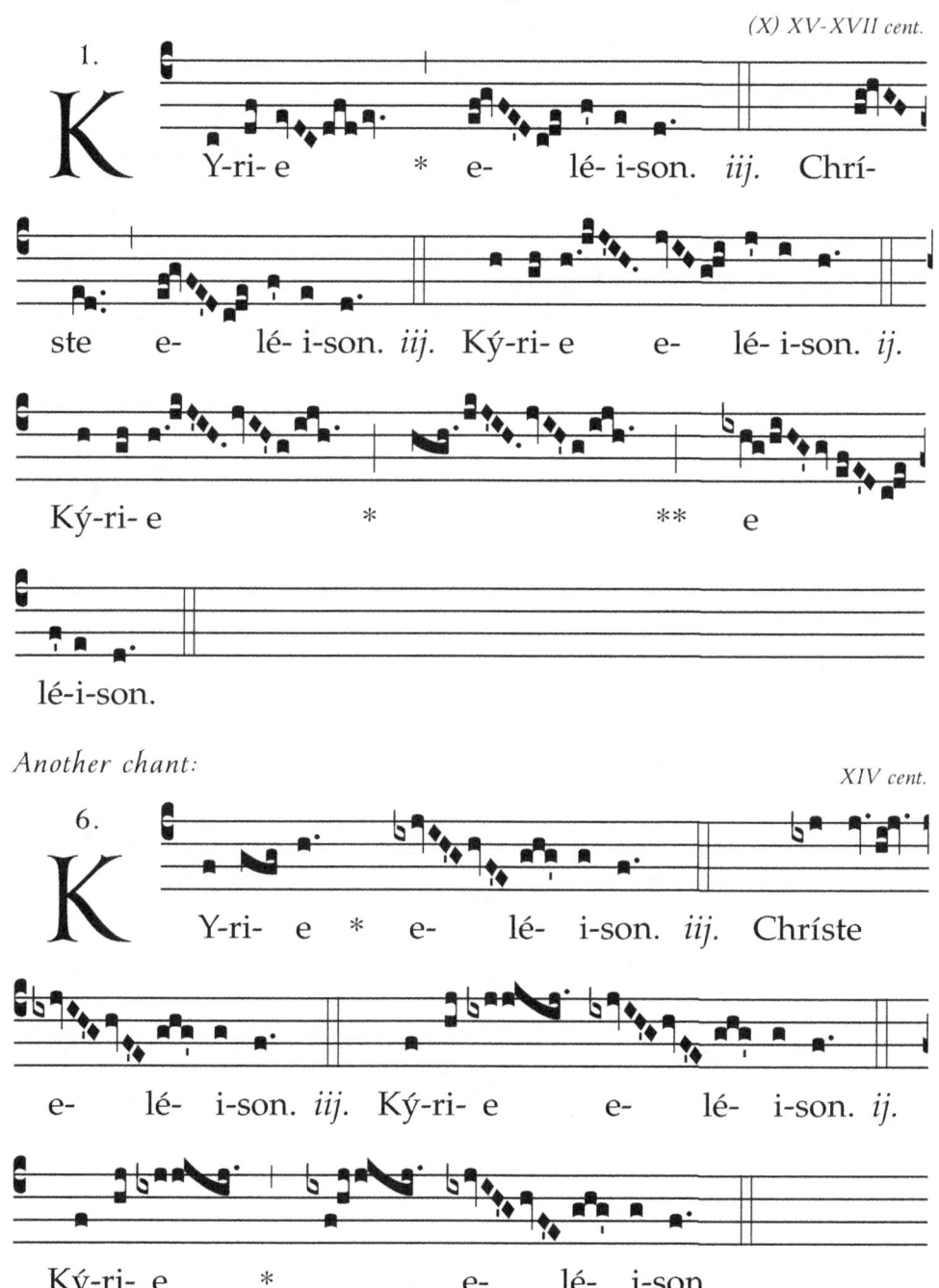

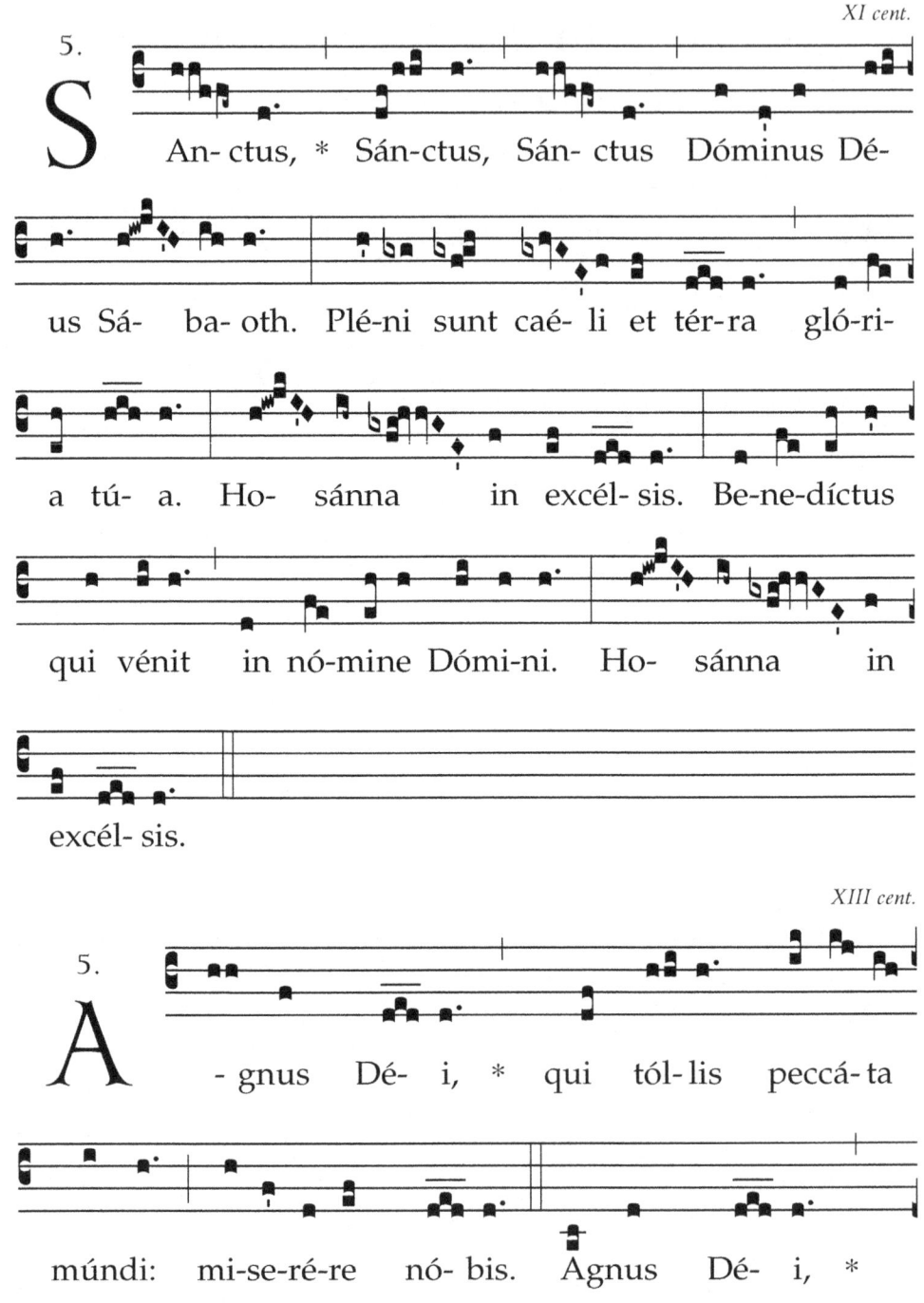

XI cent.

5.
SAn-ctus, * Sán-ctus, Sán- ctus Dóminus Dé-
us Sá- ba- oth. Plé-ni sunt caé- li et tér-ra gló-ri-
a tú- a. Ho- sánna in excél- sis. Be-ne-díctus
qui vénit in nó-mine Dómi-ni. Ho- sánna in
excél- sis.

XIII cent.

5.
A - gnus Dé- i, * qui tól- lis peccá- ta
múndi: mi-se-ré-re nó- bis. Agnus Dé- i, *

qui tól- lis peccá- ta múndi: mi-se-ré-re nó- bis.

A-gnus Dé- i, * qui tól- lis peccá- ta múndi: dóna

nóbis pá- cem.

4.

I —te, mis-sa est. ℟. De–o grá–ti–as.

XVIII. – *Deus Genitor alme.*

In feriis Adventus et Quadragesimæ.

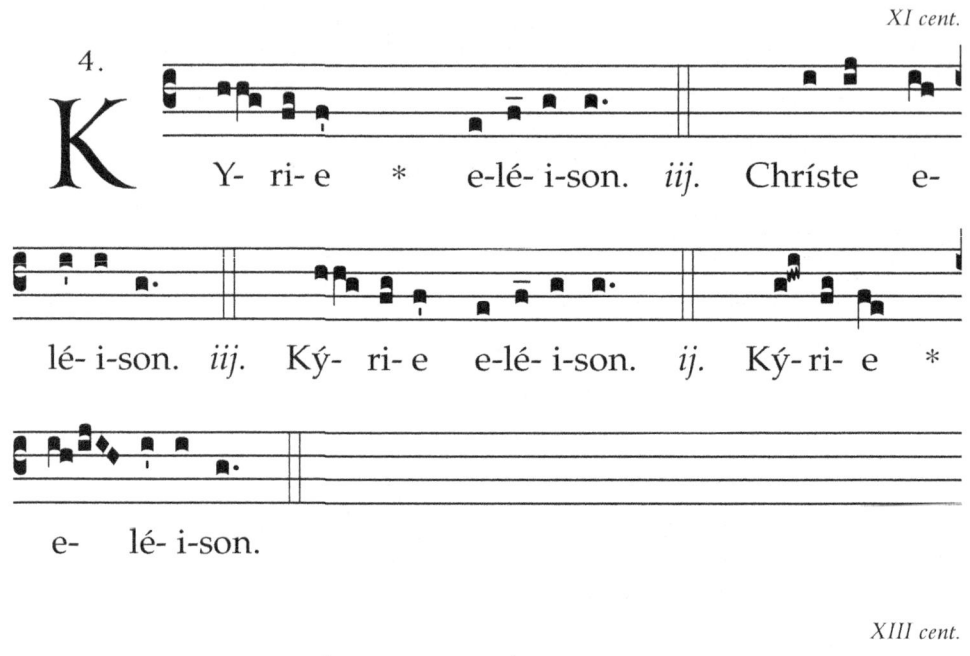

XI cent.

4.

K Y- ri- e * e-lé- i-son. *iij.* Chríste e-

lé- i-son. *iij.* Ký- ri- e e-lé- i-son. *ij.* Ký-ri- e *

e- lé- i-son.

XIII cent.

S Anctus, * Sánctus, Sánctus Dóminus Dé-us

Sába-oth. Pléni sunt caéli et térra gló-ri- a tú-a.

Hosánna in excélsis. Benedíctus qui vénit in nómine

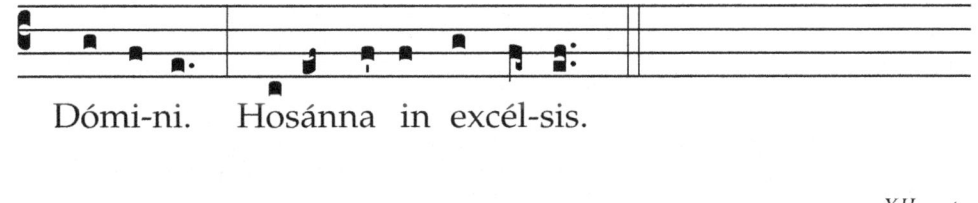

Dómi-ni.   Hosánna in excél-sis.

XII cent.

A gnus Dé- i, * qui tóllis peccá-ta múndi:

mi-se-ré-re nó-bis.   Agnus Dé- i, * qui tóllis pec-

cá-ta múndi: mi-se-ré-re nó-bis.   Agnus Dé- i, *

qui tóllis peccá-ta múndi: dóna nóbis pá-cem.

From the Vatican Edition of the Kyriale (1905):

¶ Qualislibet cantus hujus Ordinarii superius
in una Missa positus adhiberi potest etiam in
alia, feriis tamen exceptis.

*¶ This Ordinary is not meant to be a matter of hard
and fast rule: chants from one Mass may be used
together with those from others, the Ferial Masses
excepted.*

I. – *Credo.*

XI cent.

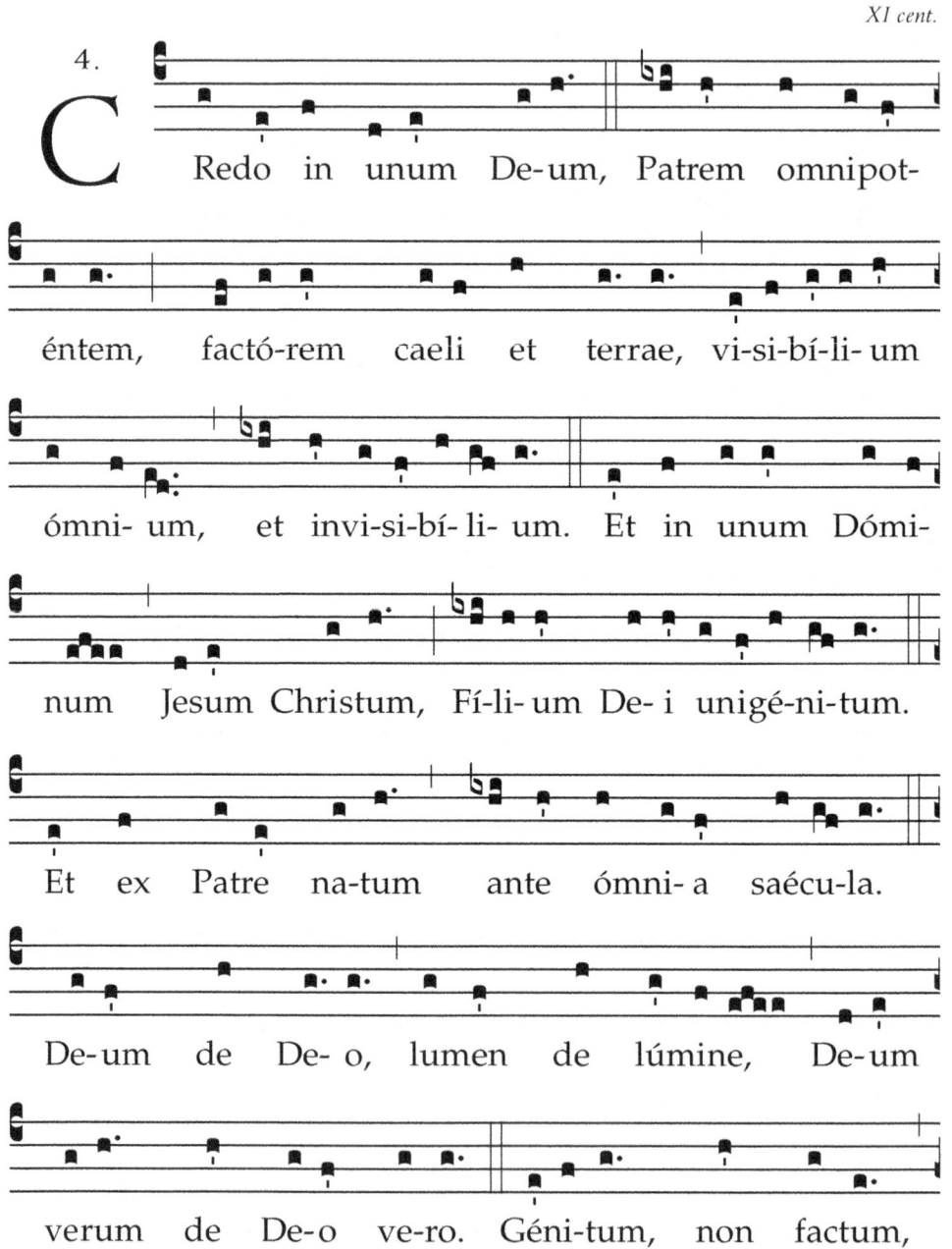

4.

C Redo in unum De-um, Patrem omnipot-

éntem, factó-rem caeli et terrae, vi-si-bí-li- um

ómni- um, et invi-si-bí- li- um. Et in unum Dómi-

num Jesum Christum, Fí-li- um De- i unigé-ni-tum.

Et ex Patre na-tum ante ómni- a saécu-la.

De-um de De- o, lumen de lúmine, De-um

verum de De-o ve-ro. Géni-tum, non factum,

consubstanti- á-lem Patri: per quem ómni- a facta

sunt. Qui propter nos hómines et propter nostram

sa-lú-tem descéndit de cae-lis. Et incarná-tus est

de Spí-ri-tu Sancto ex Ma-rí- a Vírgi-ne: Et

homo factus est. Cru-ci-fíxus ét-i- am pro nobis:

sub Pónti- o Pi-lá-to passus, et sepúltus est.

Et resurré-xit térti- a di- e, secúndum Scriptúras.

Et ascéndit in caelum: sedet ad déxte-ram

Patris. Et í-terum ventúrus est cum gló-ri- a,

judi-cá-re vivos et mórtu- os: cu-jus regni non e-rit

fi-nis. Et in Spí-ri-tum Sanctum, Dómi-num, et

vi-vi-fi-cántem: qui ex Patre Fi-li- óque procé-dit.

Qui cum Patre et Fí-li- o simul adorá-tur, et

conglo-ri-fi-cá-tur: qui locútus est per Prophé-tas.

Et unam sanctam cathó-li-cam et apostó-li-cam

Ecclé-si- am. Confí-te- or unum baptísma in remis-

si- ónem pecca-tó-rum. Et exspécto resurrecti- ónem

mortu-ó-rum. Et vi-tam ventú-ri saé-cu-li.

A- men.

¶ *In place of the foregoing original chant, the following may be used.*

II. – *Credo.*

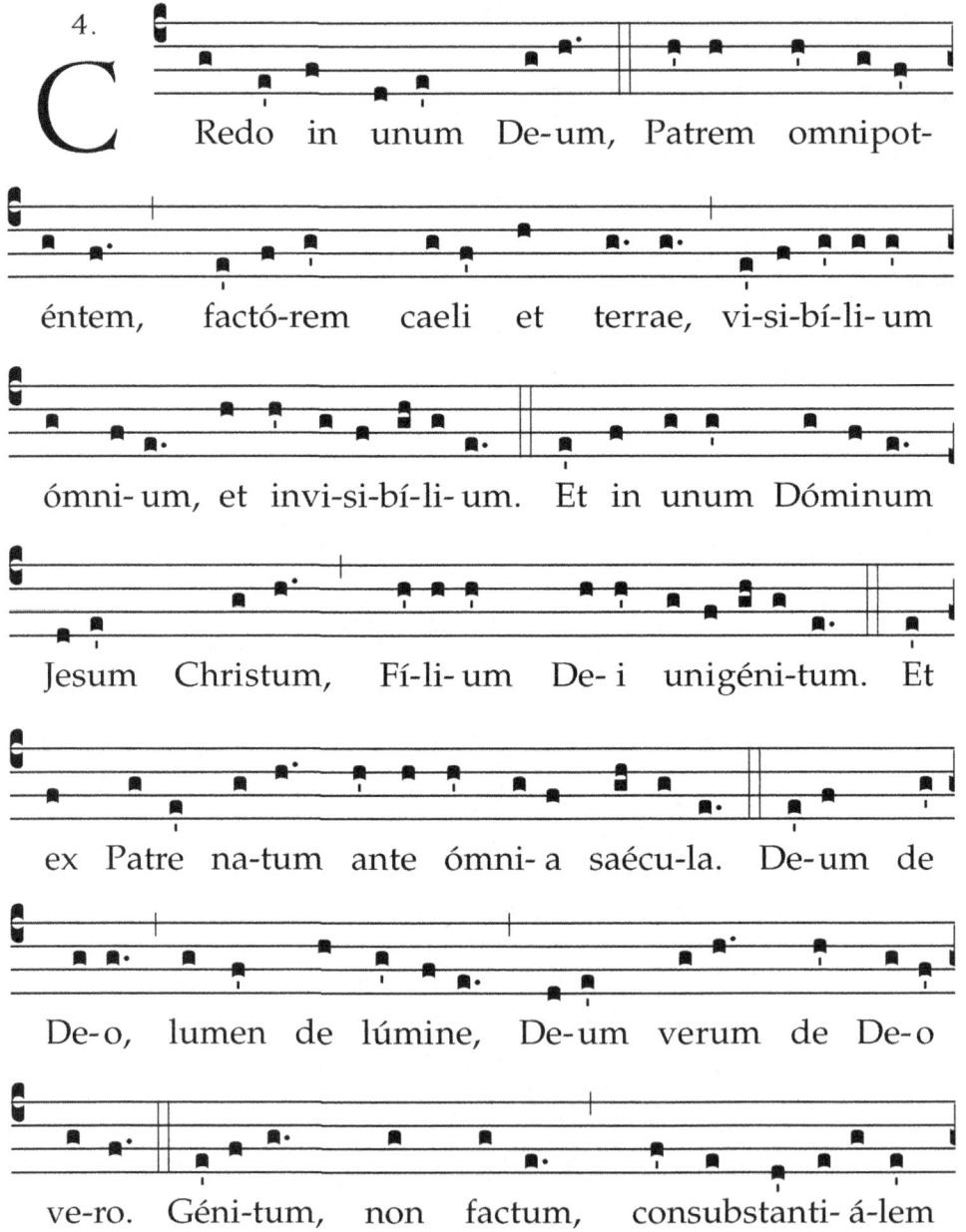

4.

CRedo in unum De-um, Patrem omnipot-

éntem, factó-rem caeli et terrae, vi-si-bí-li- um

ómni- um, et invi-si-bí-li- um. Et in unum Dóminum

Jesum Christum, Fí-li- um De- i unigéni-tum. Et

ex Patre na-tum ante ómni- a saécu-la. De-um de

De-o, lumen de lúmine, De-um verum de De-o

ve-ro. Géni-tum, non factum, consubstanti- á-lem

Patri: per quem ómni- a facta sunt. Qui propter nos

hómines, et propter nostram sa-lú-tem descéndit de

cae-lis. Et incarná-tus est de Spí-ri-tu Sancto ex

Ma-rí- a Vírgine: Et homo factus est. Cru-ci-fíxus

ét-i- am pro nobis: sub Pónti- o Pi-lá-to passus,

et sepúltus est. Et resurré-xit térti- a di- e,

secúndum Scriptúras. Et ascéndit in caelum:

sedet ad déxte-ram Patris. Et í-terum ventúrus

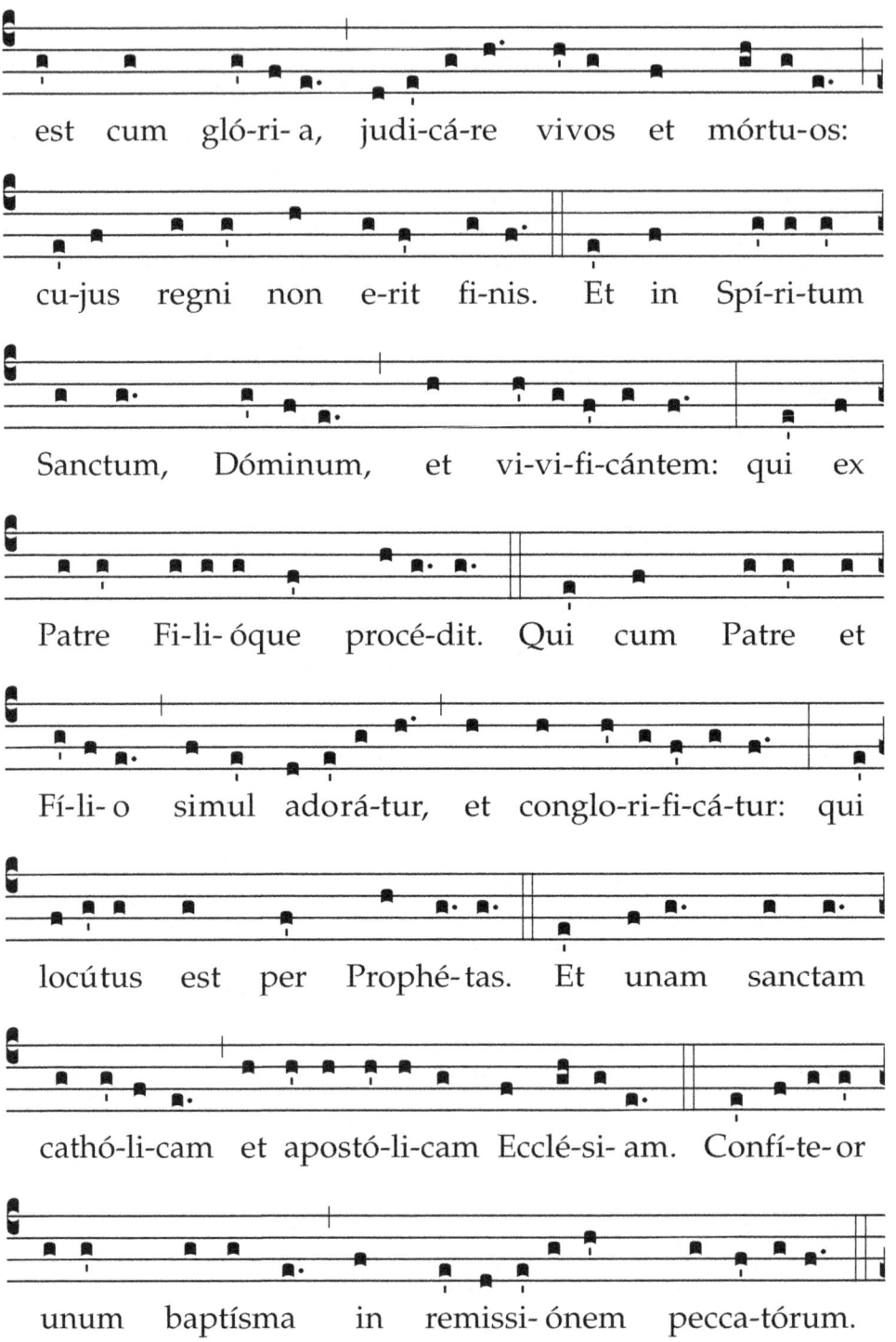

est cum gló-ri- a, judi-cá-re vivos et mórtu-os:

cu-jus regni non e-rit fi-nis. Et in Spí-ri-tum

Sanctum, Dóminum, et vi-vi-fi-cántem: qui ex

Patre Fi-li- óque procé-dit. Qui cum Patre et

Fí-li- o simul adorá-tur, et conglo-ri-fi-cá-tur: qui

locútus est per Prophé- tas. Et unam sanctam

cathó-li-cam et apostó-li-cam Ecclé-si- am. Confí-te- or

unum baptísma in remissi- ónem pecca-tórum.

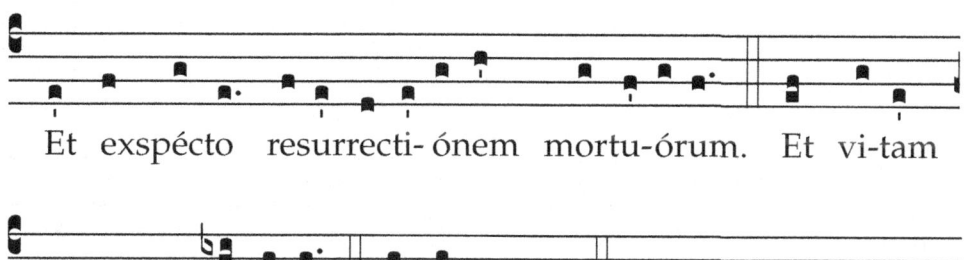

Et exspécto resurrecti- ónem mortu-órum. Et vi-tam

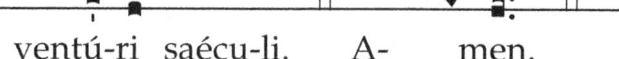

ventú-ri saécu-li. A- men.

III. — *Credo.*

XVII cent.

5. **C**Redo in unum De- um, Patrem omnipot-

éntem, factó-rem caeli et terrae, vi-si-bí-li-um

ó- mni-um, et invi-si-bí- li-um. Et in unum Dómi-

num Je-sum Christum, Fí-li-um De-i unigéni-tum.

Et ex Patre na- tum ante ómni-a saé-cu-la. De-um

de De-o, lumen de lúmine, De-um verum de De-o

ve-ro. Géni-tum, non fac-tum, consubstanti- á-lem

Patri: per quem ómni- a facta sunt. Qui propter nos

hómines, et propter nostram sa-lú-tem descéndit de

caelis. Et incarná-tus est de Spí-ri-tu Sancto ex

Ma-rí- a Vírgine: Et homo factus est. Cru-ci-fí- xus

ét-i- am pro nobis: sub Pónti- o Pi-lá-to passus,

et sepúl- tus est. Et resurré-xit térti- a di-e,

secúndum Scriptú-ras. Et ascéndit in cae- lum:

sedet ad déxte-ram Pa- tris. Et í-terum ventúrus

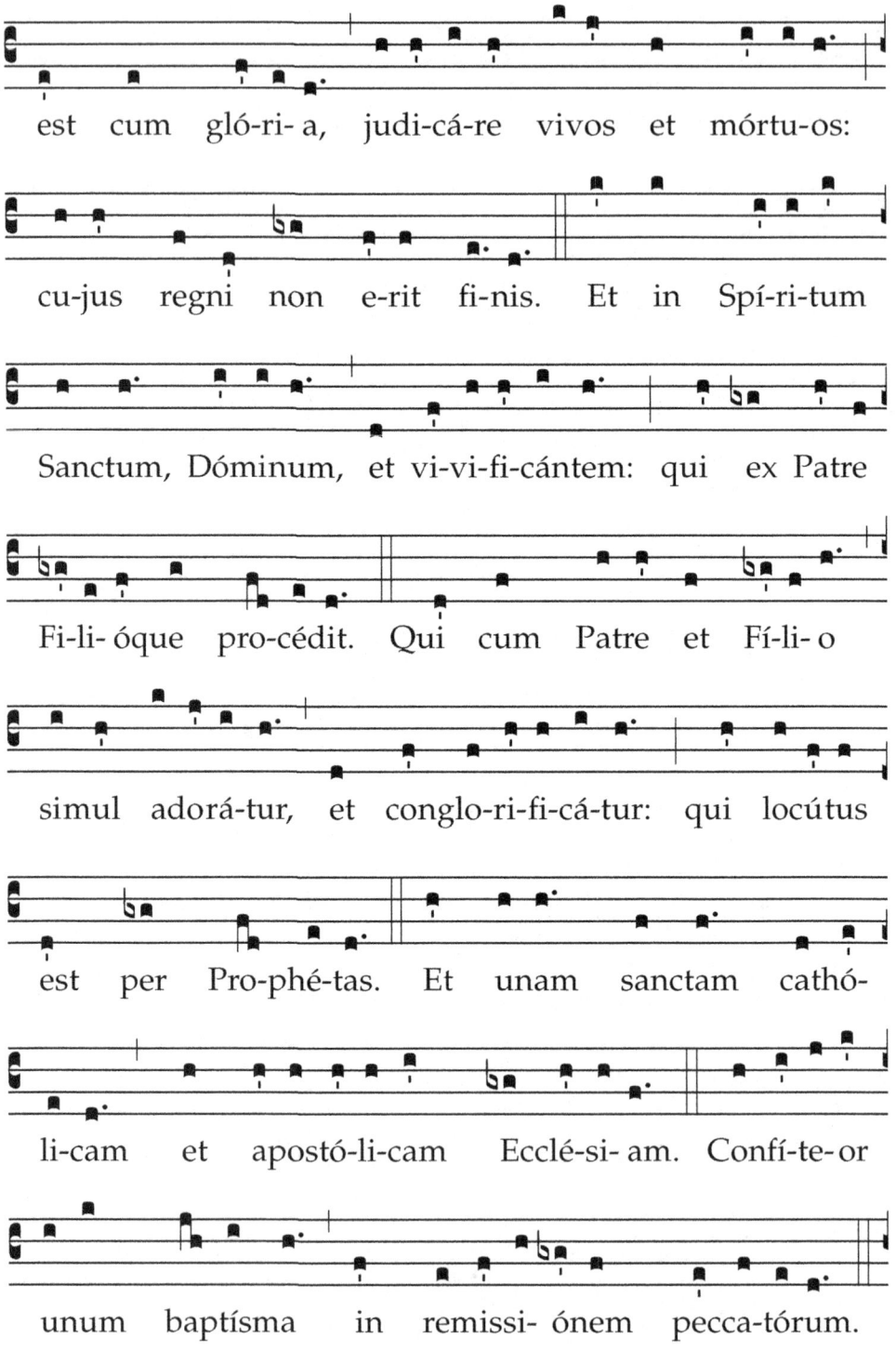

est cum gló-ri- a, judi-cá-re vivos et mórtu-os:

cu-jus regni non e-rit fi-nis. Et in Spí-ri-tum

Sanctum, Dóminum, et vi-vi-fi-cántem: qui ex Patre

Fi-li- óque pro-cédit. Qui cum Patre et Fí-li- o

simul adorá-tur, et conglo-ri-fi-cá-tur: qui locútus

est per Pro-phé-tas. Et unam sanctam cathó-

li-cam et apostó-li-cam Ecclé-si- am. Confí-te-or

unum baptísma in remissi- ónem pecca-tórum.

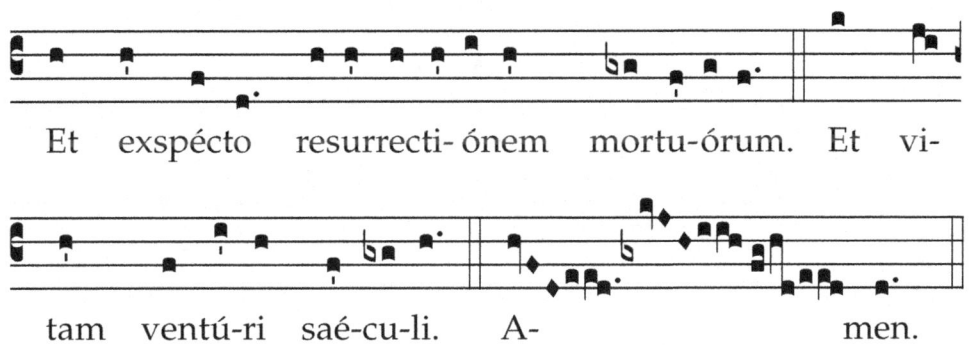

Et exspécto resurrecti- ónem mortu-órum. Et vi-

tam ventú-ri saé-cu-li. A- men.

ET ITERUM VENTURUS EST CUM GLORIA

CREDO IN DEUM

NON SERVIAM

IV. – Credo.

XV cent.

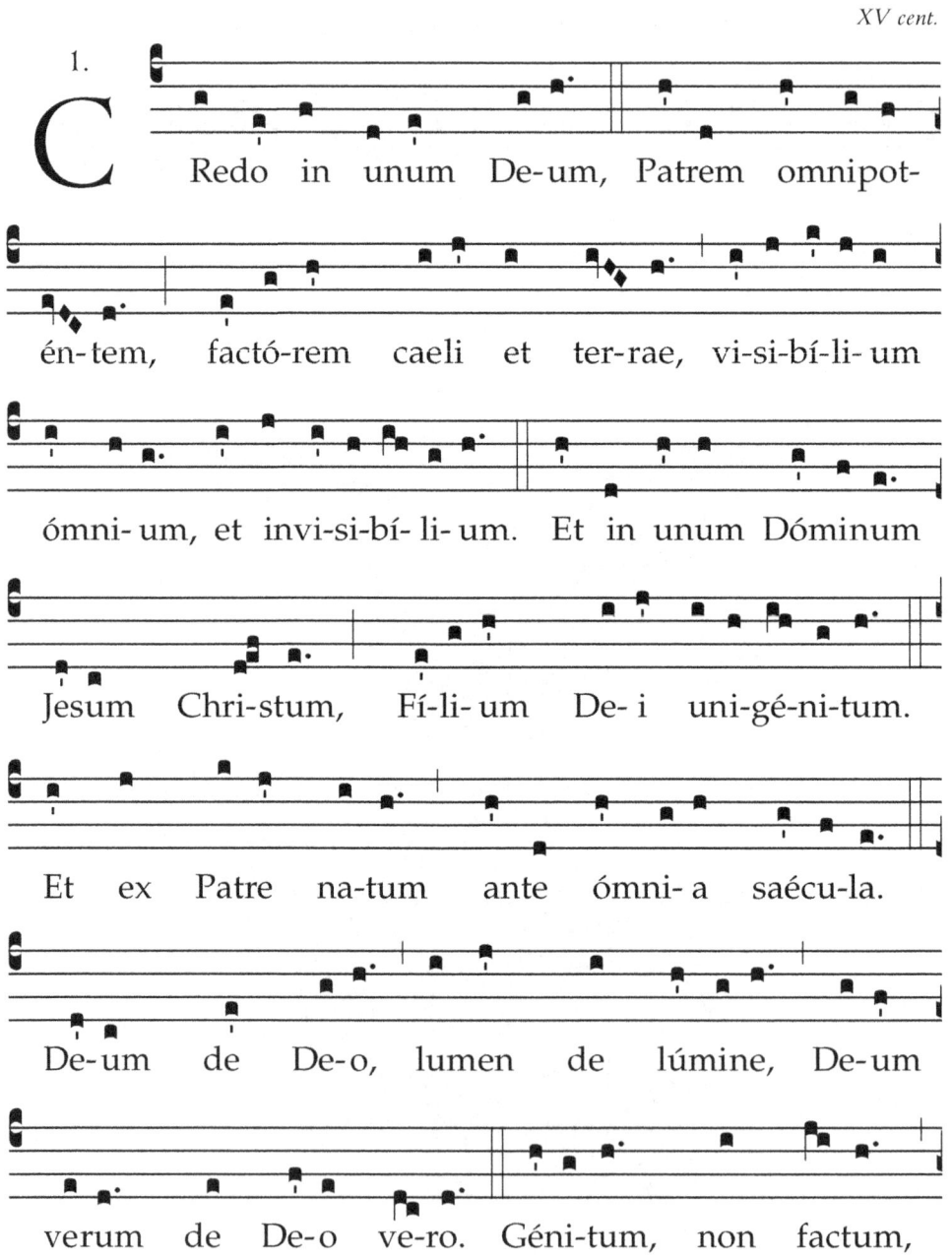

1.

Credo in unum De-um, Patrem omnipot-

én-tem, factó-rem caeli et ter-rae, vi-si-bí-li- um

ómni- um, et invi-si-bí- li- um. Et in unum Dóminum

Jesum Chri-stum, Fí-li- um De- i uni-gé-ni-tum.

Et ex Patre na-tum ante ómni- a saécu-la.

De-um de De-o, lumen de lúmine, De-um

verum de De-o ve-ro. Géni-tum, non factum,

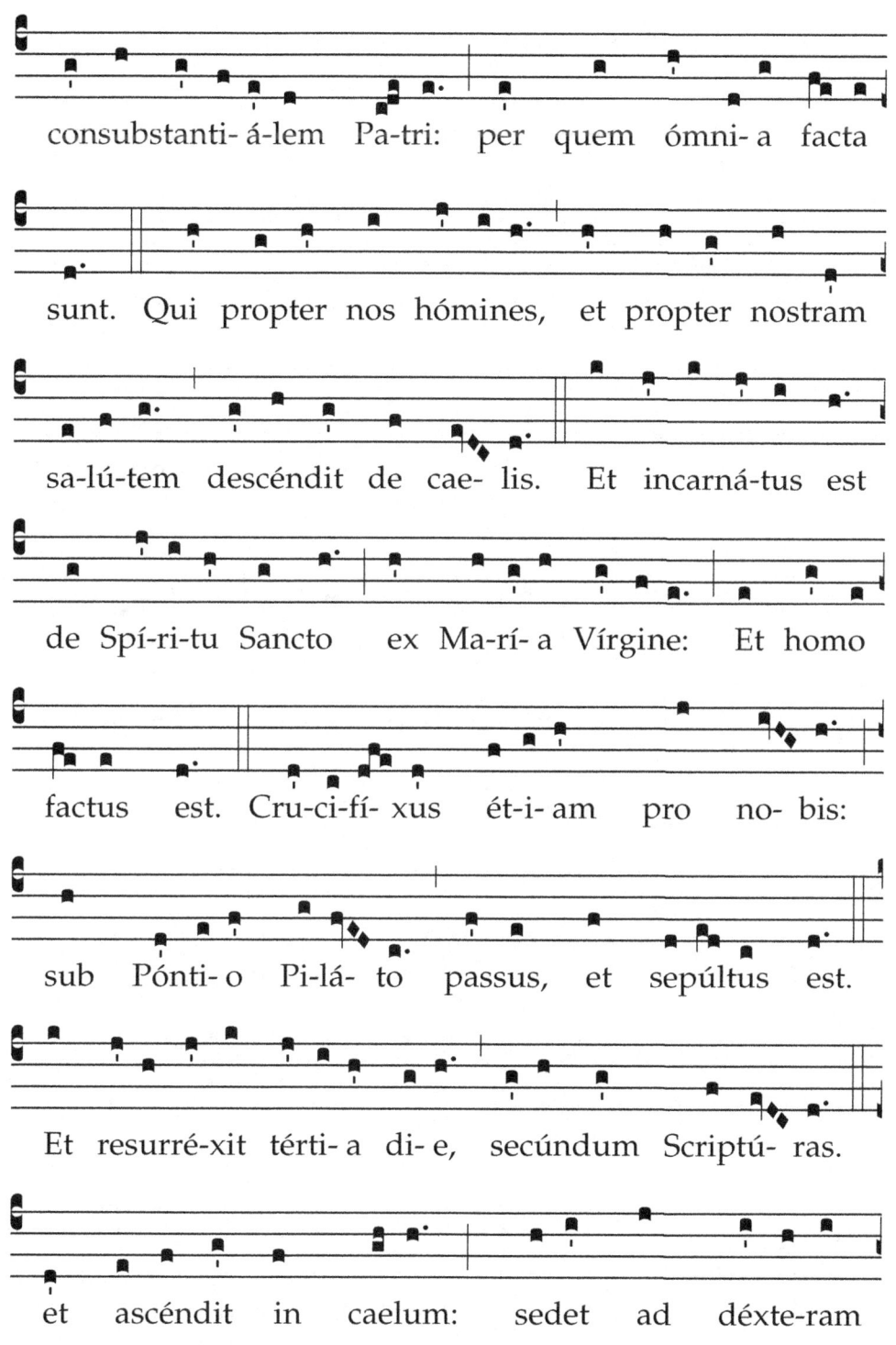

consubstanti- á-lem Pa-tri: per quem ómni- a facta

sunt. Qui propter nos hómines, et propter nostram

sa-lú-tem descéndit de cae- lis. Et incarná-tus est

de Spí-ri-tu Sancto ex Ma-rí- a Vírgine: Et homo

factus est. Cru-ci-fí- xus ét-i- am pro no- bis:

sub Pónti- o Pi-lá- to passus, et sepúltus est.

Et resurré-xit térti- a di- e, secúndum Scriptú- ras.

et ascéndit in caelum: sedet ad déxte-ram

Patris. Et í-terum ventúrus est cum gló-ri- a,

judi-cá- re vivos et mórtu-os: cu-jus regni non e-rit

fi-nis. Et in Spí-ri-tum Sanctum, Dóminum, et

vi-vi-fi-cántem: qui ex Patre Fi-li- óque pro-cé-dit.

Qui cum Patre et Fí-li- o simul adorá-tur, et

conglo-ri-fi-cá-tur: qui locútus est per Prophé-tas.

Et unam sanctam cathó-li-cam et apostó-li-cam

Ecclé-si- am. Confí-te- or unum baptísma in remis-

si- ónem pecca-tó- rum. Et exspécto resurrecti- ónem
mortu-ó- rum. Et vi-tam ventú-ri saécu-li. A-
men.

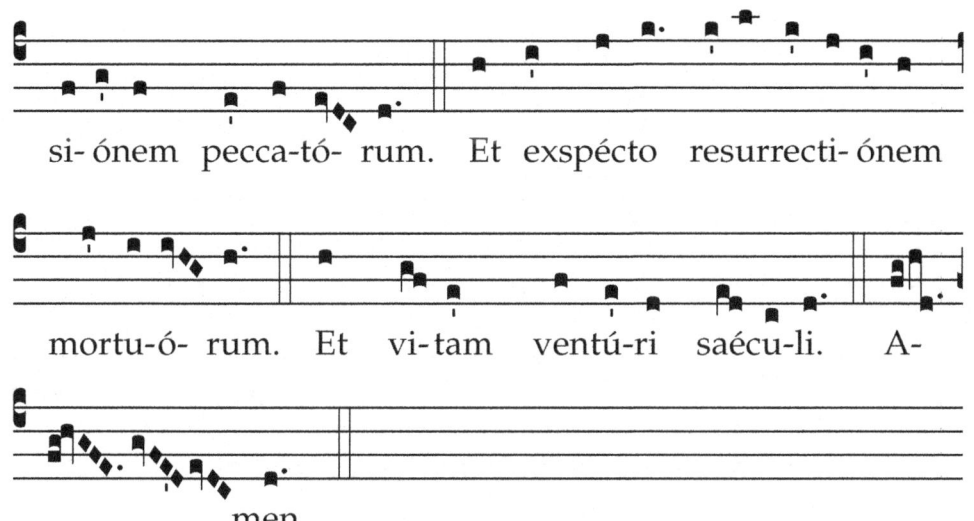

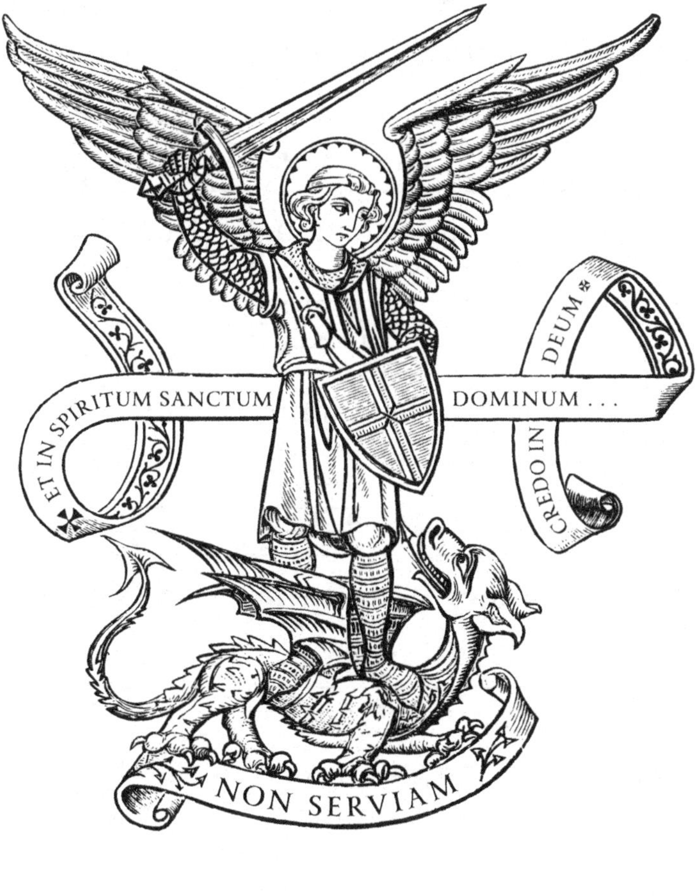
ET IN SPIRITUM SANCTUM
DOMINUM . . .
CREDO IN DEUM
NON SERVIAM

V. – *Credo.*

XII cent.

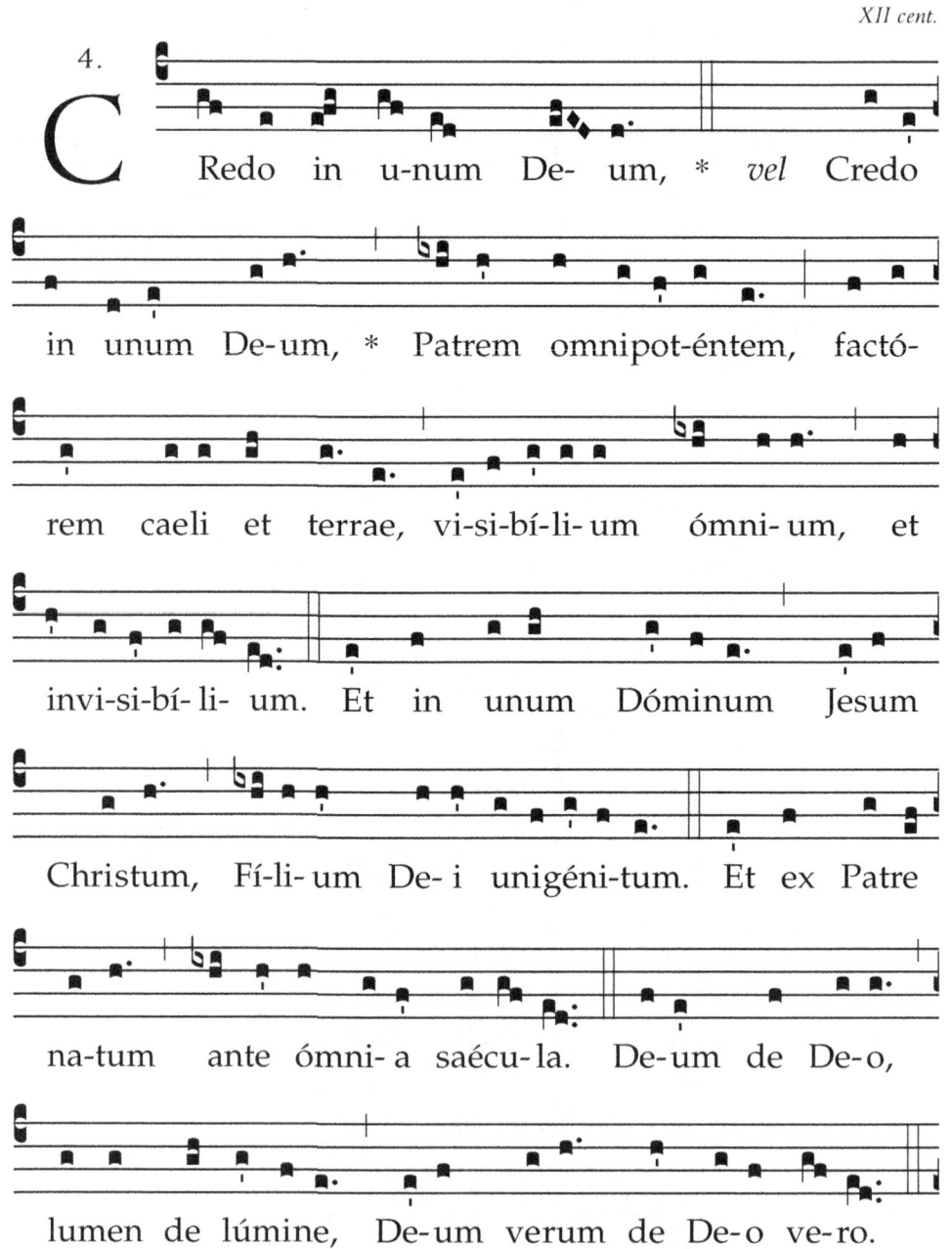

4.

CRedo in u-num De- um, * *vel* Credo

in unum De-um, * Patrem omnipot-éntem, factó-

rem caeli et terrae, vi-si-bí-li- um ómni- um, et

invi-si-bí- li- um. Et in unum Dóminum Jesum

Christum, Fí-li- um De- i unigéni-tum. Et ex Patre

na-tum ante ómni- a saécu- la. De-um de De-o,

lumen de lúmine, De-um verum de De-o ve-ro.

Géni-tum, non factum, consubstanti- á-lem Patri:

per quem ómni- a facta sunt. Qui propter nos

hómines, et propter nostram sa-lú-tem descéndit de

cae-lis. Et incarná-tus est de Spí-ri-tu Sancto ex

Ma-rí- a Vírgi-ne: Et ho-mo factus est. Cru-ci-fíxus

ét-i- am pro nobis: sub Pónti- o Pi-lá-to passus,

et sepúltus est. Et resurré-xit térti- a di- e,

secúndum Scriptú-ras. et ascéndit in caelum:

sedet ad déxte-ram Patris. Et í-terum ventúrus

est cum gló-ri- a, judi-cá-re vivos et mórtu- os:

cu-jus regni non e-rit fi- nis. Et in Spí-ri-tum

Sanctum, Dóminum, et vi-vi-ficántem: qui ex Patre

Fi-li- óque pro-cé-dit. Qui cum Patre et Fí-li- o

simul adorá-tur, et conglo-ri-fi-cá- tur: qui locútus

est per Prophé- tas. Et unam sanctam cathó-li-cam

et apostó-li-cam Ecclé-si- am. Confí-te- or unum bap-

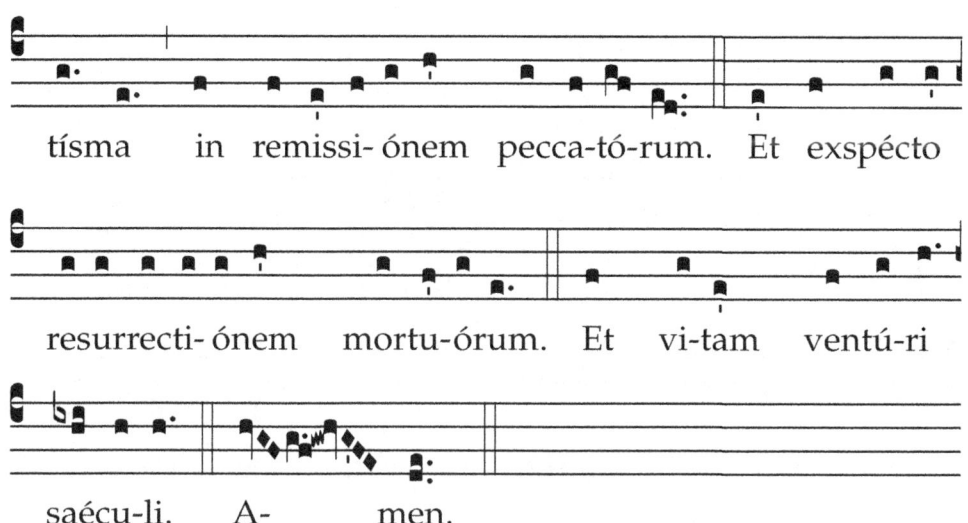

tísma   in   remissi- ónem   pecca-tó-rum.   Et   exspécto

resurrecti- ónem   mortu-órum.   Et   vi-tam   ventú-ri

saécu-li.   A-   men.

VI. – *Credo.*

XI cent.

4.

Redo in u-num De-um, * *vel* Credo in unum De-um * Patrem omnipot-én-tem, factó-rem cae-li et ter-rae, vi-si-bí-li- um ómni- um, et invi-si- bí- li- um. Et in u-num Dóminum Jesum Chri-stum, Fí-li- um De- i unigé-ni-tum. Et ex Pa-tre na-tum ante ómni- a saécu-la. De- um de De- o, lu-men de lúmine, De-um ve-rum de De-o ve- ro.

Géni-tum, non factum, consubstanti- á-lem Pa-tri:

per quem ómni- a facta sunt. Qui propter nos

hómines, et propter nostram sa-lú-tem descéndit

de cae- lis. Et incarná-tus est de Spí-ri-tu

Sancto ex Ma-rí- a Vírgi-ne: Et homo factus

est. Cru-ci- fí-xus ét-i- am pro no-bis: sub Pónti- o

Pi-lá-to passus, et sepúltus est. Et resurré-xit

térti- a di- e, secúndum Scriptú- ras. Et ascéndit

in cae-lum: sedet ad déxte-ram Pa- tris. Et í-terum

ventúrus est cum gló-ri- a, judi-cá-re vivos et

mórtu- os: cu-jus re-gni non e-rit fi- nis. Et in

Spí-ri-tum Sanctum, Dóminum, et vi-vi-fi-cán-tem:

qui ex Pa-tre Fi-li- ó-que procé- dit. Qui cum Pa-tre

et Fí-li- o simul ado-rá- tur, et conglo-ri-fi-cá- tur:

qui locútus est per Prophé- tas. Et u-nam sanctam

cathó-li-cam et apostó-li-cam Ecclé-si- am. Confí-te- or

u-num baptísma in remissi- ó-nem pecca-tó- rum.

Et exspécto resurrecti- ó-nem mortu-ó- rum. Et

vi- tam ventú-ri saécu-li. Amen.

Cantus ad libitum.

Orbis factor. *In dominicis per annum.*

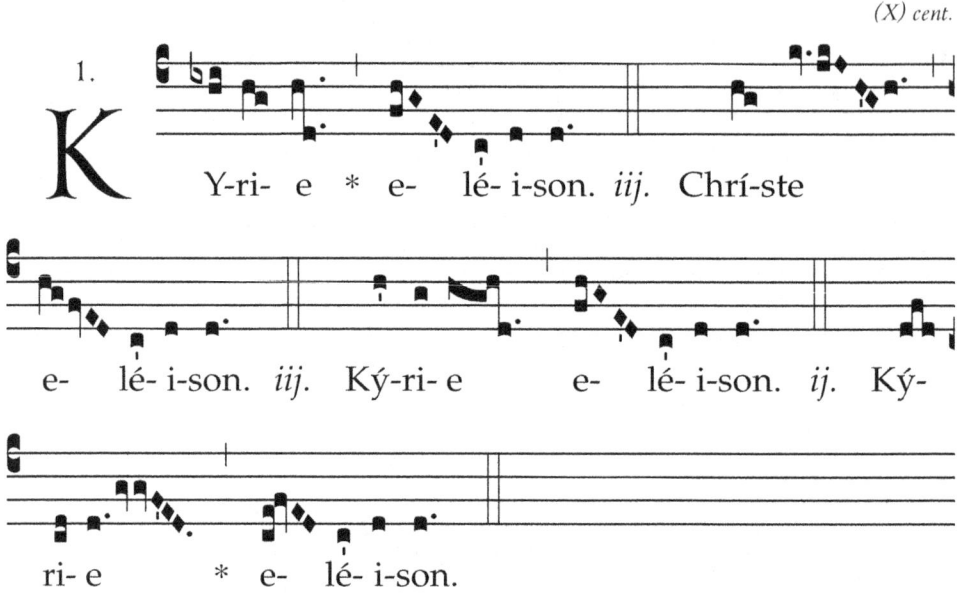

(X) cent.

1. KY-ri- e * e- lé- i-son. *iij.* Chrí-ste
e- lé- i-son. *iij.* Ký-ri- e e- lé- i-son. *ij.* Ký-
ri- e * e- lé- i-son.

Kyrie Salve. *In dominicis Adventus et Quadragesimæ.*

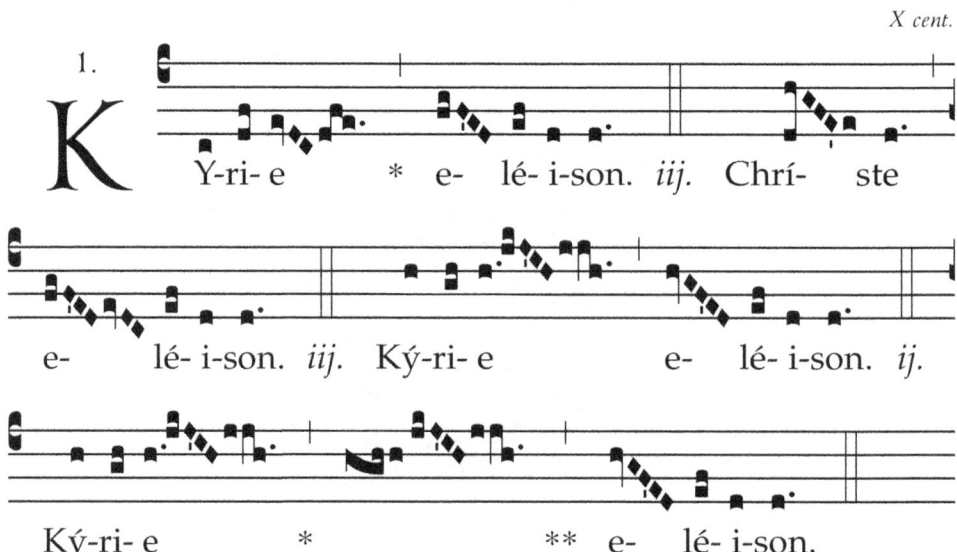

X cent.

1. KY-ri- e * e- lé- i-son. *iij.* Chrí- ste
e- lé- i-son. *iij.* Ký-ri- e e- lé- i-son. *ij.*
Ký-ri- e * ** e- lé- i-son.

Missa pro Defunctis.

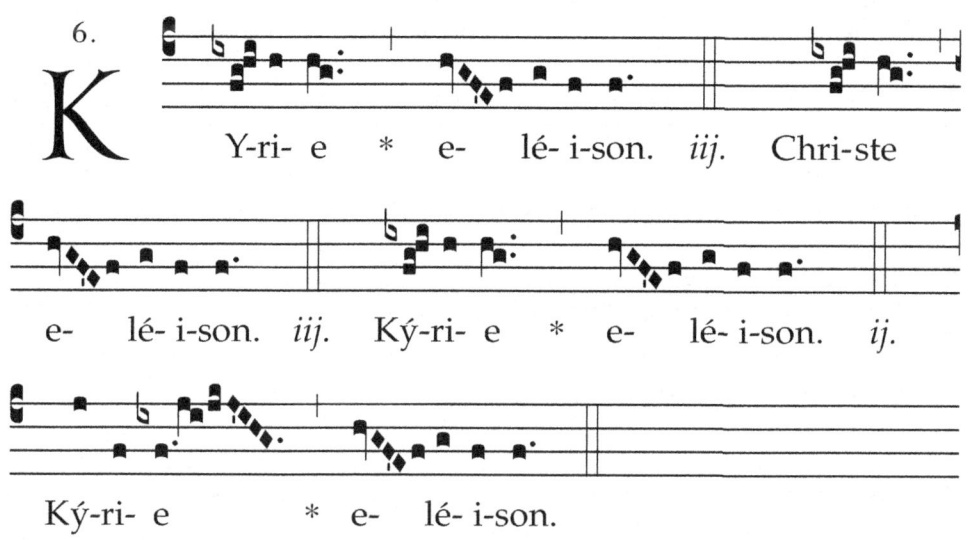

6.

K Y-ri- e * e- lé- i-son. *iij.* Chri-ste

e- lé- i-son. *iij.* Ký-ri- e * e- lé- i-son. *ij.*

Ký-ri- e * e- lé- i-son.

XIII cent.

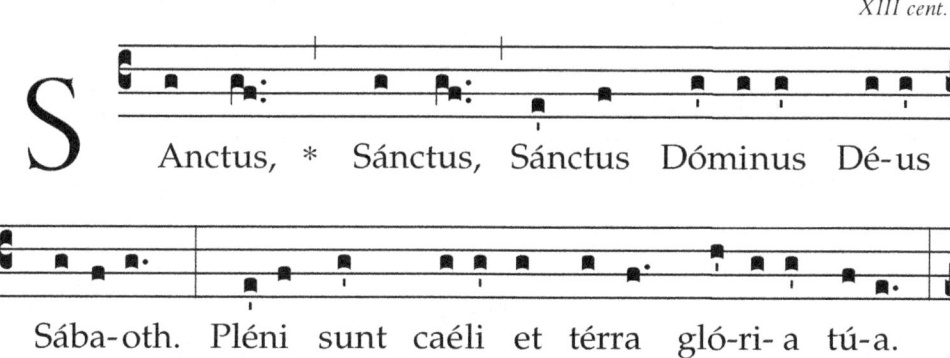

S Anctus, * Sánctus, Sánctus Dóminus Dé-us

Sába-oth. Pléni sunt caéli et térra gló-ri- a tú-a.

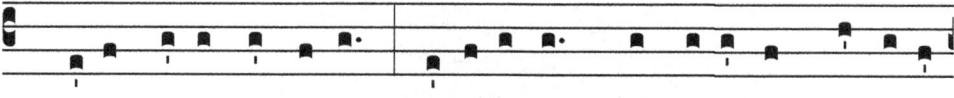

Hosánna in excélsis. Benedíctus qui vénit in nómine

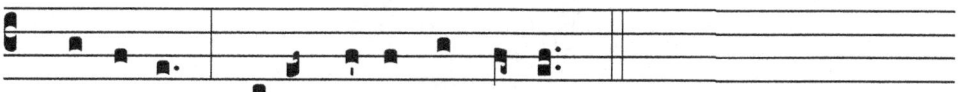

Dómi-ni. Hosánna in excél-sis.

A gnus Dé- i, * qui tóllis peccá-ta múndi:

dóna é- is réqui- em. Agnus Dé- i, * qui tóllis pec-

cá-ta múndi: dóna é- is réqui- em. Agnus Dé- i, *

qui tóllis peccá-ta múndi: dóna é- is réqui- em **

sempi-térnam.

Pie Jesu Domine

APPENDIX

Excerpts from the
St. Edmund Campion Hymnal

Hark, A Herald Voice Is Calling 477

Tune: MERTON (87 87)   Text: En clara vox redarguit

1. Hark, a her-ald voice is call-ing; "Christ is nigh," it
2. Star-tled at the sol-emn warn-ing, Let the earth-bound
3. Lo, the Lamb so long ex-pect-ed, Comes with par-don

seems to say; "Cast a-way the dreams of dark-ness,
soul a-rise; Christ her Sun, all sloth dis-pel-ling,
down from heav'n; Let us haste, with tears of sor-row,

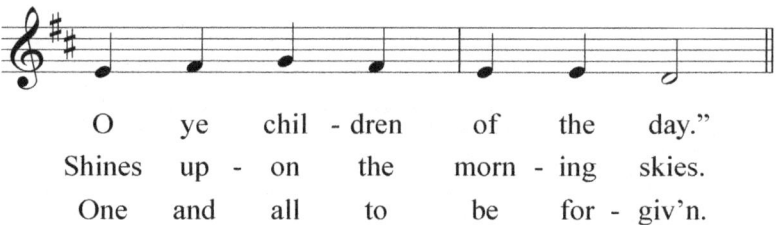

O ye chil-dren of the day."
Shines up-on the morn-ing skies.
One and all to be for-giv'n.

4. So when next he comes with glory,
   Wrapping all the earth in fear,
   May he then as our defender
   Of the clouds of heav'n appear.

5. Honor, glory, virtue, merit,
   To the Father and the Son,
   With the co-eternal Spirit,
   While eternal ages run.

Melody by William Monk (†1889).   English Translation (alt.) by
Fr. Edward Caswall (†1878), Priest of the Oratory of St. Philip Neri.   ADVENT

478 My Song Is Love Unknown

Tune: LOVE UNKNOWN (66 66 44 44)   Text: Samuel Crossman (†1683)

1. My song is love un-known, My Sav-ior's love to me;
2. Christ came from heav-en's throne Sal-va-tion to be-stow;
3. Some-times they strew His way, And His sweet prais-es sing;

Love to the love-less shown, That they might
But peo-ple scorned, and none The longed-for
Re-sound-ing all the way Ho-san-nas

love-ly be. O who am I, that for my
Christ would know: But O! my Friend, my Friend in-
to their King: Then "Cru-ci-fy!" is all their

sake My Lord should take, frail flesh and die?
deed, Who at my need His life did spend.
breath, And for His death they thirst and cry.

4. They rise, and needs will have / My dear Lord made away;
   A murderer they saved, / The Prince of life they slay,
   Yet cheerful He to suffering goes,
   That He His foes from thence might free.

5. Here might I stay and sing, / No story so divine;
   Never was love, dear King! / Never was grief like Thine.
   This is my Friend, in Whose sweet praise
   I all my days could gladly spend.

Crux Fidelis ... Faithful Cross 479

Tune: EARLS (87 87 87)   Text: Pange Lingua ... certaminis

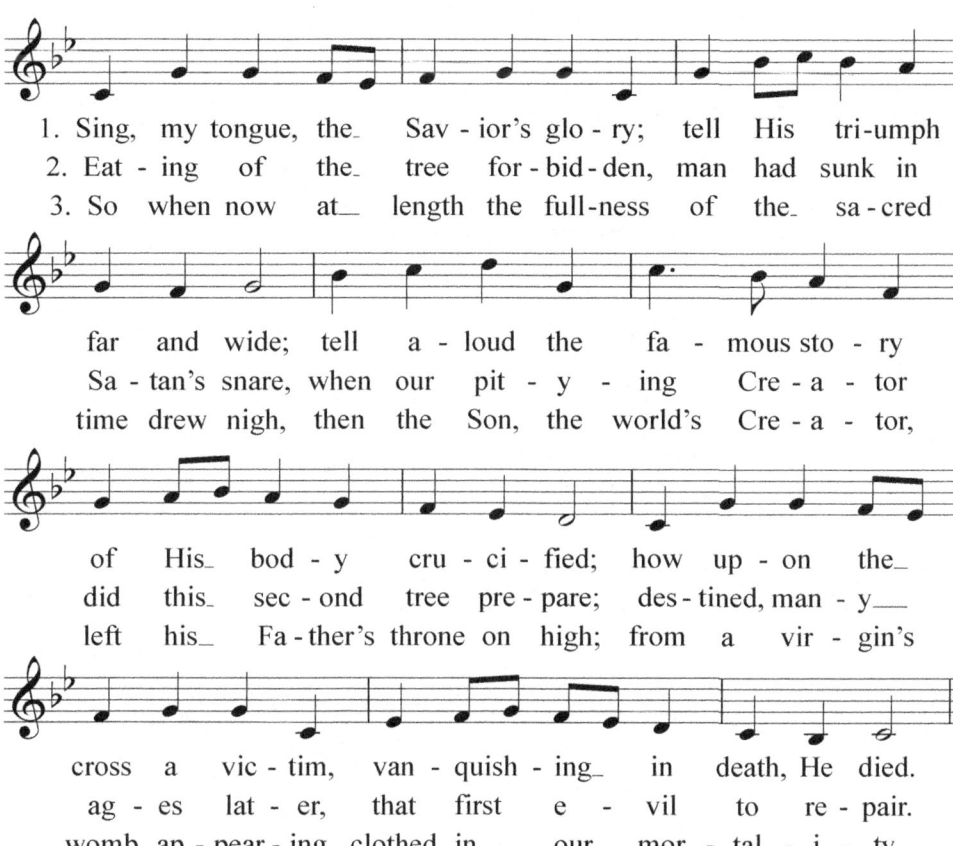

1. Sing, my tongue, the Sav-ior's glo-ry; tell His tri-umph
2. Eat-ing of the tree for-bid-den, man had sunk in
3. So when now at length the full-ness of the sa-cred

far and wide; tell a-loud the fa-mous sto-ry
Sa-tan's snare, when our pit-y-ing Cre-a-tor
time drew nigh, then the Son, the world's Cre-a-tor,

of His bod-y cru-ci-fied; how up-on the
did this sec-ond tree pre-pare; des-tined, man-y
left his Fa-ther's throne on high; from a vir-gin's

cross a vic-tim, van-quish-ing in death, He died.
ag-es lat-er, that first e-vil to re-pair.
womb ap-pear-ing, clothed in our mor-tal-i-ty.

4. All within a lowly manger,
lo, a tender babe He lies!
see his gentle Virgin Mother
lull to sleep his infant cries!
while the limbs of God incarnate
round with swathing bands she ties.

5. Thus did Christ to perfect manhood
in our mortal flesh attain:
then of His free choice He goeth
to a death of bitter pain;
as a lamb, upon the altar
of the cross, for us is slain.

6. Faithful Cross! above all other,
one and only noble Tree!
None in foliage, none in blossom,
none in fruit thy peers may be;
sweetest wood and sweetest iron!
Sweetest Weight is hung on thee!

7. Lofty tree, bend down thy branches,
to embrace thy sacred load;
oh, relax the native tension
of that all too rigid wood;
gently, gently bear the members
of thy dying King and God.

Melody by Fr. Claude Earls.   English Translation by Fr.
Caswall (†1878).   The complete hymn has eleven verses.

LENT & HOLY WEEK

480 Pange Lingua – *Holy Thursday Procession*

Pan - ge, lin - gua, glo - ri - ó - si cór - po - ris my - sté - ri - um,___
san - gui - nís - que pre - ti - ó - si, quem in mun - di pré - ti - um___
fru - ctus ven - tris ge - ne - ró - si rex ef - fú - dit___ gén - ti - um.

1. Sing, O my tongue, and praise the mystery of the glorious body
and the most precious blood, shed to save the world
by the King of the nations, the fruit of a noble womb.

No - bis da - tus,___ no - bis na - tus ex___ in - ta - cta Vír - gi - ne,___
et in mun - do con - ver - sá - tus, spar - so ver - bi sé - mi - ne,___
su - i mor - as in - co - lá - tus mi - ro clau - sit___ ór - di - ne.

2. Unto us he was given, he was born unto us of a Virgin untainted and pure;
he dwelt among us in the world, sowing the seeds of God's word;
and he ended the time of his stay on earth in the most wondrous of fashions.

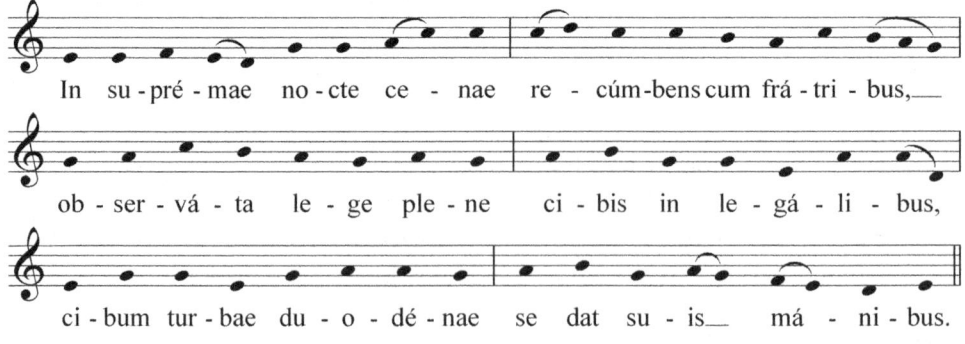

In su - pré - mae no - cte ce - nae re - cúm - bens cum frá - tri - bus,___
ob - ser - vá - ta le - ge ple - ne ci - bis in le - gá - li - bus,
ci - bum tur - bae du - o - dé - nae se dat su - is___ má - ni - bus.

3. On his last night at supper, reclining at table in the midst of his brethren disciples,
He fully observed the Ancient Law and partook of the Passover meal;
and then, with his own hands, he gave himself up as food for the group of the Twelve.

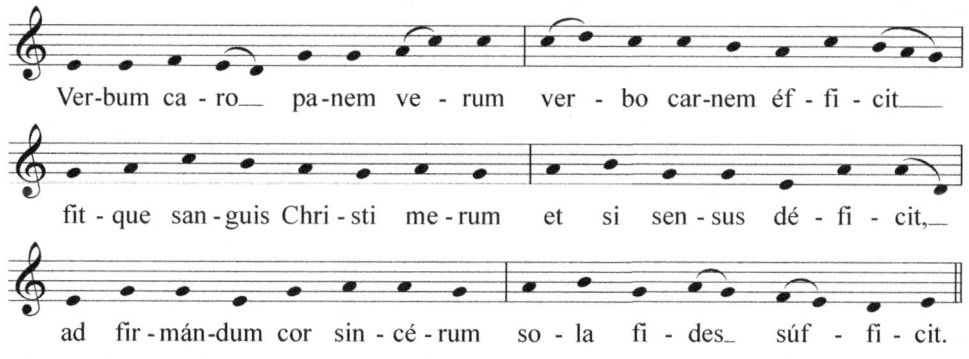

Ver-bum ca - ro__ pa-nem ve - rum ver - bo car-nem éf - fi - cit__

fit - que san-guis Chri - sti me - rum et si sen - sus dé - fi - cit,__

ad fir-mán-dum cor sin-cé-rum so - la fi - des_ súf - fi - cit.

4. The Word made flesh, by a simple word, makes of his flesh the true bread;
the blood of Christ becomes our drink; and though senses cannot perceive,
for confirming pure hearts in true belief, faith alone suffices.

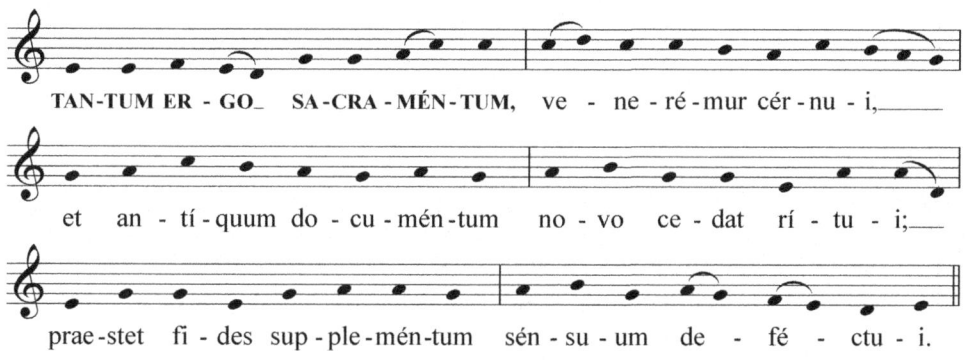

TAN-TUM ER - GO__ SA-CRA-MÉN-TUM, ve - ne - ré-mur cér - nu - i,_____

et an - tí - quum do - cu - mén-tum no - vo ce - dat rí - tu - i;__

prae-stet fi - des sup-ple-mén-tum sén - su - um de - fé - ctu - i.

5. In face of so great a mystery, therefore, let us bow down and worship;
let precepts of the Ancient Law give way to the new Gospel rite;
and let faith assist us and help us make up for what senses fail to perceive.

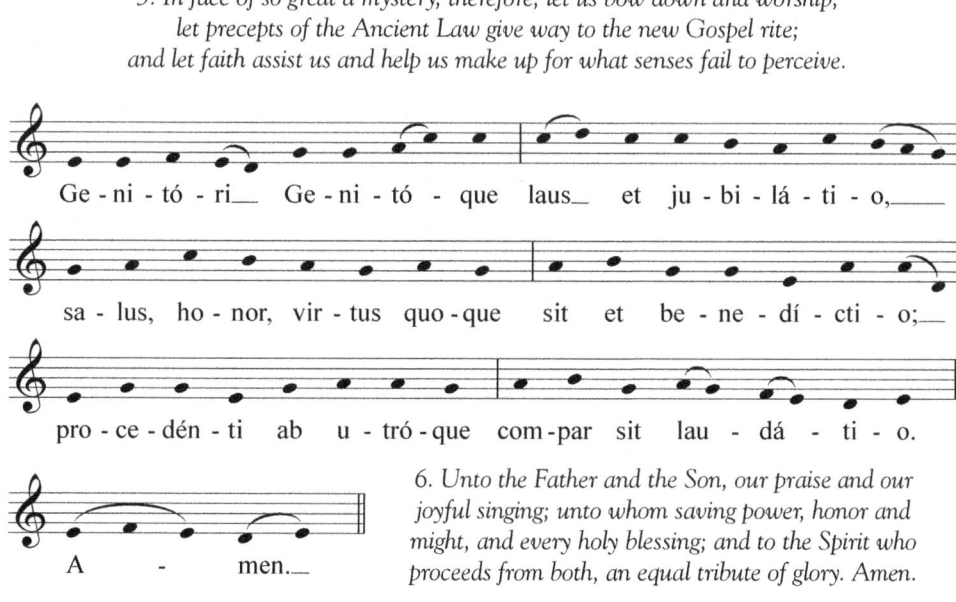

Ge - ni - tó - ri__ Ge - ni - tó - que laus_ et ju - bi - lá - ti - o,__

sa - lus, ho - nor, vir - tus quo-que sit et be - ne - dí - cti - o;__

pro - ce - dén - ti ab u - tró - que com-par sit lau - dá - ti - o.

A - men.__

6. Unto the Father and the Son, our praise and our
joyful singing; unto whom saving power, honor and
might, and every holy blessing; and to the Spirit who
proceeds from both, an equal tribute of glory. Amen.

482 In Our Risen Lord Rejoice

Tune: ROCKINGHAM (LM)   Text: Aurora cælum purpurat

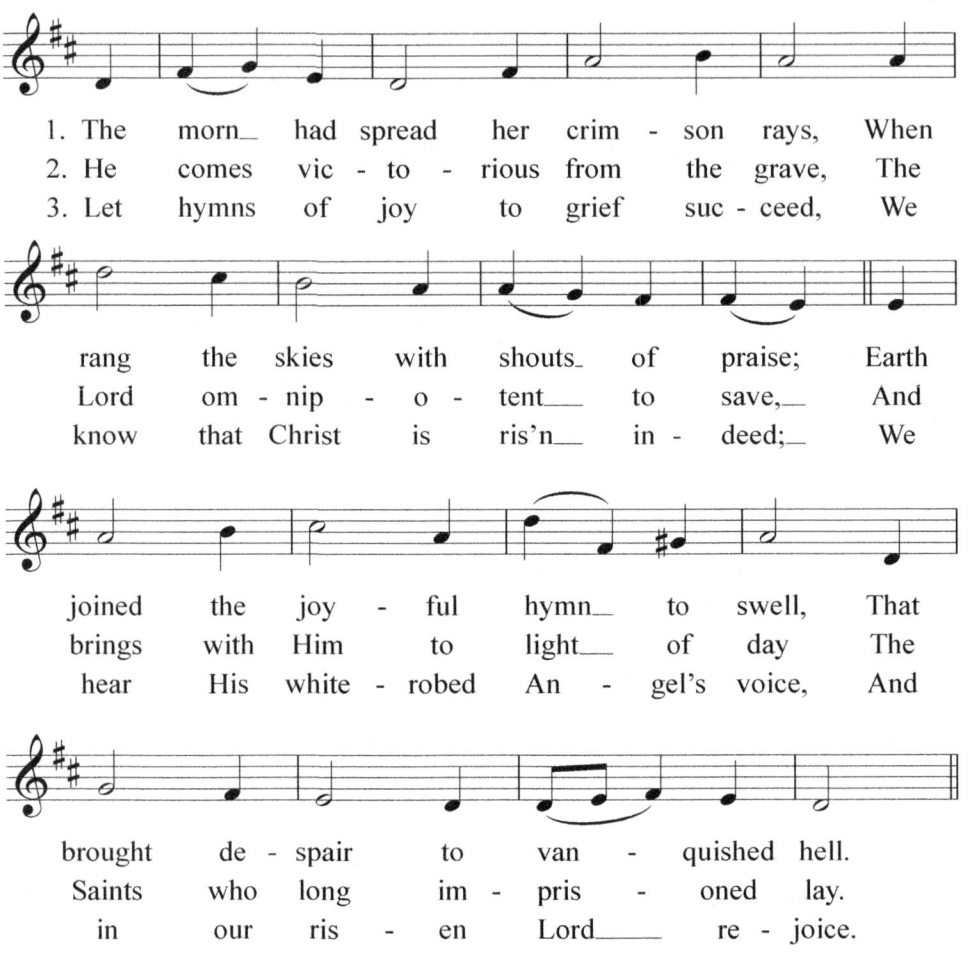

1. The morn had spread her crim - son rays, When
2. He comes vic - to - rious from the grave, The
3. Let hymns of joy to grief suc - ceed, We

rang the skies with shouts of praise; Earth
Lord om - nip - o - tent to save, And
know that Christ is ris'n in - deed; We

joined the joy - ful hymn to swell, That
brings with Him to light of day The
hear His white - robed An - gel's voice, And

brought de - spair to van - quished hell.
Saints who long im - pris - oned lay.
in our ris - en Lord re - joice.

4. With Christ we died, with Christ we rose,
   When at the font His Name we chose;
   Oh, let not sin our robes defile,
   And turn to grief the paschal smile.

English Translation by Robert Campbell (†1868).
Melody by Edward Miller (†1807).

O Christ, Who Mountest Up The Sky   483

Tune: BRESLAU (LM)   Text: Nobis, olympo redditus

1. O Christ, who mount - est up the sky
2. There gifts to all thou dost af - ford,
3. With eye un - veiled and sat - ed heart

To deck fair thrones for___ us on high,
Thy - self shall be our___ great re - ward;
We there shall see thee___ as thou art,

Thine ex - iled sons in love re - store
How brief be - low our time of pain!
And tell in hymns of sweet ac - cord

Un - to their na - tive land once more.
How long our pleas - ure shall re - main!
Our love and praise of thee, O Lord.

4. Lest we be orphaned of thy love, / Send down from thy high halls above
   The Spirit of adoption sweet, / Salvation's pledge, the Paraclete.

5. O Christ, to thee our anthems tend / Who shalt be judge at time's last end;
   To God the Father equal praise / And Holy Ghost through endless days.

English Translation by Alan McDougall (†1965).
German Melody (c. 1452).   V5 alt.   ASCENSION

484 Thee, O Christ, The Prince Of Ages

Tune: LAUDA ANIMA (87 87 87)

1. Thee, O Christ, the Prince of ag - es,
2. Come, O Lord, as - sure Thy King - ship,
3. From our own dear land, O Sav - ior,

Thee, the na - tions' glo - rious King,
Re - bel hearts Thy pow'r can gain;
Drive the night of her - e - sy

Praise we now with ex - ul - ta - tion,
Bend the stub - born will of rul - ers,
That, in ho - ly Church u - nit - ed,

Men and An - gels an - swer - ing,
Who from hom - age still re - frain:
All may love and wor - ship Thee:

And to Thee with meek de - vo - tion,
In the home as in the cit - y
Who, up - on the Cross up - lift - ed

Hearts and minds and sens - es bring.
Be su - preme, O Christ, and reign.
Draw - est all in char - i - ty.

Traditional Text as found in the St. Pius X Hymnal (1952).
CHRIST, OUR KING
Melody by John Goss (†1880).

To The Name Of Our Salvation 485

Tune: REGENT SQUARE (87 87 87)   Text: Gloriosi Salvatoris

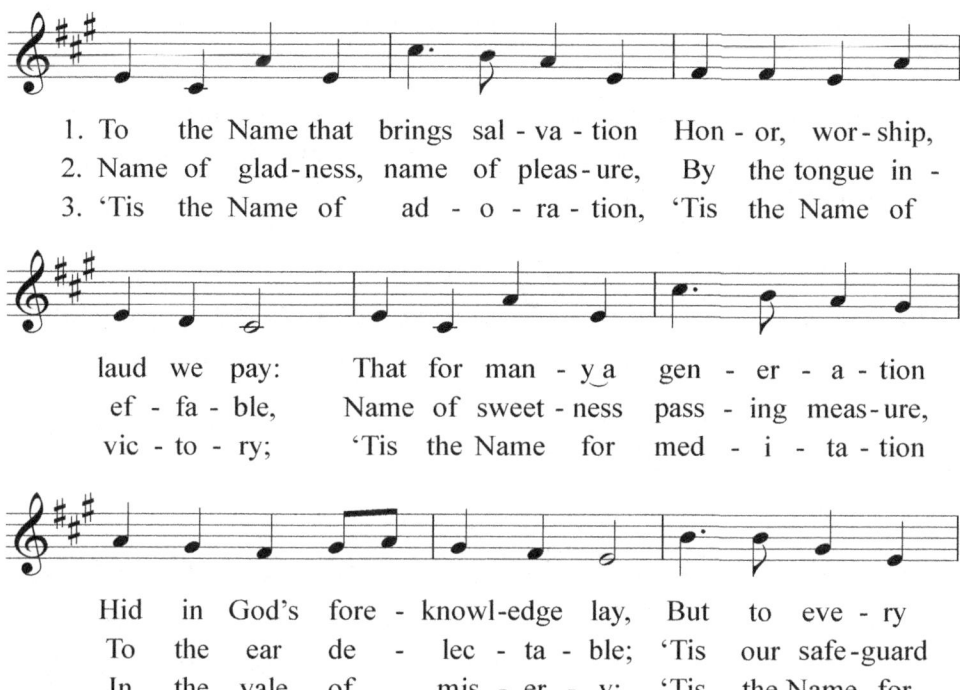

1. To the Name that brings sal - va - tion Hon - or, wor - ship,
2. Name of glad-ness, name of pleas-ure, By the tongue in -
3. 'Tis the Name of ad - o - ra - tion, 'Tis the Name of

laud we pay: That for man - y a gen - er - a - tion
ef - fa - ble, Name of sweet - ness pass - ing meas-ure,
vic - to - ry; 'Tis the Name for med - i - ta - tion

Hid in God's fore - knowl-edge lay, But to eve - ry
To the ear de - lec - ta - ble; 'Tis our safe-guard
In the vale of___ mis - er - y; 'Tis the Name for

tongue and na - tion Ho - ly Church pro - claims to - day.
and our treas-ure, 'Tis our help 'gainst sin and hell.
ven - er - a - tion By the cit - i - zens on high.

4. 'Tis the Name by right exalted / Over every other name:
That when we are sore assaulted / Puts our enemies to shame:
Strength to them that else had halted / Eyes to blind and feet to lame.

5. Jesu, we thy Name adoring, / Long to see Thee as Thou art:
Of Thy clemency imploring / So to write it in our heart,
That hearafter, upward soaring, / We with angels may have part.

English Translation by Dr. John Neale (†1866).
Melody by Henry Smart (†1879).   MOST HOLY NAME

486 Hail, Holy Wounds Of Jesus, Hail

Tune: ARUNDEL (LM)   Text: Salvete Christi vulnera

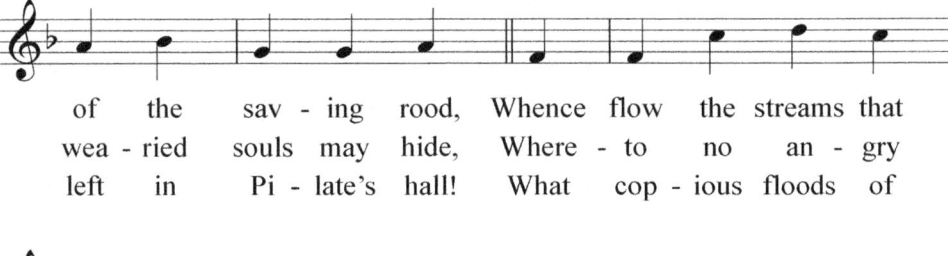

1. Hail, ho - ly Wounds of Je - sus, hail, Sweet pledg - es
2. Por - tals ye are to that dear home Where - in our
3. What count - less stripes our Je - sus bore, All na - ked

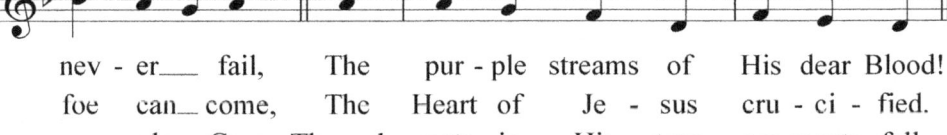

of the sav - ing rood, Whence flow the streams that
wea - ried souls may hide, Where - to no an - gry
left in Pi - late's hall! What cop - ious floods of

nev - er__ fail, The pur - ple streams of His dear Blood!
foe can__ come, The Heart of Je - sus cru - ci - fied.
pur - ple__ Gore Through rents in His torn gar - ments fall.

4. His beauteous Brow, oh, shame and grief,
   By the sharp throny crown is riv'n;
   Through Hands and Feet, without relief,
   The cruel nails are rudely driv'n.

5. In full atonement of our guilt,
   Careless of self, the Saviour trod—
   E'en till his Heart's best Blood was spilt—
   The wine-press of the wrath of God.

6. Come, bathe you in the healing flood,
   All ye who mourn, by sin oppressed;
   Your only hope is Jesus' Blood,
   His sacred Heart your only rest.

English Translation by Henry Oxenham (†1888).
Text and Melody from Arundel Catholic Hymnal (1898).

PRECIOUS BLOOD

Blessed Lamb, On Calvary's Mountain   487

Tune: LAUDA ANIMA (87 87 87)

1. Bless - ed Lamb! on Cal - v'ry's moun - tain
2. Bless - ed Lamb! – vouch - safe us par - don,
3. So shall Peace– sweet peace be giv - en,

Slain to take our sins a - way: Let the
In thy love our souls con - fide: By Thy
Pur - chase of Thy pre - cious pain; So shall

drops of that rich foun - tain Our tre - men - dous
groans with - in the Gar - den, By the death which
earth but lead to Heav - en, Since for us the

ran - som pay: Sa - cred Sav - ior! Sa - cred
Thou hast died– Let Thy Pas - sion– let Thy
Lamb was slain: Dear Re - deem - er! dear Re -

Sav - ior! Low - ly at Thy feet we pray.
Pas - sion Ev - er more with us a - bide!
deem - er! Thou canst not have died in vain.

Text by Matthew Bridges (†1894), disciple of Blessed
Cardinal Newman.   Melody by John Goss (†1880).   PRECIOUS BLOOD

488 All Ye Who Would The Christ Descry

Tune: DUGUET (LM)   Text: Quicumque Christum quæritis

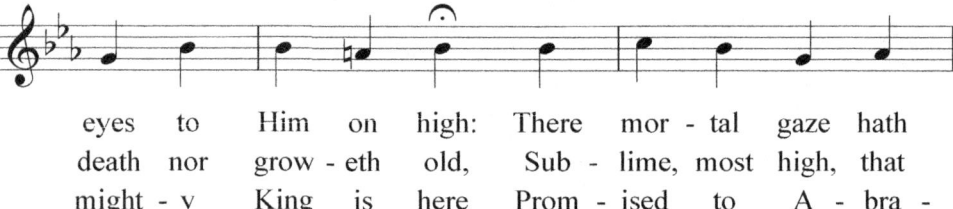

1. All ye who would the Christ de-scry, Lift up your
2. A won-drous sign we there be-hold, That knows not
3. Here is the King the Gen-tiles fear, The Jews' most

eyes to Him on high: There mor-tal gaze hath
death nor grow-eth old, Sub-lime, most high, that
might-y King is here Prom-ised to A-bra-

strength to__ see The to-ken of His maj-es-ty.
can-not__ fade, That was ere earth and heav'n were made.
ham of__ yore, And to his seed for-ev-er-more.

4. 'Tis He the Prophets words foretold,
   And by their signs shown forth of old;
   The Father's witness hath ordained
   That we should hear with faith unfeigned.

5. O Lord, to Thee our praise we pay,
   To little ones revealed today,
   With Father and Blest Spirit One
   Until the ages' course is done.

English Translation by Alan McDougall (†1965).
Melody by Abbé Duguet (†1767). V5 alt.

TRANSFIGURATION

Light Of The Anxious Heart 489

Tune: DOMINICA (SM)   Text: Lux alma, Jesu, mentium

1. Light of the anx - ious heart, O Lord, Thou
2. Joy - ous is he, with whom, God's Word, Thou
3. Bright - ness of God a - bove! Un - fath - om -

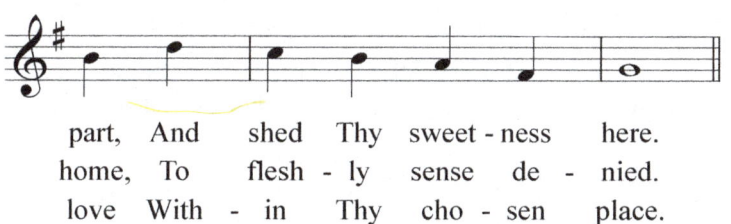

dost ap - pear, To bid the gloom of guilt de -
dost a - bide; Sweet Light of our e - ter - nal
a - ble grace! Thy Pres - ence be a fount of

part, And shed Thy sweet - ness here.
home, To flesh - ly sense de - nied.
love With - in Thy cho - sen place.

4. To Thee, whom children see,
   The Father ever blest,
   The Holy Spirit, One and Three,
   Be endless praise addressed.

*English Translation by Blessed Cardinal Newman (†1890),
Priest of the Oratory of St. Philip Neri.
Melody by Herbert Oakeley (†1903). VI alt.*

TRANSFIGURATION

490 Christ In The Highest

Tune: ISTE CONFESSOR (11 11 11 5)   Text: Christe supreme dominator alme

1. Christ in the high-est, ho-ly Lord of all___ things,
   Con-quer-or and Sov-'reign, wor-ship-ful Re-deem-er,
   Hear us in mer-cy, whom with price most won-drous
   Thou hast re-deem-èd.

2. Praise and thanks-giv-ing ju-bi-lant and meet-est
   Of-fer we pray-ing, sweet-est King and kind-est,
   Whom by the pour-ing of thy blood thou sav-edst
   On Rood vic-to-rious.

3. Once of old time the an-cient foe had lured us
   Un-to his pris-on by a tree's temp-ta-tion,
   But through the ho-ly wood of Christ he wail-eth
   Bound through the ag-es.

4. Now doth the serpent mourn his fangs, no longer
   Able to harm, his poison reft for ever,
   Now doth he weep, hell harrowed, and his people / Called to the heavens.

5. So through the cross, O Crucified, most precious,
   So through the price unpriced of thy fair lifeblood,
   Deign in thy mercy now to save thy servants / From death eternal.

6. Glory to God who reigneth in the highest,
   Praise to the Son who reigns with him for ever,
   Laud to the Holy Spirit coeternal, / Equal in Godhead.

HOLY CROSS

English Translation by Alan McDougall (†1965).
Melody from the Poitiers Antiphoner (1746).

Blessed Are The Sons Of God 491

Tune: DIX (77 77 77)

1. Bless - èd___ are the sons of God, They are bought with
2. They are___ lights up - on the earth, Chil - dren of a
3. With them_ num-ber'd may we be, Now and thro' e -

Christ's own Blood, They are___ harm - less, meek, and
heav'n - ly birth; Born of___ God, they hate all
ter - ni - ty! Though they___ suf - fer much on

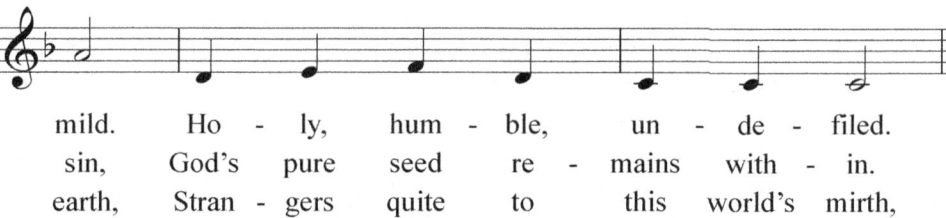

mild. Ho - ly, hum - ble, un - de - filed.
sin, God's pure seed re - mains with - in.
earth, Stran - gers quite to this world's mirth,

℟. With them num-ber'd may we be, Now and thro' e - ter - ni - ty!

4. They alone are truly blest,
   Heirs of God, joint heirs with Christ;
   They with love and peace are filled,
   They are by his Spirit sealed. ℟.

Text (alt.) by Joseph Humphreys (b. 1720).
Melody by Conrad Kocher (†1872).

SAINTS

492 Who Are These, Like Stars Appearing

Tune: ALL SAINTS (87 87 77)

1. Who are these like stars ap - pear - ing, These be - fore God's
2. Who are these of daz - zling bright-ness, These in God's own
3. These are they who have con - tend - ed For their Sav - ior's

throne who stand? Each a gold - en crown is wear - ing;
truth ar - rayed, Clad in robes of pur - est white - ness,
hon - or long, Wres-tling on till life was end - ed,

Who are all this glo - rious band? Al - le - lu - ia!
Robes whose lus - tre ne'er shall fade, Ne'er be touched by
Fol- l'wing not the sin - ful throng; These who well the

Hark, they sing, Prais - ing loud their heav'n - ly King.
time's rude hand? Whence come all this glo - rious band?
fight sus - tained, Tri - umph through the Lamb have gained.

4. These are they whose hearts were riven, / Sore with woe and anguish tried,
   Who in pray'r full oft have striven / With the God they glorified;
   Now, their painful conflict o'er, / God has bid them weep no more.

5. These, like priests, have watched and waited, / Off'ring up to Christ their will;
   Soul and body consecrated, / Day and night to serve Him still:
   Now in God's most holy place / Blest they stand before His face.

German Text by Heinrich Schenk (†1727). English Translation by
Frances Cox (†1897). German Melody (†1698).

SAINTS

For All Thy Saints, O Lord   493

Tune: FESTAL SONG (SM)

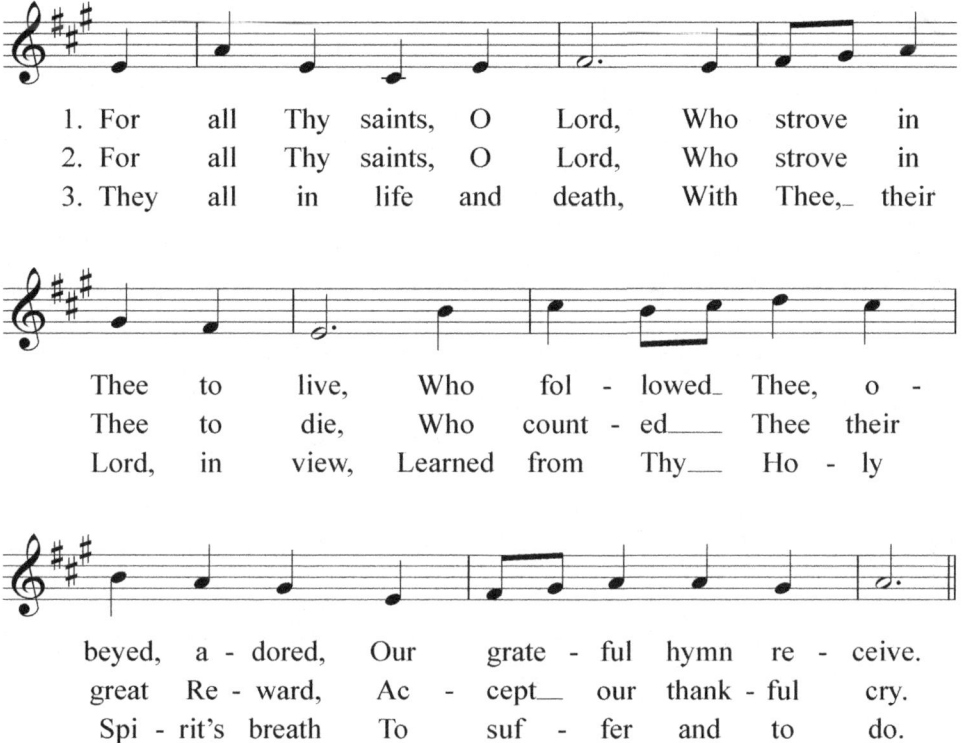

1. For all Thy saints, O Lord, Who strove in
2. For all Thy saints, O Lord, Who strove in
3. They all in life and death, With Thee, their

Thee to live, Who fol - lowed Thee, o -
Thee to die, Who count - ed Thee their
Lord, in view, Learned from Thy Ho - ly

beyed, a - dored, Our grate - ful hymn re - ceive.
great Re - ward, Ac - cept our thank - ful cry.
Spi - rit's breath To suf - fer and to do.

4. For this Thy name we bless
   And humbly pray that we
   May follow them in holiness
   And live and die in Thee.

5. All might, all praise, be thine,
   Father, co-equal Son,
   and Spirit, bond of love divine,
   while endless ages run.

Text (alt.) by Richard Mant (†1848).
Melody by William Walter (†1893).

SAINTS

494 O Thou, The Martyrs' Glorious King

Tune: BRESLAU (LM)   Text: Rex gloriose martyrum

1. O Thou, the Mar - tyrs' glo - rious King!
   Of con - fes - sors the crown and prize;
   Who dost to joys ce - les - tial bring
   Those who the joys of earth de - spise.

2. By all the praise Thy Saints have won;
   By all their pains in days gone by;
   By all the deeds which they have done;
   Hear Thou Thy sup - pliant peo - ple's cry.

3. Thou dost a - mid Thy Mar - tyrs fight;
   Thy Con - fes - sors Thou dost for - give;
   May we find mer - cy in Thy sight,
   And in Thy sa - cred pres - ence live.

4. To God the Father glory be,
   And to His sole-begotten Son;
   And glory, Holy Ghost, to Thee!
   While everlasting ages run.

SAINTS

English Translation by Fr. Edward Caswall (†1878), Priest of the Oratory of St. Philip Neri. German Melody (c. 1452).

Author Of Man's Salvation   495

Tune: UFFINGHAM (LM)   Text: Auctor salutis hominum

1. Au - thor of man's sal - va - tion, blest
2. That he for whose dear sake we cry
3. Ex - ceed - ing bless - èd is that town;

Je - su, our ref - uge and our rest,
Be joined to cit - i - zens on high
The full - ness of the God - head shown

We fall be - fore thy face in prayer,
Where pa - tri - ar - chal choirs, his need
In thy Je - ru - s'lem makes it fair,

Thy ser - vants, worth - less of thy care,
Know - ing and pit - ying, in - ter - cede.
For man - y heav'n - ly stones are there:

4. And in that hall, with merits stored
   Of prophets, may he find reward,
   Whom lovingly and faithfully,
   Lord Jesus, we commend to thee.

English Translation by Alan McDougall (†1965).
Melody by Jeremiah Clarke (†1707).

ALL SOULS & FUNERAL

496 Holy Father, Great Creator

Tune: REGENT SQUARE (87 87 87)

1. Ho - ly Fa - ther, great Cre - a - tor, Source of mer - cy,
2. Ho - ly Je - sus, Lord of glo - ry, Whom an - gel - ic
3. Ho - ly Ghost, Thou Sanc - ti - fi - er, Come with unc - tion

love and peace, Look up - on the Me - di - a - tor,
hosts pro - claim, While we hear Thy won - drous sto - ry,
from a - bove, Raise our hearts to rap - tures high - er,

Clothe us with His_ right-eous - ness; Heav'n - ly Fa - ther,
Meet and wor - ship_ in Thy Name, Dear Re - deem - er,
Fill them with the_ Sav - ior's love. Source of com - fort,

heav'n - ly Fa - ther, Through the Sav - ior hear and bless!
dear Re - deem - er, In our hearts Thy peace pro - claim.
source of com - fort, Cheer us with the Sav - ior's love.

4. God the Lord, through every nation
   Let Thy wondrous mercies shine,
   In the song of Thy salvation
   Every tongue and race combine,
   Thou Almighty, God Eternal,
   Form our hearts and make them Thine.

HOLY TRINITY

Text (alt.) by Alexander Griswold (†1843)
Melody by Henry Smart (†1879).

Firmly I Believe And Truly   497

Tune: HALTON HOLGATE (87 87)

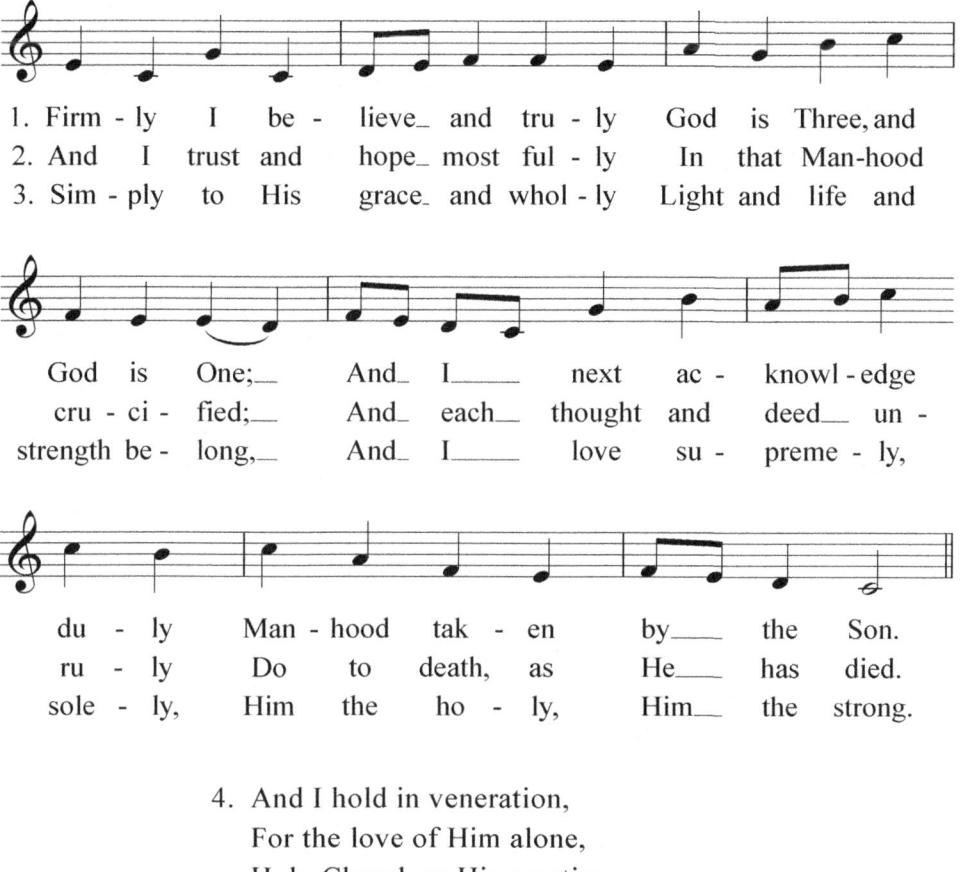

1. Firm - ly I be - lieve_ and tru - ly God is Three, and
2. And I trust and hope_ most ful - ly In that Man-hood
3. Sim - ply to His grace_ and whol - ly Light and life and

God is One;__ And_ I____ next ac - knowl - edge
cru - ci - fied;__ And_ each__ thought and deed__ un -
strength be - long,__ And_ I____ love su - preme - ly,

du - ly Man - hood tak - en by__ the Son.
ru - ly Do to death, as He__ has died.
sole - ly, Him the ho - ly, Him__ the strong.

4. And I hold in veneration,
   For the love of Him alone,
   Holy Church as His creation,
   And her teachings are His own.

5. And I take with joy whatever
   Now besets me, pain or fear,
   And with a strong will I sever
   All the ties which bind me here.

6. Adoration aye be given,
   With and through th'angelic host,
   To the God of earth and Heaven,
   Father, Son and Holy Ghost.

Text by Blessed Cardinal Newman (†1890), Priest of the Oratory of St. Philip Neri. Melody by William Boyce (†1779).

HOLY TRINITY

498 Come Holy Ghost, Who Ever One

Tune: WHITEHALL (LM)   Text: Nunc Sancte nobis Spiritus

1. Come, Holy Ghost, who ev - er One
2. Let flesh, and heart, and lips, and mind,
3. Grant this, O Fa - ther, ev - er One

Art with the Fa - ther and the Son,
Sound forth our wit - ness to man - kind;
With Christ, Thy sole - be - got - ten Son,

It is the hour, our souls pos - sess
And love light up our mor - tal frame,
And Ho - ly Ghost, whom all a - dore,

With Thy full flood of ho - li - ness.
Till oth - ers catch the liv - ing flame.
Reign - ing and blest for - ev - er - more.

HOLY GHOST

English Translation by Blessed Cardinal Newman (†1890), Priest of the Oratory of St. Philip Neri. Melody by Henry Lawes (†1662).

Holy Light On Earth's Horizon 499

Tune: HYMN TO JOY (87 87D)   Text: Alma lux

1. Ho - ly light on earth's ho - ri - zon Star of hope to
2. Moth - er of the world's Re - deem - er Prom - ised from the
3. Earth be - low and high - est heav - en Praise the splen - dor

fall - en man, Light a - mid a world of shad - ows,
dawn of time: How could one so high - ly fa - vored
of thy state, Thou who now art crowned in glo - ry

Dawn of God's re - demp - tive plan. Cho - sen
Share the guilt of Ad - am's crime? Sun and
Wast con - ceived im - mac - u - late. Hail, be -

from e - ter - nal__ ag - es, Thou a - lone of
moon and stars a - dorn thee, Sin - less__ Eve, tri -
lov - èd of the__ Fa - ther, Moth - er__ of his

all our race, By thy Son's a - ton - ing mer - its
um - phant sign; Thou art she who crushed the ser - pent,
on - ly Son, Mys - tic bride of Love e - ter - nal,

Wast con - ceived in per - fect grace.
Mar - y, pledge of life di - vine.
Hail, thou fair and spot - less one!

Translation by Fr. Edward Caswall (†1878), Priest of the Oratory of St. Philip Neri.   Melody by Ludwig van Beethoven (†1827).

OUR LADY

500 Prayer To The Mother Of Christ

Tune: RUSTINGTON (87 87D)   Text: Pulchra tota sine nota

1. Thou, when deep-est night in-fer-nal Had for ag-es
2. Thine the prov-ince to de-liv-er Souls that deep in
3. Teach thy chil-dren, ho-ly Moth-er, How to con-quer

shroud-ed man, Gav-est us that light e-ter-nal Prom-ised
bond-age lie: Thine to crush, and crush for ev-er, Life-de-
ev-'ry sin, How to love and help each oth-er, How e-

since the world be-gan. God in thee hath show-ered
stroy-ing her-e-sy. Thine to show that earth-ly
ter-nal life to win. Thou to whom a Child was

plen-ty On the hun-gry and the weak; Send-ing
pleas-ures, All the world's en-chant-ing bloom, Are out-
giv-en, Great-er than the sons of men, Com-ing

back the might-y emp-ty, Set-ting up on high the meek.
ri-valled by the treas-ures Of the glo-rious life to come.
down from high-est Heav-en To cre-ate this world a-gain.

4. Oh, by that Almighty Maker / Whom thyself a virgin bore;
   Oh, by thy supreme Creator / Linked with thee for evermore;
   By the hope thy name inspires; / By our doom, reversed through thee,
   Help us, Queen of Angel choirs, / Now and through eternity.

OUR LADY

*English Text by Fr. Edward Caswall (†1878), Priest of the
Oratory of St. Philip Neri.   Melody by Charles Parry (†1918).*

Remember Me Before The Lord 501

Tune: BRESLAU (LM)   Text: O Maria piissima

1. O Mar - y, Star that lov - ing - ly
2. Re - mem - ber me be - fore the Lord,
3. Grant me from eve - ry ill re - lease,

In fair light shin - est____ o'er the sea,
Je - sus thy Son, the____ Christ of God;
Of eve - ry vir - tue____ grant in - crease,

Moth - er of per - fect clem - en - cy
My soul from eve - ry e - vil guard,
Be - stow on me thy per - fect peace,

And hall of pur - est chas - ti - ty,
And bring me to thy blest re - ward.
And keep my heart in qui - et - ness.

4. And when my life is ending here, / Do thou before mine eyes appear,
That with thy counsel I may know / To 'scape the terror of the foe.

5. O Maid, vouchsafe to lead my feet / Unto the Father's blissful seat,
Lest Satan by some envious wile / My steps from the right way beguile.

6. That from my many stains abhorred / Of sinning I may be restored
To Michael, of the heavenly guard / The Archangelic prince and lord,

7. Whose might in the ce-les-tial tow'r / Is strong from every evil pow'r
To save the faithful and the blest, / And bring them to eternal rest.

English Translation by Alan McDougall (†1965).
German Melody (c. 1452).

OUR LADY

502 Our Lady Of The Most Holy Rosary

Tune: DUGUET (LM)   Text: Te gestientem gaudiis

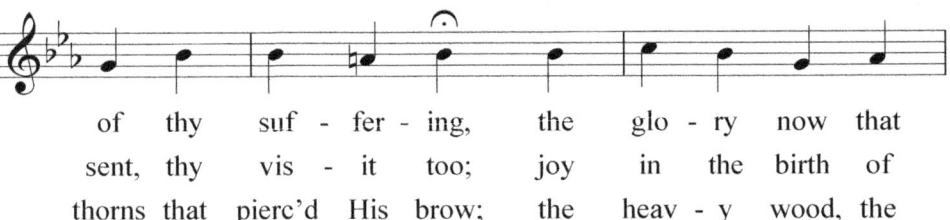

1. The glad - ness of thy Moth - er - hood, the an - guish
2. Hail, bless - èd Moth - er, full of joy in thy con-
3. Hail, sor - r'wing in His ag - o - ny— the blows, the

of thy suf - fer - ing, the glo - ry now that
sent, thy vis - it too; joy in the birth of
thorns that pierc'd His brow; the heav - y wood, the

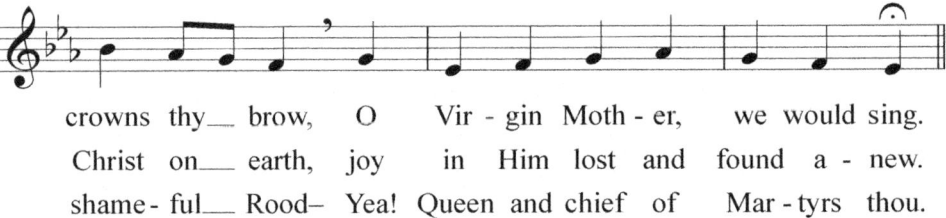

crowns thy＿ brow, O Vir - gin Moth - er, we would sing.
Christ on＿ earth, joy in Him lost and found a - new.
shame - ful＿ Rood– Yea! Queen and chief of Mar - tyrs thou.

4. Hail, in the triumph of thy Son, / the quickening flames of Pentecost;
shining a Queen in light serene, / when all the world is tempest-tost.

5. O come, ye nations, roses bring, / culled from these mysteries divine,
and for the Mother of your King / with loving hands your chaplets twine.

6. We lay our homage at Thy feet, / Lord Jesus, Thou the Virgin's Son,
With Father and with Paraclete, / Reigning while endless ages run.

*Text by Fr. Augustine Ricchini, O.P. (†1779). English Translation by
Abbot Oswald Hunter-Blair (†1939). Melody by Abbé Duguet (†1767).*

OUR LADY

The Two Worlds 503

Tune: SONG 67 (CM)

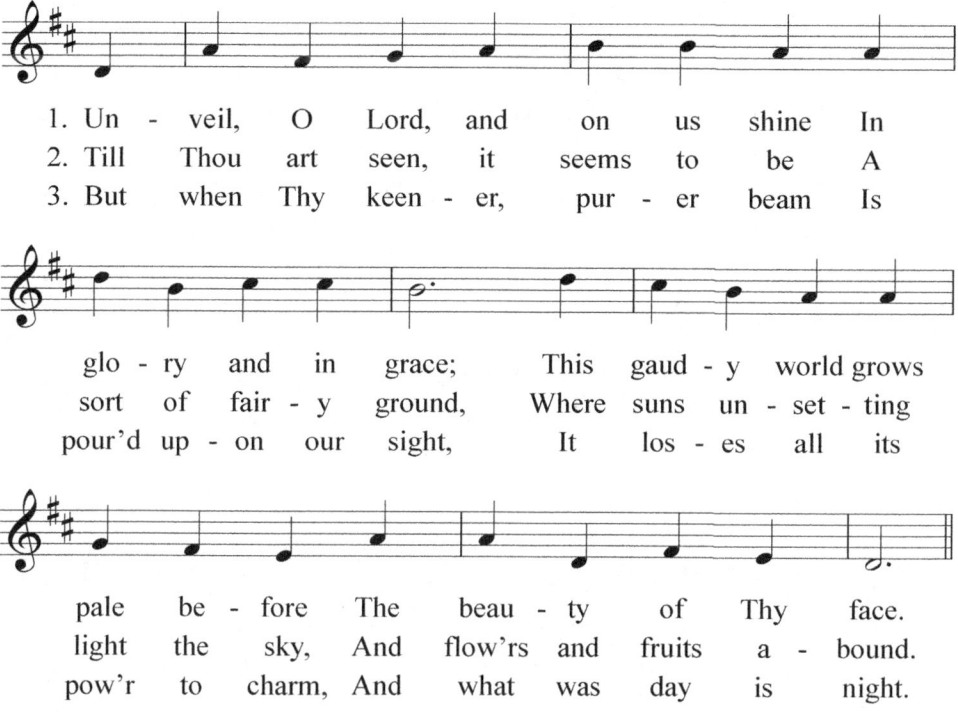

1. Un - veil, O Lord, and on us shine In
2. Till Thou art seen, it seems to be A
3. But when Thy keen - er, pur - er beam Is

glo - ry and in grace; This gaud - y world grows
sort of fair - y ground, Where suns un - set - ting
pour'd up - on our sight, It los - es all its

pale be - fore The beau - ty of Thy face.
light the sky, And flow'rs and fruits a - bound.
pow'r to charm, And what was day is night.

4. Its noblest toils are then the scourge
Which made Thy blood to flow;
Its joys are but the treach'rous thorns
Which circled 'round Thy brow.

5. And thus, when we renounce for Thee
Its restless aims and fears,
The tender mem'ries of the past,
The hopes of coming years,

6. Poor is our sacrifice, whose eyes
Are lighted from above;
We offer what we cannot keep,
What we have ceased to love.

Text by Blessed Cardinal Newman (†1890).
Melody by Orlando Gibbons (†1625).

GENERAL

504 I Heard The Voice Of Jesus Say

Tune: KINGSFOLD (DCM)

1. I__ heard the voice of Je-sus say, "Come un-to me__ and
   rest; lay_ down, thou wea-ry one, lay down thy__
   head up-on__ my breast." I__ came to Je-sus as I
   was, so__ wea-ry,__ worn, and sad; I__ found in
   him__ a__ rest-ing place, and__ he has made me glad.

2. I__ heard the voice of Je-sus say, "Be-hold, I free-ly
   give the_ liv-ing wa-ter; thirst-y one, stoop
   down and drink, and live." I__ came to Je-sus, and I
   drank of__ that life-giv-ing stream; my__ thirst was
   quenched, my_ soul re-vived, and_ now I live_ in him.

3. I__ heard the voice of Je-sus say, "I__ am this dark_ world's
   light; look un-to me, thy morn shall rise, and_
   all thy day_ be bright." I__ looked to Je-sus, and I
   found in__ him my_ Star, my Sun; and_ in that
   light_ of__ life I'll walk till_ trav-'ling days are done.

Lord Of All Hopefulness   505

Tune: SLANE (10 11 11 11)

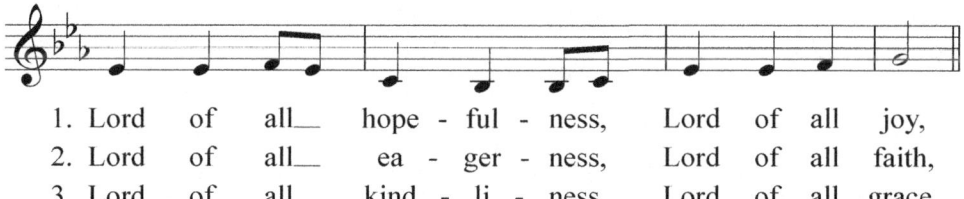

1. Lord of all__ hope - ful - ness, Lord of all joy,
2. Lord of all__ ea - ger - ness, Lord of all faith,
3. Lord of all__ kind - li - ness, Lord of all grace,

Whose trust, ev - er child- like, no cares could de - stroy,
Whose strong hands were skilled at the plane and the lathe,
Your__ hands swift to wel- come, your arms to em - brace,

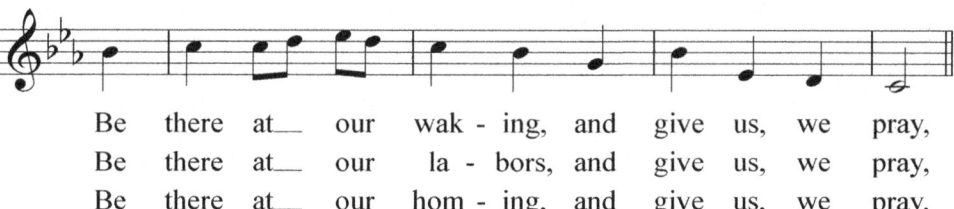

Be there at__ our wak - ing, and give us, we pray,
Be there at__ our la - bors, and give us, we pray,
Be there at__ our hom - ing, and give us, we pray,

Your bliss in our hearts, Lord, at the break of the day.
Your strength in our hearts, Lord, at the noon of the day.
Your love in our hearts, Lord, at the eve of the day.

4. Lord of all gentleness, Lord of all calm,
Whose voice is contentment, whose presence is balm,
Be there at our sleeping, and give us, we pray,
Your peace in our hearts, Lord, at the end of the day.

GENERAL

506 O God Of Loveliness

Tune: SCHÖNSTER HERR JESU (568 558)

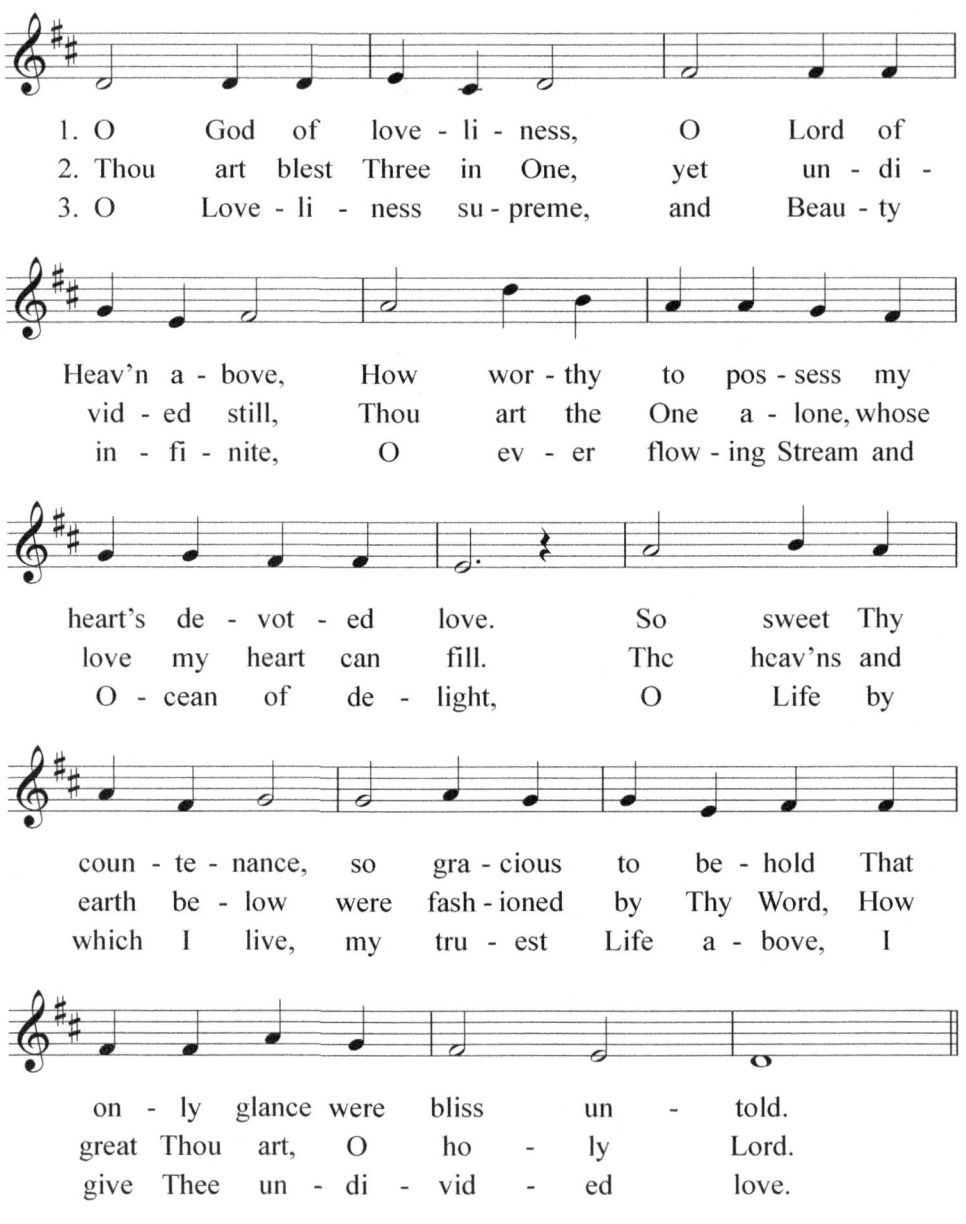

1. O God of love - li - ness, O Lord of
2. Thou art blest Three in One, yet un - di -
3. O Love - li - ness su - preme, and Beau - ty

Heav'n a - bove, How wor - thy to pos - sess my
vid - ed still, Thou art the One a - lone, whose
in - fi - nite, O ev - er flow - ing Stream and

heart's de - vot - ed love. So sweet Thy
love my heart can fill. The heav'ns and
O - cean of de - light, O Life by

coun - te - nance, so gra - cious to be - hold That
earth be - low were fash - ioned by Thy Word, How
which I live, my tru - est Life a - bove, I

on - ly glance were bliss un - told.
great Thou art, O ho - ly Lord.
give Thee un - di - vid - ed love.

Italian Text by St. Alphonsus Ligouri (†1787). English Translation
(alt.) by Fr. Edmund Vaughan (†1908), Priest of the Congregation
of the Most Holy Redeemer. Traditional Melody.

GENERAL

O Salutaris Hostia / O Saving Victim   507

Tune: DUGUET (LM)   Text: St. Thomas Aquinas (†1274)

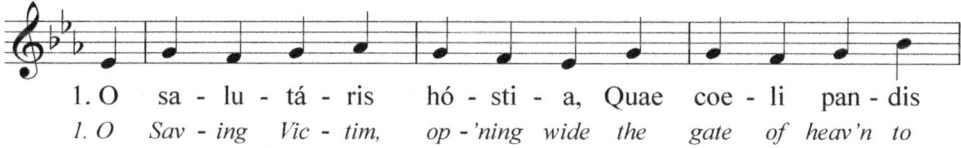

1. O   sa - lu - tá - ris   hó - sti - a,   Quae   coe - li   pan - dis
1. O   Sav - ing   Vic - tim,   op -'ning   wide   the   gate   of   heav'n   to

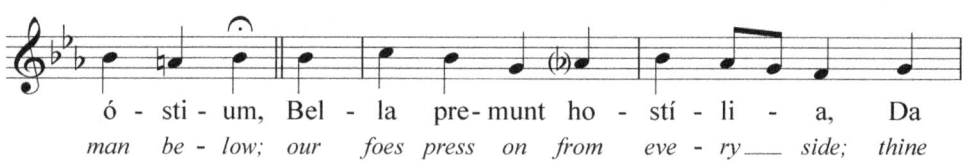

ó - sti - um,   Bel - la   pre - munt   ho - stí - li - a,   Da
man   be - low;   our   foes   press   on   from   eve - ry___ side;   thine

ro - bur,   fer   au - xí - li - um.   2. U - ni   tri -
aid   sup - ply,   thy   strength   be - stow.   2. To   thy   great

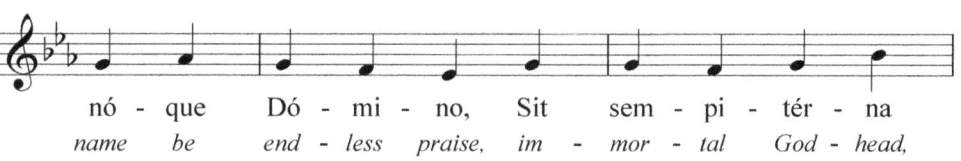

nó - que   Dó - mi - no,   Sit   sem - pi - tér - na
name   be   end - less   praise,   im - mor - tal   God - head,

gló - ri - a: Qui   vi - tam   si - ne   tér - mi - no   No -
one   in   three!   O   grant   us   end - less   length   of___ days,   in

bis   do - net   in   pá - tri - a.   A - men.
our   true   na - tive   land   with   thee.   A - men.

508 Tantum Ergo / Down In Adoration

Tune: ST. THOMAS (87 87 87)   Text: St. Thomas Aquinas (†1274)

1. Tan-tum er-go Sa-cra-mén-tum Ve-ne-ré-mur cér-nu-i:
1. Down in ad-o-ra-tion fall-ing, Lo! the sa-cred Host we hail,

Et an-tí-quum do-cu-mén-tum No-vo ce-dat rí-tu-i:
Lo! o'er an-cient forms de-part-ing New-er rites of grace pre-vail;

Præ-stet fi-des sup-ple-mén-tum Sén-su-um de-fé-ctu-i.
Faith for all de-fects sup-ply-ing, Where the fee-ble sens-es fail.

2. Ge-ni-tó-ri, Ge-ni-tó-que Laus et ju-bi-lá-ti-o,
2. To the ev-er-last-ing Fa-ther, And the Son Who reigns on high

Sa-lus, ho-nor, vir-tus quo-que Sit et be-ne-dí-cti-o:
With the Spir-it Blest pro-ceed-ing Forth from Each e-ter-nal-ly,

Pro-ce-dén-ti ab u-tró-que Com-par sit lau-dá-ti-o.
Be sal-va-tion, hon-or, bless-ing, Might and end-less maj-es-ty.

℣. Panem de caelo praestitísti eis.
℟. Omne delectaméntum in se habéntem.   Orémus:

Deus, qui nobis sub sacraménto mirábili, passiónis tuae memóriam reliquísti: tríbue, quaésumus, ita nos córporis et sánguinis tui sacra mystéria venerári; ut redemptiónis tuae fructum in nobis júgiter sentiámus. Qui vivis et regnas in saécula saeculórum. ℟. Amen.

℣. You have given them bread from heaven.   ℟. Having all sweetness within it.   Let us pray.

O GOD, who in this wonderful sacrament left us a memorial of your passion, grant, we implore you, that we may so venerate the sacred mysteries of your Body and Blood as always to be conscious of the fruit of your redemption.   You who live and reign, forever and ever. ℟. Amen.

HYMNS

Composed by Martyrs of England

The Assumption Of Our Lady 511

Tune: NACHTLIED (10 10 10 10 10 10)　　　Text: Saint Robert Southwell (†1595)

1. If sin be cap - tive, grace must find re - lease;
2. The daz - zled eye doth dim - mèd light re - quire,
3. Gem to her worth, spouse to her love as - cends,

From curse of sin the in - no - cent is free;
And dy - ing sights re - pose in shroud - ing shades;
Prince to her throne, queen to her heav'n - ly King,

Tomb pris - on is___ for sin - ners that de - crease,
But ea - gles' eyes___ to bright - est light as - pire,
Whose court with sol - emn pomp on her at - tends,

No tomb but___ throne to guilt - less doth a - gree:
And liv - ing___ looks de - light in loft - y___ glades:
And choirs of___ saints with greet - ing notes do___ sing;

Though thralls of sin lie lin - g'ring in the grave,
Faint - wing - èd fowl by ground do faint - ly fly,___
Earth ren - d'reth up her un - de - serv - èd prey,___

Yet___ fault - less corse with soul re - ward must have.
Our___ prince - ly ea - gle mounts un - to the___ sky.
Heav'n___ claims the right, and bears the prize a - way.

Text by St. Robert Southwell, S.J. (†1595), one of the Forty Martyrs of
England and Wales.　Melody by Henry Smart (†1879).　　　OUR LADY

512 The Virgin's Salutation

Tune: YORKSHIRE (10 10 10 10 10 10)   Text: Saint Robert Southwell (†1595)

1. Spell "E - va" back and "A - ve" shall you find,
2. O vir - gin bless'd! the heav'ns to thee in - cline,
3. With haugh - ty mind to God - head man as - pired,

The first be - gan, the last re - versed our harms;
In thee their joy and sov -'reign they ag - nize;
And was by pride from place of pleas - ure chased;

An an - gel's witch - ing words did E - va blind,
Too mean their glo - ry is to match with thine,
With lov - ing mind our man - hood God de - sired,

An an - gel's "A - ve" dis - en - chants the charms:
Whose chaste re - ceipt God more than heav'n did prize.
And as by love in great - er pleas - ure placed;

Death first by wom - an's weak - ness en - ter'd in,
Hail! fair - est heav'n, that heav'n and earth did bless,
Man la - b'ring to as - cend pro - cured our fall,

In wom - an's vir - tue life doth now be - gin.
Where vir - tue's star God's sun of jus - tice is!
God yield - ing to de - scend cut off our thrall.

OUR LADY

Text by St. Robert Southwell, S.J. (†1595), one of the Forty Martyrs of
England and Wales. Melody by John Wainwright (†1768).

O Christ, The Glorious Crown   513

Tune: FITZALAN (66 66 44 44)   Text: Saint Philip Howard (†1595)

1. O Christ, the glo-rious Crown Of vir-gins that are
2. All char-i-ty of those Whose souls Thy love doth
3. The sky, the land, the sea. And all on earth be-

pure, Who does a love and thirst for Thee With-
warm; All sim-ple pleas-ures of such minds As
low. The glo-ry of Thy wor-thy Name, Do

in their minds pro-cure; Thou art the Spouse of those
think no kind of harm; All sweet de-lights where-with
with their prais-es show. The win-ter yields Thee praise.

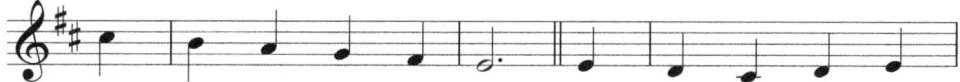

That chaste and hum-ble be, The hope, the life, the
The pa-tient hearts a-bound, Do blaze Thy Name, and
And sum-mer doth the same; The sun, the moon, the

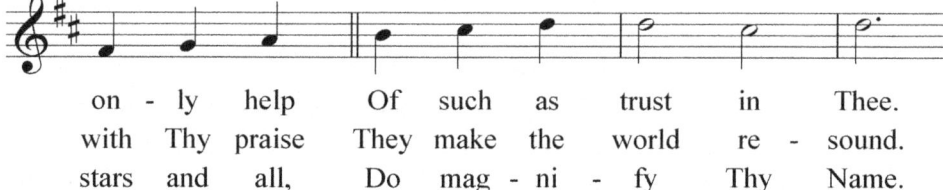

on-ly help Of such as trust in Thee.
with Thy praise They make the world re-sound.
stars and all, Do mag-ni-fy Thy Name.

4. The roses that appear / So fair in outward sight; | The violets which, with their scent, /
Do yield so great delight; | The pearls, the precious stones, / The birds, Thy praise do
sing; | The woods, the wells, and all delights / Which from this earth do spring.

5. What creature, O sweet Lord, / From praising Thee can stay? | What earthly thing, but
filled with joy, / Thine honor doth betray? | Let us therefore with praise, / Thy mighty
works express, | With heart and hand, with mind and all / Which we from Thee possess.

Text written in the Tower of London by
St. Philip Howard (†1595), Earl of Arundel and Martyr of Jesus Christ.
Melody from a Yorkshire Manuscript, as printed in the Arundel Catholic Hymnal.   GENERAL

514   Let Folly Praise What Fancy Loves

Tune: ELLACOMBE (76 76D)   Text: Saint Robert Southwell (†1595)

1. Let fol - ly praise what fan - cy loves, I
2. Love's sweet - est mark, laud's high - est theme, Man's
3. Though young, yet wise; though small, yet strong; though

praise and love that Child, Whose heart no thought, Whose
most de - sir - èd light, To love Him, life; to
man, yet God He is: As wise, He knows; as

tongue no word, Whose hand no deed, de - filed. I praise Him
leave Him, death; To live in Him, de - light. He mine by
strong, He can; as God, He loves to bless. His knowl-edge

most, I love Him best, all praise and love is His; While
gift, I His by debt, thus each to oth - er due, First
rules, His strength de - fends, His love doth cher-ish all; His

Him I love, in Him I live, And can - not live a - miss.
friend He was, best friend He is, all times will find Him true.
Birth our joy, His Life our light, His death our end of thrall.

4. Alas! He weeps, He sighs, He pants, / Yet do His angels sing;
   Out of His tears, His sighs and throbs, / Doth bud a joyful spring.
   Almighty Babe, Whose tender Arms / Can force all foes to fly,
   Correct my faults, protect my life, / Direct me when I die!

German Melody (1784) from the Arundel Hymnal (1898).
Text by St. Robert Southwell (†1595), Priest of the Society of Jesus
and one of the Forty Martyrs of England and Wales.

CHRISTMAS

Tune: MOZART (DCM) *   Text: Saint Robert Southwell (†1595)

1. As I in hoar-y win-ter's night Stood shiv-'ring in the
2. Who, scor-chèd with ex-ces-sive heat, Such floods of tears did
3. "My fault-less Breast the fur-nace is, The fu-el wound-ing

snow, Sur-prised I was with sud-den heat, Which
shed, As though His floods should quench His flames Which
thorns, Love is the fire, and sighs the smoke, The

made my heart to glow; And lift-ing up a fear-ful
with his tears were fed. "A-las!" quoth He, "but new-ly
ash-es shame and scorns; The fu-el Jus-tice lay-eth

eye To view what fire was near, A pret-ty Babe, all
born, In fier-y heats I fry, Yet none ap-proach to
on, And mer-cy blows the coals, The met-als in this

burn-ing bright, Did in the air ap-pear.
warm their hearts, Or feel my fire but I!"
fur-nace wrought Are men's de-fil-èd souls."

4. "For which, as now on fire I am, / To work them to their good,
So will I melt into a bath, / To wash them in My Blood."
With this He vanished out of sight / And swiftly shrunk away,
And straight I callèd unto mind / That it was Christmas Day!

* FOREST GREEN can also be used as the Tune.

Arundel Melody by Wolfgang Amadeus Mozart (†1791).
Text by St. Robert Southwell (†1595), Priest of the Society of Jesus
and one of the Forty Martyrs of England and Wales.

CHRISTMAS

516   New Prince, New Pomp

Tune: SONG 67 (CM)   Text: Saint Robert Southwell (†1595)

1. Be - hold a sim - ple ten - der Babe, In freez - ing win - ter night, In home - ly man - ger trem - bling lies, A - las! A pit - eous sight.

2. The inns are full; no man will yield This lit - tle Pil - grim bed; But forced He is with see - ly beasts In crib to shroud his head.

3. De - spise Him not for ly - ing here, First what He is in - quire: An o - rient pearl is of - ten found In depth of dirt - y mire.

4. Weigh not His crib, His wooden dish, / Nor beasts that round Him press;
   Weigh not His Mother's poor attire, / Nor Joseph's simple dress.

5. This stable is a Prince's Court, / The crib His chair of state;
   The beasts are parcel of His pomp, / The wooden dish His plate.

6. The persons in that poor attire / His royal liv'ries wear;
   The Prince Himself is come from Heav'n, / This pomp is prizèd there.

7. With joy approach, O Christian soul, / Do homage to thy King;
   And highly praise His humble pomp, / Which He from Heav'n doth bring.

Melody by Orlando Gibbons (†1625).
Text by St. Robert Southwell (†1595), Priest of the Society of Jesus
and one of the Forty Martyrs of England and Wales.

CHRISTMAS

Come To Your Heaven 517

Tune: ST CATHERINE (88 88 88)   Text: Saint Robert Southwell (†1595)

1. Come to your heav'n, you heav'n-ly choirs, Earth hath the heav'n of your de - sires; Re - move your dwell - ing to your God, A stall is now His best a - bode; Since men their hom - age do de - ny, Come, An - gels, all their faults sup - ply.

2. This lit - tle Babe so few days old, Is come to ri - fle Sa - tan's fold; All hell doth at His pres - ence quake, Though he him - self for cold do shake; For in this weak, un - arm - èd wise, The gates of hell He will sur - prise.

3. With tears He fights and wins the field, His na - ked breast stands for a shield; His bat - t'ring shot are ba - bish cries, His ar - rows, looks of weep - ing eyes, His mar - tial en - signs, cold and need, And fee - ble flesh His war - rior's steed.

4. His camp is pitchèd in a stall, / His bulwark but a broken wall;
   His crib His trench, hay stalks His stakes, / Of shepherds He His muster makes;
   And thus, as sure His foe to wound, / The angels' trumps alarum sound.

5. My soul, with Christ join thou in fight; / Stick to the tents that He hath pight;
   Within His crib is surest ward, / This little Babe will be thy guard;
   If thou wilt foil thy foes with joy, / Then flit not from the heavenly boy.

Melody by Henri Hemy (†1888).
Text by St. Robert Southwell (†1595), Priest of the Society of Jesus
and one of the Forty Martyrs of England and Wales.   CHRISTMAS

518 The Painful Cross Of Christ

Tune: NIORT (10 10 10 10 10 10 10)   Text: Saint Thomas More (†1535)

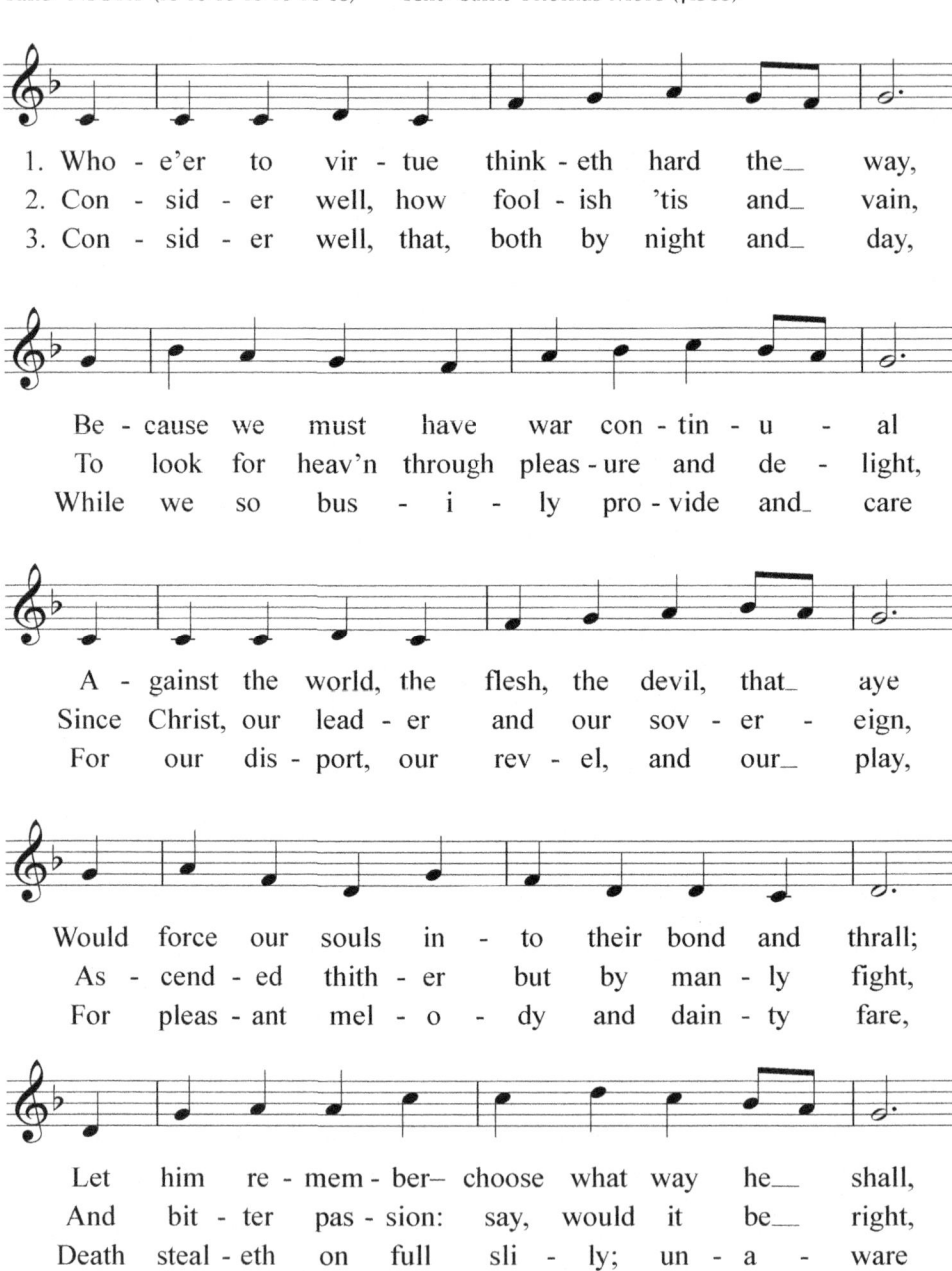

1. Who - e'er to vir - tue think - eth hard the_ way,
2. Con - sid - er well, how fool - ish 'tis and_ vain,
3. Con - sid - er well, that, both by night and_ day,

Be - cause we must have war con - tin - u - al
To look for heav'n through pleas - ure and de - light,
While we so bus - i - ly pro - vide and_ care

A - gainst the world, the flesh, the devil, that_ aye
Since Christ, our lead - er and our sov - er - eign,
For our dis - port, our rev - el, and our_ play,

Would force our souls in - to their bond and thrall;
As - cend - ed thith - er but by man - ly fight,
For pleas - ant mel - o - dy and dain - ty fare,

Let him re - mem - ber— choose what way he_ shall,
And bit - ter pas - sion: say, would it be_ right,
Death steal - eth on full sli - ly; un - a - ware

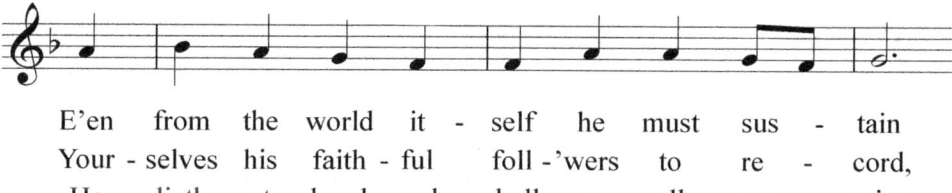

E'en	from	the	world	it - self	he	must	sus - tain
Your - selves	his	faith - ful	foll -'wers	to	re - cord,
He	lieth	at	hand, and	shall	us	all	sur - prise,

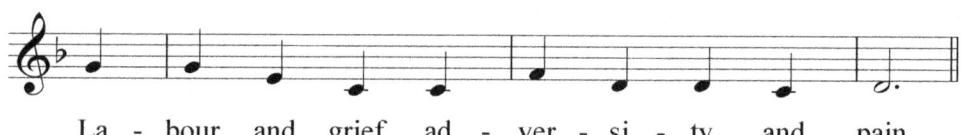

La - bour	and	grief,	ad - ver - si - ty	and	pain.
Yet	stand	on	terms	far	bet - ter	than	your	Lord?
We	know	not	when,	nor	where,	nor	in	what	wise.

4. Thy God hath formed thee, and hath ransom'd both,
   To Him full many a blessing dost thou owe;
   Though thou hast often mov'd him to be wrath,
   Yet hath he kept, and brought thee up till now,
   And daily calleth on thee to his bliss;
   How mayst thou then to Him unloving be,
   Who still hath been so loving unto thee?

5. When fierce temptations threat thy soul with loss,
   Think on his Passion and the bitter pain,
   Think on the mortal anguish of the Cross,
   Think on Christ's blood let out at every vein,
   Think of his precious heart all rent in twain:
   For thy redemption think all this was wrought;
   Nor be that lost which He so dearly bought!

Text by St. Thomas More (†1535), Lord Chancellor of England and martyr. Melody by Fr. Antonin Lhoumeau (†1920).

LENT & PASSIONTIDE

520 Sin's Heavy Load

Tune: YORKSHIRE (10 10 10 10 10 10)   Text: Saint Robert Southwell (†1595)

1. O Lord, my sins doth o - ver-charge thy breast,
2. This globe of earth doth thy one fin - ger prop,
3. O Sin! how huge and heav - y is thy weight,

The poise there - of doth force thy knees to bow;
The world thou dost with - in thy hand em - brace;
That weigh - est more than all the world be - side;

Yea, flat thou fall - est with my faults op - press'd,
Yet all this weight of sweat drew not a drop,
Of which when Christ had tak - en in His freight,

And blood - y sweat runs trick - ling from thy brow:
Nor made thee bow, much less fall on thy face;
The poise there - of His flesh could not a - bide.

But had they not to earth thus press - èd thee,
But now thou hast a load so heav - y found,
A - las! if God Him - self sink un - der sin,

Much more they would, in hell, have pes - ter'd me.
That makes thee bow, yea fall flat to the ground.
What will be - come of man that dies there - in?

Text by St. Robert Southwell, S.J. (†1595), one of the Forty Martyrs of England and Wales. Melody by John Wainwright (†1768).

LENT & PASSIONTIDE